STRANGER IN CHINA

COLIN McCULLOUGH

STRANGER IN CHINA

WILLIAM MORROW & COMPANY, INC.
New York, 1973

Illustrations follow page 118

McCullough, Colin.
    Stranger in China.

    1. China—Description and travel—1949–   I. Title.
    DS711.M18   915.1′04′5   74-182954
    ISBN 0-688-00137-8

For Regina and Katharine

FOREWORD

THE first thing that strikes a Western visitor to China is the harsh poverty of the country. Of course he knows the Chinese leaders insist publicly that China is a poor and backward country, but that doesn't prepare him for the initial shock of seeing sweating men and women straining at rope harnesses to pull a rough wooden cart loaded with bricks. Nor does it prepare him for the curious contrast of very modern office buildings occupied by people wearing an almost uniform dress of patched and faded cotton jackets and trousers. And it is a bit frightening to realize that the peaks of prosperity in Chinese society have truly been scraped away, leaving a giant unrelieved flatland where everyone walks, eats and works at the same level.

There are some Westerners who think the vista is magnificent; they romantically see the Chinese political experiment as producing The New Man, a selfless creature who works unstintingly for his fellow man personified by the state. Others who know the old China are prepared to argue about the methods the Communists have used to transform the country, but not about the results; they saw too many Chinese children die of disease and starvation in the streets. But however a visitor feels about what has happened and is happening, he finds it difficult to reconcile what he sees with the ominous warnings that Peking is poised to engulf the world. Plainly, China is too poor to do much more than try to take care of its own problems.

That will not always be true. Economically China is moving ahead quickly, despite being jerked into setbacks occasionally by what seems to some Westerners to be a kind of political flagellation. Real international power, represented by economic strength rather than sheer weight of people, will eventually come to China. But it is people who in the end will matter, the people who will govern China when Mao Tse-tung, Chou En-lai and the other old guerrillas have gone.

No foreigner can really know the Chinese of today, never mind tomorrow. He can say that the Chinese have a sense of continuity and identity derived from the links of family and ancient civilization. And he can suggest the inner satisfaction and superiority this gives the ordinary Chinese. All probably true, though that same ordinary Chinese wouldn't know what the foreigner was talking about.

Essentially, a foreigner is a stranger in China, and the Chinese can never regard him in any other way. He is not Chinese; there is nothing more to say. But he can describe what it is like to be a foreigner in China, which is what this book tries to do. It is about a minuscule but crucial portion of Chinese Communist history. Politically, the importance of the Cultural Revolution cannot be overestimated. But it was also the first time since the Communists came to power that the Chinese masses had the opportunity to show openly their feelings toward foreigners. Their behaviour is worth remembering in these days of rapprochement between China and the West.

By that I do not mean that the excesses of the Cultural Revolution should be regarded as typical of the nation; but neither should they be forgotten in the euphoria being generated about China these days. Westerners often have a strange determination to see China in one light, either good or bad. Unfortunately, the Chinese seem to have the same optic affliction when they look toward the West. I have no pretensions about this book, but I do hope it will at least widen the view from this side of a people and country that for the first time in centuries have a vitality and sense of purpose that is lacking in most nations today.

Colin McCullough

London, 1972

STRANGER IN CHINA

1

It all begins at Lo Wu, which indeed is an unimpressive place for anything to begin. But Lo Wu is the end of the line; it's as far as you can go directly north on the train from Hong Kong, about forty miles away. Beyond Lo Wu is China.

Back in Hong Kong, in the thick-carpeted lobby of the Hilton Hotel, there is a large sign just beside the cigar stand. It looks a bit peculiar amid comfortable reminders of home such as *Life* magazine, Halo shampoo, the *Wall Street Journal,* and feel-sharp-be-sharp Gillette razor blades. The sign says: SEE RED CHINA.

A lot of people do. Every morning the tourists, mostly Americans, gather around the sign, cameras at the ready. They've paid for the tour and now they're waiting for the guide to pick them up. There is an unmistakable undercurrent of excitement. They are going to see the land of the enemy, perhaps even the enemy himself, and the whole idea has the delicious flavour of danger. Their guide knows better, of course, but why should he spoil a good thing? He arrives, assures everyone that pictures can be taken of

[1]

China, and shepherds the group down the escalator to the waiting bus. Within a few hours, they will have travelled into the New Territories where, from a hillside, they can see China in the distance. With a little imagination, and a little prompting from their guide, they will be able to make out the tiny figures of Communists far away.

They do not go to Lo Wu. Probably they have never even heard of it, and certainly the Hong Kong Chamber of Commerce won't tell them about it. British authorities don't consider Lo Wu a tourist attraction. In fact, it is forbidden to snap photographs of the whitewashed stucco station building, the surrounding tangle of protective barbed wire, the nearby pillbox observation post, the Gurkha and English soldiers patrolling behind sandbag emplacements. Most of all, the British don't want to risk the possibility of anyone creating an incident by focusing a camera on Chinese Red Army soldiers who, with rifles slung over their shoulders, are standing just fifty yards away in the covered bridge that leads into China.

This modest steel and wood bridge spanning a small stream is the gateway into China. If you are not going to use it, then the British don't want you to go to Lo Wu—though there is nothing to prevent you from buying a ticket for the inexpensive (fifty cents) and beautiful train ride from Kowloon to Lo Wu. It is a venerable old train, its first-class section outfitted with ceiling fans and compartments large enough for six passengers. There are lots of passengers, neatly dressed students on their way to the Chinese University of Hong Kong, Chinese men wearing brightly coloured shirts and natty trousers on their way to play golf. The train slowly clatters past breathtaking scenery: great sweeps of rugged mountains and blinding blue coastal inlets where clusters of anchored junks gracefully ride the ocean swells. Then flatter land, with rice paddy fields worked by women of the

[2]

Hakka race, who wear broad-brimmed straw hats fringed with black cloth.

The train stops at little villages along the way. Old Chinese women run alongside the train from open window to open window, trying to hawk a wild assortment of goods to passengers: plastic hair curlers, slippers, hot water bottles, umbrellas, Wrigley's chewing gum. One by one the passengers leave, the students to their studies, the golfers to their tees. As the train nears Sheung Shui, the station before Lo Wu, Hong Kong police walk slowly along the aisles inspecting passengers' papers. If you don't have a special police pass or a visa into China, you are ordered to get off at Sheung Shui. When the train starts moving again toward Lo Wu, the last stop, the only persons left in the first-class section are a couple of ubiquitous China Travel Service men, wearing white bus driver caps and shining red Mao Tse-tung badges, and perhaps one or two foreigners on their way into China—an embassy courier with a sealed diplomatic bag on the seat beside him, and a morose journalist like myself. The travelogue ends at Lo Wu.

The crossing into China is as dramatic as your imagination wants it to be, but admittedly there is something both lonely and final about it. This is because of the bridge. It has railway tracks, but no train takes you across the border. Such luxury transportation is reserved for the thousands of squealing pigs and tons of vegetables and other produce that are daily carried by freight cars from China's communes to Hong Kong's markets and fine restaurants.

You walk into China by yourself, carrying your own suitcases, your footsteps sounding hollowly on the wood planking of the bridge. At the end, eyeing you impassively, are three Chinese soldiers wearing the baggy brown cotton uniforms of the People's Liberation Army, a red felt star sewn on their caps. One of them looks at the visa in your passport, hands it back, and wordlessly waves you on. Just beyond the end of the bridge is a long roofed patio. Two Chinese women in long white gowns are seated behind a table that has an array of test tubes and hypodermic syringes. A soldier standing beside the desk steps forward and the China Travel Service man, who has been trailing behind you, whispers that it is time to have your immunization certificate inspected.

The soldier studies each page carefully, as though suspecting a forgery, then stares you straight in the eye and demands: 'Are you healthy?" If the question doesn't startle you into flubbing the answer—a confused diplomat once spent an hour there assuring the soldier he meant to say yes when he said no—you are allowed to pocket your medical papers and walk into the large white building nearby where you will go through customs and have lunch.

Two things happen as you struggle along with your suitcases. The restaurant waitresses, who have been watching from an upstairs window, quickly slip a record on the turntable and from the thirty loudspeakers around the building blares the music: "Sailing the seas depends on the helmsman, making revolution depends on Mao Tse-tung." At the same time your guide, who is unencumbered by anything more weighty than the speech he has memorized for this moment, trots along beside you shouting a monologue on the iniquities of the capitalist system and the glories of Chinese communism.

Your stay in China has begun. In my case, it lasted a year and a half.

2

SIX weeks in Peking. I hated the city that I did not know. The yellow wind had come, blowing down across the Gobi Desert and collecting tons of powderlike sand that penetrated the apartment despite tightly closed windows. A fine dust covered the floor and every piece of furniture. The papers on my desk felt gritty; my typewriter was clogged with it and the keys stuck together when I tried to write a story. The sand even seeped into the closets; little clouds of dust popped out of the seams of my suit jacket when I put it on.

I hated the Chinese plumbers. They had cut off the hot water in the apartment for a month so they could clean the boilers. "They do it twice a year," said my Nepalese neighbour cheerfully. "You get used to it." But four weeks to clean boilers? "They're very thorough"—he smiled.

I hated the Peking traffic license division. I had successfully passed the required physical examination for drivers at the Anti-Imperialist Hospital—eyes, ears, blood pressure, reflexes—but I still didn't have a driver's license. The special police in the license bureau, a tiny one-storey building in a muddy courtyard, had taken my Province of Ontario driver's license, but refused to give me a Peking license—for the time being, anyhow. The problem, they explained, was that Canada didn't have diplomatic relations with China so they and their comrades would have to consider the question for a while—a favourite Chinese expression that means don't call us, we'll call you. They still hadn't called, and in my wilder moments I had visions of Premier Chou En-lai personally weighing the international implications of approving a driver's license for me.

Anyhow, the Volkswagen's Chinese battery had gone dead.

I hated the Chinese painters. They announced they were going to paint my five-room apartment and that the cost would be $400 in advance. I said it didn't need painting. They said it was required by the lease. I said I wouldn't pay until the job was finished. They said it was against the regulations. I said the price was too high. They said it was non-negotiable. I said I wouldn't pay unless I could have some colour other than white. They said that might be possible but it couldn't be discussed until after I'd paid. I said I wouldn't pay $400 if they were again going to use white-wash that rubbed off on your clothes when you leaned against a wall. They said it was suitable paint for foreigners' flats. I said I didn't have $400 and that my office would never give me that amount of money. They went away.

I hated the Diplomatic Service Bureau, for a variety of reasons. I complained to my Nepalese neighbour, who said philosophically: "Ah, the Service Bureau giveth and the Service Bureau taketh away."

"Yeah," I protested, "but the Service Bureau hasn't giveth me anything, but it's taketh away everything." I was beginning to hate him too.

The Service Bureau provided hired help to foreigners in Peking. Within the first week of my arrival, the two amahs

[6]

and cook who had worked for my predecessor had resigned and left—on the orders of the Service Bureau. Before that, and afterwards too, I had written pleading letters to the bureau asking that they be allowed to stay on. No answer. I telephoned, but the man who answered would speak only Chinese—though I knew from other foreigners that he spoke English.

With the combination of the Yellow Wind and absent amahs, my apartment was beginning to resemble a giant sandbox. I practically gave up trying to clean it; my weak efforts simply raised miniature dust storms. Anyhow, I was busy with ironing and with washing underwear and socks and shirts—in cold water. Occasionally, I would even find time to write a story.

The loss of the cook was annoying, but I certainly wasn't starving. I had brought in some tinned sardines, soups, and meats from Hong Kong and these, combined with the stock my predecessor had left behind, kept me adequately fed. There were lots of markets in Peking, of course, but I didn't know where they were then and there didn't seem much point in trying to find out. I had no way of getting to them (even if I had known the telephone number of the taxi stand, I wouldn't have been able to tell the driver where to go in Chinese), and I had no way of telling the storekeeper what I wanted to buy, nor did I know anything about Chinese food.

The closest restaurant was about three miles away.

These were but minor problems and most of them could have been solved if I had had a translator. More important, without an interpreter I was having extreme difficulty doing my job. Two of the correspondents, Hans Bargmann of the West German news agency DPA and Mihailo Saranovic of the Yugoslavian news agency Tanjug, were very helpful, not only in driving me to various functions but also in letting me see translations produced by their translators. But I couldn't impose on their kindness every day, nor could I let them continually run the risk of losing their own translators by helping me. There was a very real chance of that happening. After all, if I didn't have a translator, then it was because the Diplomatic Service Bureau didn't want me to have one. That, at least, was the consensus among the diplomats and correspondents. They figured that the Chinese, in their usual oblique way, were showing their disapproval of *The Globe and Mail* correspondent. They further reasoned that I hadn't been in China long enough to do anything that would annoy the Chinese, so the Chinese were obviously angry with my predecessor, David Oancia.

I was much taken with this explanation. It fitted perfectly with my Western ideas of Oriental deviousness: somewhere in the Diplomatic Service Bureau lurked the cunning and inscrutable Dr. Fu Man Chu.

Later, much later, I learned that there was a much simpler explanation for the bureau's failure to produce a translator: there wasn't one available. By then I had learned to be somewhat skeptical of the deductive powers of both diplomats and foreign correspondents who sometimes arrived at momentous judgments of China and the Chinese on the basis of minuscule scraps of information gleaned from the almost undecipherable jargon of government propaganda.

This is not to say that the Chinese—and the Diplomatic Service Bureau in particular—could not be devious, or, more accurately, petty.

A Finnish diplomat, for instance, fired his Chinese cook after a one-month trial period. The Service Bureau official was incredulous at the diplomat's explanation that the fellow just couldn't cook, and said the question of sending another cook would have to be considered. A month later, the diplomat called the bureau and was told the search for a cook was still going on. Still another month passed, and the inquiring diplomat was given the same answer.

"Look here," said he, "when am I going to get a cook?"

"We are still searching," said the official gently, "but it is most difficult to find a cook who meets your high standards."

"Oh," sighed the diplomat. He got the message.

A year later he still didn't have a cook, but it should be noted that he got one immediately when he called the bureau and explained that he urgently needed a cook because his wife was returning to Finland for three months and he had nobody to prepare food for his young daughter.

The Service Bureau was also adept at twisting the knife a little.

Hungarian correspondent Charles Patock had tried unsuccessfully for a year to get a translator (he used his embassy's translations, paying forty cents a page). At the end of that time, his visa was not renewed because he had written "distorted" stories and the Foreign Ministry told him he had three days to get out of China. The next day, a man appeared at Patock's apartment door and announced he was a translator sent by the Diplomatic Service Bureau.

By that time though, it was evident that the Chinese did indeed have a shortage of translators—one of the many manifestations of the Cultural Revolution. There were two reasons.

For the two years before I arrived in Peking, all universities and institutes of international languages had ceased academic operations. Most schools were closed, and those that remained open were given over to Cultural Revolution activities—some of which were approved, such as the criticism of bourgeois academic authorities and the revamping of curricula; and others which were unapproved, such as open fighting between student factions.

[9]

In any case, the result was that China's schools were producing no new translators.

The second reason for the shortage was that many of the translators working for foreigners were suspected of harbouring bourgeois tendencies. Under especially harsh criticism were those Chinese who had been educated in the United States or the United Kingdom. They were, of course, older men and women and thus were not products of the "new" state. Even worse, most of them were the children of very wealthy Chinese—i.e., the exploiting class—otherwise they would never have been able to study abroad. The experience that made them excellent translators—their education, cultural background, and their understanding of Western life and idiomatic language—was the very thing that made them vulnerable to attacks from jealous colleagues who were very proletarian and very inadequate. Ironically, these "Westernized" Chinese had sufficient wealth to get out of China at the time the Communists took over in 1949. But they were young people who were dismayed at the corruption of the old system—in which their parents had often been involved—and wanted to play a role in building the new China.

One translator told me he had been studying at an American university (he wouldn't say which one) when he heard that Chiang Kai-shek had fled to Formosa. He returned to China immediately, disobeying his parents, and joined other idealistic young people who wanted to serve their country. He disappeared one day, just as other expert translators disappeared one by one from the embassies in Peking and were replaced by Chinese often barely able to cope with English. Even the Pakistanis, who could do no wrong in Chinese eyes, lost their best translator. Some translators left at the end of a workday, and simply never reappeared.

Others gave one day's notice or, as in the case of Mrs. Mai, one hour's notice.

Mrs. Mai was a tiny, pretty woman, perhaps forty-five. Her thick black hair was cropped short and, of course, she wore no makeup. Her only concession (if it could be called that) to her background was her scrupulous cleanliness and her neatly pressed clothes. Since she always wore the same grey cotton trousers and brown jacket in the three weeks that I saw her, she must have pressed them every evening. She often quoted Mao Tse-tung at me, but turned aside any questions that did not relate to translations or to housekeeping problems. Her favourite comment was: Live simply and work hard; this is the road to greatness for China.

Mrs. Mai, a graduate of an American university, spoke excellent English. She was also a comfortable person to be with. Whatever the disaster might be, she would smile cheerfully and set it right; her experience as translator for *The Globe and Mail* correspondents for almost four years meant there was no problem she had not encountered before—except one.

Usually, Mrs. Mai started work at ten in the morning. She would seat herself at the small desk set up in a corner of the dining room and translate the headlines of the Chinese newspapers I received daily. After lunch, I would look at the headlines and ask her to translate one or two of the stories that seemed interesting.

But one morning Mrs. Mai arrived at 9 A.M. She maintained her usual outward calm, but she was clearly very nervous. Tiny beads of perspiration lined her upper lip and her forehead. She had, she said, been given "new responsibilities" and was quitting. She had two hours to clean up her affairs before returning to the Service Bureau. The next 120 minutes were hectic, as we rushed by taxi to the bank, the hospital, the cable office and other places where I had

[11]

business that could only be done with the help of a translator. Along the way, I kept asking her if anything was wrong, if there was any kind of trouble, if she knew what her new job would be. No, nothing was wrong. No, there was no trouble. No, she didn't know what her new job would be. In the taxi, I gave Mrs. Mai her severance pay of about three hundred dollars—money which I knew she would have to turn over to the Service Bureau—and she asked to be let out at a street corner. It was the last time I saw her.

What became of Mrs. Mai? The East Europeans, always morbid about China and perhaps conditioned by experiences in their own countries, were convinced that Mrs. Mai and the other English-language translators had been sent out to work in the rice fields or even imprisoned because of their close association with foreigners. The Pakistanis, always the apologists for the Chinese, thought the translators had simply been seconded to work in more important jobs.

The truth probably lay somewhere in between. Certainly many of the translators probably went through gruelling self-criticism sessions. Their sins—in the eyes of their envious fellow workers—were many. They had been friends to the foreigners, even exchanging family visits. They had accepted gifts, usually small but identifiably foreign articles such as cigarets or old clothing. The latter especially aroused anger because cotton was rationed. Some of the women translators even wore lipstick and curled their hair. Very bourgeois.

All of these misdeeds, plus the more subtle crimes of "thinking" in a Western way or of somehow showing by word or action that they felt superior to other Chinese, would have to be confessed over and over again. It is difficult for a Westerner to comprehend the psychological effect that a self-criticism has on a Chinese. It has to do with the centuries-old Chinese concept of individual respect and status

[12]

among his fellow men. To lose that—in other words, to lose face—is to lose everything. Chinese history and literature are filled with the stories of men and women who committed suicide or even murder for this reason. During the Cultural Revolution a number of professors and politicians killed themselves rather than face the humiliation of being marched through the streets wearing a dunce cap, or of being forced to beg contritely for forgiveness at mass meetings.

The translators would probably have to stand before a hundred of their fellow workers and abjectly "confess" their bourgeois crimes—not once, but hundreds of times during the course of a meeting. These would not be quiet sessions. People would shout and scream at them from all sides; their pleas of sorrow would be rejected as false; their best friends, carefully watched for the slightest indication of sympathy, would be the loudest in denouncing them; their slightest proletarian deviation over the last ten or twenty years would be brought to account; their parents and brothers and sisters and children would be forced to confront them with accusations.

They might, if lucky, face only one such session. On the other hand, they might be dragged to self-criticism meetings two or three times a week for a month or longer.

Most of the translators would also have to go through a period of manual labour. This might mean a month or two of sweeping streets, or gathering night soil, or working at a nearby commune. This, supposedly, would rid them of their "air of superiority" and make them realize the real worth and equality of China's peasants and workers.

I am convinced that eventually Mrs. Mai and nearly all the other translators returned to their old work, but not for foreigners. The inconvenience caused to the diplomats and the handful of correspondents was of small concern to the Chinese Government, and rightly so. It needed expert translators to work in the various ministries and, more particularly, to take the place of translators in the propaganda and economic departments who had openly fought to depose Mao Tse-tung. I feel certain that is what happened to Mrs. Mai, but I don't know. I never saw her again.

I did, however, see the cook Chen, and the two amahs, Wu and Ouyang.

They marched in the door of the apartment exactly three weeks after they had walked out (each taking one month's severance pay). I rushed over to greet them, leaving behind the trousers I had been pressing in preparation for a dinner at the Finnish Embassy. There was much shaking of hands and broad smiles. They chattered at me in Chinese, and I replied happily in English. Chen kept scratching his black spiky hair, a sign that he was immensely pleased with the world; Wu, who was tall and thin, headed for the overflowing laundry basket; and the short and fat Ouyang waddled over to the ironing board to take over the job I had started. Nobody seemed to notice or care that I was wearing only underwear.

I retreated to my office elated, and typed out two messages. The first was a cable informing the office that the domestic staff had returned but that there was no sign of a translator. The second was a letter to the Foreign Ministry requesting an interview as soon as possible. It was time to face Mr. Wong.

3

MR. WONG was the first government official I met in China. A few days after my arrival in Peking, I was invited to the Foreign Ministry for a formal introduction to officials of the Information Department. This was standard procedure for all new correspondents, the only difference being the level of government official who attended and the length of the meeting. And these two factors were, of course, determined by the state of relations between China and the journalist's country. At the top of the scale was the Albanian correspondent, who would receive an audience of at least one hour with the Director of the Information Department. At the bottom were the Russians, who would get no more than fifteen minutes with a minor functionary. I received exactly thirty minutes, no more, no less, with one of the deputy directors, Mr. Wong. Several times during our meeting, when two and three minutes would pass by when nobody spoke, I made a modest effort to leave.

"Well," I said, shifting my weight in the chair, "I don't want to take up any more of your time."

"Not at all," said Mr. Wong through an interpreter. "We have many things yet to discuss."

We hadn't, of course. This was purely a formal meeting, as I quickly discovered. Mr. Wong was very courteous and very patient when I tried to raise matters related to my work as a journalist in China. But he wasn't answering any questions, and he wasn't allowing the meeting to break up until my officially allotted thirty minutes had passed.

I had arrived precisely three minutes before our meeting was to take place, driving along old Legation Street where foreign countries, including the United States, had once had their embassies. All but the Rumanian Embassy now house government offices. Even St. Michael's Catholic Church, where Han Suyin attended mass as a child, has become a primary grade school. Inside there are pictures and busts of Mao Tse-tung but, strangely, there is still a cross on the church spire.

The People's Liberation Army soldiers armed with rifles and bayonets stood guard by the gateway in the high grey brick walls around the Foreign Ministry. This was the French Embassy in the old days, and inside were eight large grey brick buildings set around a circular drive and, surprise of surprises, neatly clipped green lawns. Grass, I should explain, is rare in Peking. The boulevarded streets, the parks, the areas around apartment buildings—are all a bald brown. If a blade of grass pokes through the tightly packed earth, the Chinese immediately scrape it off.

"But why?" I asked one Chinese. Well, he said, grass harbours insects and is not very clean. Get rid of the grass and you can easily sweep the earth with straw brooms, keeping everything neat and tidy. He was politely skeptical when I suggested that grass might help reduce the constant swirl of dust in Peking.

I drove past the guards without showing any identification,

or even slowing the car. They knew the car; they knew who I was. The Information Department is in a three-storey house that had been the residence of the French counsellor. A white-jacketed youth held open the screen door and led me into what had once been a living room. Hanging on the walls were large colour portraits of Mao Tse-tung and, in gold Chinese characters on a red background, facsimiles of his quotations in his own writing. Six large easy chairs and four chesterfields, all wrapped in beige cotton slipcovers, were ranged around the room. The arms and backs of the chairs were decorated with crocheted doilies. A single bulb hung from the center of the ceiling by a long cord.

The white-jacketed boy came into the room carrying a tray of cigarets, matches and Chinese tea mugs, each with its own lid. A minute later Mr. Wong came into the room with two men. One was a secretary who wrote down every word we said; the other was a translator, who smilingly performed the introductions.

After we had settled in our chairs and lighted cigarets, Wong quietly spoke at some length in Chinese. It gave me an opportunity to study him. He was tiny, almost fragile, and the dark blue cotton boiler suit hung limply on his body. His thin aesthetic face was dominated by a very high forehead that swept back to a few thin strands of grey hair. His eyes, partly obscured by thick steel-rimmed glasses, seemed as gentle as his voice. He sat very straight, his arms folded.

"Mr. Wong bids you welcome to China, and he expresses the hope that the Information Department will have the same warm relations with you that it had with your predecessor," said the translator.

I looked closely at Mr. Wong but saw no flicker of amusement in his eyes. My predecessor had been waiting for three weeks for Mr. Wong to give him an exit visa and in the past

[17]

had been hauled before the Foreign Ministry and police for "serious" warnings.

"Mr. Wong would like to know if you have any questions concerning your future work in China."

"Where am I allowed to take photographs in Peking?" I promptly asked, since I had already heard several stories of foreigners who had films seized when taking pictures of street scenes.

Mr. Wong's reply was translated. "You may take photographs wherever you are permitted to go."

I thought that over while we all had another sip of tea, and decided to try another tack.

"Will it be possible for me to travel in China?" I asked, knowing that no journalists or diplomats had been able to visit other parts of the country since the Cultural Revolution had begun two years earlier. Indeed, the correspondents hadn't even been able to visit a hospital, museum, art gallery, school or factory in that time.

"Mr. Wong suggests that you submit an application to the Foreign Ministry specifying which places you wish to visit," said the translator.

I glumly asked a couple of other questions, which were laboriously translated into Chinese for Mr. Wong, and I listened to his noncommittal answers translated into English. Finally, I just gave up, lighted a cigaret and leaned back in the chair. A full minute of silence passed, during which I studied a big portrait of Mao Tse-tung, whose face carried not one line of age and had the ruddy flesh tones of a seventeen-year-old boy.

At last Mr. Wong spoke again. He wanted to know if I had any further questions concerning my work in China, explained the translator. I replied, with what I hoped was obvious sarcasm, that I was sure that I couldn't possibly think of any questions that hadn't already been fully an-

us stratagems and feeling
n into a corner, he was
sive face. It was my first
officials: you can try to
out if the game is played

ampened for very long.
enjoyed himself at my
y had little enough to
matter was that I would
in. We had worried that
give a visa to my wife,
alized Canadian citizen,
ich had been taken over
the Second World War.
Chinese might say no to
-Soviet relations. As it
y; nor did my successor,
orn in the United States
a few months before they

eginning of April, plan-
New Delhi, Tokyo and
o various diplomats and
nterpretation of events in
had lunch with British
either of us knew it at
in a few months when
d'Affaires, replacing Sir

travelling pace, and be-
arine miss three months
at they should come to
d a short time when we

swered. Mr. Wong nodded gravely, but there was a slight smile on his thin lips.

He glanced at his watch and rose from the chair to shake hands. As we walked to the door he said, in perfect English: "I understand that your wife and young daughter will be joining you in Peking eventually. I trust that they and you will enjoy your stay in China."

The rascal could speak English. I was so startled that I barely managed to stammer a thank you as I was ushered out of the door.

That was two months ago, though, and as I drove to the Foreign Ministry for a second meeting with Wong I was determined to get some straight answers out of him—assuming, of course, that he would still be there. After my first meeting with him, I learned from other correspondents that he hadn't been seen by them for more than a year. They had taken it for granted that he was one of the many government officials who had fallen victim to the Cultural Revolution. I was curious to see whether he had been taken off the shelf and dusted off for my benefit—he had also given the formal welcome to previous *Globe and Mail* correspondents—or had in fact managed to hold his position as Deputy Director of the Foreign Ministry's Information Department.

Sure enough, Mr. Wong was on hand to meet me along with the same translator, a handsome young man named Chi who wore run-down shoes and a patched and faded blue cotton Chinese boiler suit. I didn't know it then, but that was to be the last time I would see Mr. Wong.

The conversation this time was much more businesslike; that is, this wasn't an official welcoming session and the interview didn't have to last a certain number of minutes. Nonetheless, it went slowly. There were two questions that I felt I had to force Mr. Wong to answer before I left the Foreign Ministry. The first was whether or not I was going

[19]

to get a translator. The second was whether or not
nese were going to issue visas to my wife and daughte
answers were no, or more likely negatively equivoc
it was certain that I would have to leave China and
newspaper would probably have to close the bure
porarily.

On the first question, concerning a translator, I
success in budging Wong in the first ten minutes.

Would the Foreign Ministry undertake to supply
a translator? The Foreign Ministry did not have the
sibility and I should apply to the Diplomatic Service

I had already done that, twice, and since I still
have a translator could the Foreign Ministry do sc
about it? The Foreign Ministry did not have thi
sibility and I should apply again.

Did the Foreign Ministry think it possible I wo
get a translator? This was the problem of the D
Service Bureau, which was a government office not c
in the least with the Information Department.

At this point, I made a lengthy speech on the c
I was having without a translator, and added that
was so seriously impaired that it seemed doubtful
be able to stay in Peking. Mr. Wong did not lool
larly grieved at this thought, so I tried another tack

Could the Information Department, whose resp
did not cover this matter, possibly speak to the D
Service Bureau about the problems I was having?
proach seemed to satisfy the rules of Chinese logi
Wong smiled slightly and allowed that he indeed
this was possible.

I moved on to the next matter. Would my wife a
ter be given a visa to enter and stay in China?
unhappily as Mr. Wong carefully explained tha
applications must be submitted through the Chi

[20]

it. So while I was employing var
terribly clever at having talked
grinning broadly behind his imp
lesson about Chinese governmen
outsmart them at their own game
in China then you will not win.

Still, my good spirits were not
It didn't matter if Mr. Wong h
expense; the poor fellow proba
amuse him in those days. What di
be seeing my wife and daughter a
the Chinese might be reluctant t
Regina. Although she was a nat
she had been born in Lithuania v
by the Russians toward the end c
There was the possibility that the
her, considering the state of Si
turned out we didn't have to wor
Norman Webster, whose wife was
and became a Canadian citizen jus
left for China.

I had set out for Peking at the
ning to stop off in London, Paris
Hong Kong along the way to talk
journalists who could give me their
China. In London, incidentally,
diplomat John Denson. Although
the time, we would meet in Pekir
he became the new British Charge
Donald Hopson.

Because of my deliberately slow
cause it seemed foolish to have Kat
of school, Regina and I decided t
Peking at the end of June. It seem

[22]

swered. Mr. Wong nodded gravely, but there was a slight smile on his thin lips.

He glanced at his watch and rose from the chair to shake hands. As we walked to the door he said, in perfect English: "I understand that your wife and young daughter will be joining you in Peking eventually. I trust that they and you will enjoy your stay in China."

The rascal could speak English. I was so startled that I barely managed to stammer a thank you as I was ushered out of the door.

That was two months ago, though, and as I drove to the Foreign Ministry for a second meeting with Wong I was determined to get some straight answers out of him—assuming, of course, that he would still be there. After my first meeting with him, I learned from other correspondents that he hadn't been seen by them for more than a year. They had taken it for granted that he was one of the many government officials who had fallen victim to the Cultural Revolution. I was curious to see whether he had been taken off the shelf and dusted off for my benefit—he had also given the formal welcome to previous *Globe and Mail* correspondents—or had in fact managed to hold his position as Deputy Director of the Foreign Ministry's Information Department.

Sure enough, Mr. Wong was on hand to meet me along with the same translator, a handsome young man named Chi who wore run-down shoes and a patched and faded blue cotton Chinese boiler suit. I didn't know it then, but that was to be the last time I would see Mr. Wong.

The conversation this time was much more businesslike; that is, this wasn't an official welcoming session and the interview didn't have to last a certain number of minutes. Nonetheless, it went slowly. There were two questions that I felt I had to force Mr. Wong to answer before I left the Foreign Ministry. The first was whether or not I was going

[19]

to get a translator. The second was whether or not the Chinese were going to issue visas to my wife and daughter. If the answers were no, or more likely negatively equivocal, then it was certain that I would have to leave China and that the newspaper would probably have to close the bureau temporarily.

On the first question, concerning a translator, I had no success in budging Wong in the first ten minutes.

Would the Foreign Ministry undertake to supply me with a translator? The Foreign Ministry did not have the responsibility and I should apply to the Diplomatic Service Bureau.

I had already done that, twice, and since I still did not have a translator could the Foreign Ministry do something about it? The Foreign Ministry did not have this responsibility and I should apply again.

Did the Foreign Ministry think it possible I would ever get a translator? This was the problem of the Diplomatic Service Bureau, which was a government office not connected in the least with the Information Department.

At this point, I made a lengthy speech on the difficulties I was having without a translator, and added that my work was so seriously impaired that it seemed doubtful I would be able to stay in Peking. Mr. Wong did not look particularly grieved at this thought, so I tried another tack.

Could the Information Department, whose responsibility did not cover this matter, possibly speak to the Diplomatic Service Bureau about the problems I was having? This approach seemed to satisfy the rules of Chinese logic, for Mr. Wong smiled slightly and allowed that he indeed did think this was possible.

I moved on to the next matter. Would my wife and daughter be given a visa to enter and stay in China? I sighed unhappily as Mr. Wong carefully explained that all visa applications must be submitted through the China Travel

Service Bureau in Hong Kong. By this time I was beginning to catch on.

Of course, I said, that was exactly what Mrs. McCullough and my daughter would do. But it was a long trip from Canada to Hong Kong, and could Mr. Wong venture an opinion on whether the applications would be successful if the passports and other relevant papers were in order.

Mr. Wong, obviously relieved that I had finally tuned into the Chinese wavelength and wasn't going to create an ugly scene by demanding a straightforward answer, ventured that he did not anticipate that there would be any difficulties concerning the visas.

I left the Foreign Ministry pleased with myself, and walked along old Legation Street to the Hsin Chiao Hotel where my friend the West German correspondent lived. As far as I was concerned I had been given a guarantee—or as much of a guarantee as one could expect—that my family would be allowed to join me. And I had also got a commitment that the Foreign Ministry would put pressure on the Diplomatic Service Bureau to provide a translator. Who knows, I thought, I might even get a translator next week.

When I arrived at Hans Bargmann's hotel room, however, I discovered that *he* had news for *me*. My amah had called his translator looking for me. The Diplomatic Service Bureau had telephoned my flat to say that I would be receiving a translator the next day. I asked Bargmann when the amah had telephoned the message.

"Exactly at noon," he said, "but what difference does that make? And what are you looking so unhappy about?"

The difference, I told him, was that the telephone call from the Diplomatic Service Bureau had been made even before I walked into the Foreign Ministry. And that meant that Mr. Wong must have known before we met that I would be getting a translator—indeed, he had probably authorized it. So while I was employing various stratagems and feeling terribly clever at having talked him into a corner, he was grinning broadly behind his impassive face. It was my first lesson about Chinese government officials: you can try to outsmart them at their own game, but if the game is played in China then you will not win.

Still, my good spirits were not dampened for very long. It didn't matter if Mr. Wong had enjoyed himself at my expense; the poor fellow probably had little enough to amuse him in those days. What did matter was that I would be seeing my wife and daughter again. We had worried that the Chinese might be reluctant to give a visa to my wife, Regina. Although she was a naturalized Canadian citizen, she had been born in Lithuania which had been taken over by the Russians toward the end of the Second World War. There was the possibility that the Chinese might say no to her, considering the state of Sino-Soviet relations. As it turned out we didn't have to worry; nor did my successor, Norman Webster, whose wife was born in the United States and became a Canadian citizen just a few months before they left for China.

I had set out for Peking at the beginning of April, planning to stop off in London, Paris, New Delhi, Tokyo and Hong Kong along the way to talk to various diplomats and journalists who could give me their interpretation of events in China. In London, incidentally, I had lunch with British diplomat John Denson. Although neither of us knew it at the time, we would meet in Peking in a few months when he became the new British Chargé d'Affaires, replacing Sir Donald Hopson.

Because of my deliberately slow travelling pace, and because it seemed foolish to have Katharine miss three months of school, Regina and I decided that they should come to Peking at the end of June. It seemed a short time when we

[22]

talked about it in Toronto, but the days in Peking dragged by slowly. Sometimes, when I sat alone in the apartment, I wondered what Katharine would think of it all.

Katharine was eight years old then, with brown hair and blue eyes. She liked school, Walt Disney movies, strawberry shortcake, ice-skating and Saturday morning television cartoons. All her life she had lived in a big house in a pleasant suburb of Toronto. In Peking she would live in a suburb where a section called San Li Tun had been set aside for foreigners, both diplomats and correspondents. It was a new and modern area, with cream brick embassies and grey brick apartment buildings.

Formal schooling had been a problem since the old convent school for diplomats' children was closed by Red Guards in August, 1966. The Russian Embassy operated a school, but it too had been closed when wives and children of officials returned to the Soviet Union. Some of the older foreign children took correspondence courses, while the French and Indian Embassies started classes for younger children. Both offered to take Katharine, and she probably would go to the French school where—as one French diplomat said with a smile—she would quickly learn a language that might be useful to her in Canada.

Strawberry shortcake, Walt Disney and television were out, but I thought she and her mother would enjoy the apartment. It was as comfortable and spacious as any I had seen in Toronto—surely luxury accommodation in Peking. Three things would surprise them: the marble-tiled hall more than six feet wide that ran the length of the apartment, with rooms opening on each side including a living room larger than the one we had at home; the huge windows (bigger than some store windows in Toronto); and the ceilings, which were more than ten feet high. Best of all, the flat was on the third of the building's six floors and Katharine would

[23]

be able to look out over the trees and count the flags of the embassies, or look down and watch the two-wheeled carts drawn by mules. Often the carts were loaded with vegetables being taken into the city from nearby communes, and often the driver would be curled up on top fast asleep—contrary to Peking traffic regulations.

Some things I knew Katharine would not understand: the words, HANG TITO THE DOG'S HEAD, painted on the wall around the Yugoslav Embassy about a block away; and, farther on, the empty Burmese Embassy with its shattered windows, still guarded by a security officer. She would soon get used to seeing security officers and learn to distinguish them from soldiers, though both wore blue trousers, and brown tunics and caps (soldiers have a red cloth star sewn on their caps while police have a red enamel badge). There were always two security officers, sometimes four, at the two gates in the iron fence around the apartment. The guards were installed a few months before I arrived, ostensibly to protect us; but in fact they effectively sealed off the foreigners, since no Chinese could enter the gates without an official pass.

As far as Katharine would be concerned, it wouldn't make much difference: Chinese children do not play with foreign children. This is something that she would discover, though she would see lots of them. The surrounding buildings were occupied by Chinese families, and every day their children would stand solemn-faced on the other side of the fence, sometimes two or three, sometimes as many as thirty, their soft black eyes staring in fascination at the foreign children. I wondered if she would get used to that.

As the time of Katharine's arrival drew closer, however, my worries about how she would take the cultural change were being replaced by concerns about her and her mother's safety. Although the violent phase of the Cultural Revolution seemingly had ended, there were signs that it might break out again. At that point in time, the spring of 1968, it was easy to be convinced by the gloomy East Europeans that another large-scale tremor could split China into a real civil war. There were reports of renewed fighting in Sinkiang, Szechwan and other provinces. These were perhaps nothing more than rumours, but it was a fact that scores of bodies, some of them bound and others with their hands cut off, were being washed up on Hong Kong's shores after apparently drifting down the Pearl River from nearby Kwantung Province.

Moreover, strife in China is historically accompanied by a wave of xenophobia, and the attitude of the Foreign Ministry toward journalists, the most vulnerable group of foreigners in Peking, gave little room for optimism. My own experience with the Chinese had not been encouraging. They had made no effort to solve any of my problems—indeed, they had added to them—despite the fact that Canada's new Prime Minister had announced he was interested in establishing diplomatic relations with China. Anthony Grey, the Reuters correspondent, was still under house arrest. Other journalists were having difficulties doing their work. Then there were Jean Vincent, the Agence France Presse man, and Keiji Samejima, correspondent for the Japanese economic newspaper, *Nihon Keizai Shimbun*.

Jean was expelled a month after I arrived. One month later, in the dead of night, soldiers entered Keiji's flat and arrested him. No one knew why. In fact, I took an early plane out of Peking that same day and didn't even know he had been arrested until I arrived in Hong Kong and saw the newspaper headlines. The next day, I was to meet Regina and Katharine at the Hong Kong airport.

[25]

4

To me the choice seemed simple. I explained it very carefully to Regina. She and Katharine would stay in Hong Kong and I would go back into China. After a month or so, if the situation in China remained the same, I would come out to Hong Kong and bring them back to Peking. In retrospect, I was being rather melodramatic, but I recall thinking that if a civil war developed, Regina and Katharine would be safer in Hong Kong while I would be able to fend for myself much better alone, and, if necessary, work my way back to the border. As agreed some months earlier, I called Toronto and talked to the newspaper's editor and managing editor, Richard Doyle and Clark Davey. Their approach to the problem was the same with me as it was with all correspondents: Since I was the man on the spot, I was best able to judge the situation; they would be satisfied with whatever decision I took. (If Reuters news agency had taken this reasonable position, incidentally, correspondent Anthony Grey would probably not have spent twenty-six months under house arrest in Peking.) Regina patiently listened to my explanation of why she and Katharine should wait in Hong

Kong, agreed that I was right, but firmly added that they were going with me anyhow—despite the disappearance of the Japanese correspondent and the news of bodies floating down the Pearl River. After three days of arguing I gave up, and on a cool grey June morning the three of us boarded the Kowloon train for Lo Wu and China.

We were the only foreigners crossing the border that day, but nothing seemed to have changed. The British emigration official wore his usual they-must-be-mad expression while he stamped our passports, and the Chinese soldiers at the other end of the bridge greeted us as glumly as ever. What I didn't know, nor did they, was that things had changed: In Peking, the leaders had decided that the Cultural Revolution had gone far enough.

Despite this lack of perception on my part—which would have eased my mind that day—our first day in China began auspiciously because of an incident involving Katharine. It was, as it turned out, an omen that we would spend a happy year and a half in Peking.

We went through customs and were ushered into the big restaurant for lunch (always the same: tea, scrambled eggs, rice, fried prawns and bamboo-shoot soup). Outside, the squeals of pigs being shipped to Hong Kong lent raucous accompaniment to the loudspeakers loudly playing revolutionary music. We were the only customers in the railway restaurant. Regina looked around the room, its walls covered with pictures of Mao Tse-tung and posters. She was wide-eyed.

"Is it always like this?" she shouted above the noise.

Katharine, who wasn't much interested in her food, asked if she could go for a walk in the building. She was completely unimpressed by her surroundings, which pleased me, and I told her she could take a walk but to come back in ten minutes. I knew no Chinese would harm her, but when she

[28]

hadn't returned after fifteen minutes, I set off to look for her.

I heard her before I saw her. As I walked down a long corridor, I could hear her voice in the distance singing "Puff, the Magic Dragon." I couldn't help smiling to myself. Only a child would be innocent enough to wander about in revolutionary China singing to herself about dragons. But she wasn't by herself, as I discovered when I got to the room at the end of the corridor. She was surrounded by smiling waitresses and men and women in customs uniforms. They applauded when she finished the song about Puff. Then they joined in a chorus of "Chairman Mao Is the Red Sun in Our Hearts" while Katharine listened attentively. She applauded enthusiastically and launched into "I'm Looking Over a Four-leaf Clover." I decided it was time to break up the singsong.

The incident at the railway station was typical of Katharine's attitude during the time we spent in China.

She quickly became used to the openmouthed stares of the Chinese, and at first even seemed to enjoy the attention. Shyer children, especially those whose parents had been harried by the Red Guards, became very nervous in crowds and refused to go shopping with their parents in the downtown area. One four-year-old girl, the daughter of a British couple, often awoke screaming in the middle of the night. For Katharine, though, the Red Guards were nothing but a name, and she adjusted to her new life with an ease that I envied. Even the constant demonstrations became routine to her after the first few weeks, and she would read a Peanuts book or paint, undisturbed by the clamour outside. At the same time the novelty of being an object of curiosity to the Chinese wore off.

One afternoon in Tientsin, where foreigners are rarely seen, the three of us had to wait on the street for about half an hour for our translator, who had gone into a nearby building to ask for directions to a garage (our car was almost out of gas). Before five minutes had passed, we were surrounded by about seventy-five Chinese of all ages, gaping and pressing ever closer. It was very hot and uncomfortable, and the smell of perspiration and garlic was becoming overpowering. Regina and I tried sign language, but the ones in front kept edging nearer as people at the back began pushing to get a look at us. Finally, Katharine took matters in hand.

"I'll get us some air," she announced, and worked her way through the crowd. Suddenly the Chinese moved away from us, and I was able to see her. She was walking along the middle of the street, followed by the curious Chinese. She went as far as the end of the block, then turned and came back with the crowd still trailing behind her. She was very pleased with herself that day.

School occupied much of Katharine's time in Peking. Officials at the French Embassy kindly allowed her to enroll in the school for their children. Actually, there wouldn't have been much for the teacher to do if the school had not taken in outside students. There were only two French students, so the rest of the twenty-student class was composed of children from a variety of nations. It was very much like a one-room country school, with the students ranging in age from five to twelve.

The school was located on the upper floor of a large two-storey red brick building that had once been the Norwegian Embassy. An armed policeman stood guard at the gate, and next door was a one-storey primary school for Chinese. Sometimes when I would arrive early to pick up Katharine (her school was downtown) I would stand on the street and listen to the children in both schools singing lustily. It made a strange contrast—on the one side, "Sur le Pont d'Avignon"; on the other side, "Socialism is Good."

Officially, Katharine's school was the French Cultural

Center. It was set up by the French shortly after France and China established diplomatic relations in 1964. In line with President Charles de Gaulle's conviction of the superiority of all things French, it was supposed to bring a touch of French culture to the Chinese. Thus there was a large library, which included all the latest French periodicals as well as recordings by French artists. And there was also a French language teacher who had new audiovisual teaching equipment at her disposal. Alas, General de Gaulle's little sortie into cultural imperialism was unsuccessful, at least during the time I was in Peking. Neither the teacher nor the librarian had one Chinese customer. They were kept fairly busy, however, by members of the foreign community who particularly liked the popular records which were ideal for dance parties.

I admired the patience and understanding of the children's teacher, Jean Sanyas. He not only had to cope with different educational levels, but also had to contend with the fact that more than half of the children began school unable to speak French. He confidently predicted that within a month they would all be speaking French fluently. He was right; but I never quite accepted as ordinary the sight of children from Mali, Guinea, Bulgaria, France, Canada, Japan, Algeria, the Congo and Cambodia happily chattering in French while they played tag in the school's backyard.

Still, it was no more disconcerting than the "parents' night" I attended at the Indian Embassy school. I sat in the audience of doting mothers and fathers, most of them armed with cameras, and watched the students go through their carefully rehearsed program. I suspect I was the only person who thought there was anything unusual about Tanzanian and Yugoslavian girls in saris doing a traditional Indian folk dance with Rumanian and Zambian boys in jodhpurs, all to the sound of a record of exotic Indian music, of course.

[31]

English was the language of instruction in the Indian school, which was located in the Indian Embassy chancery. It was a makeshift affair, since the Indians had no budget for a school and no qualified teachers. Lessons were given by the wives of Indian diplomats and also by other foreigners who volunteered. Despite the inadequacies of the school, the Indians at least tried. The Pakistanis, who had more children than any other embassy, had no school of any kind during the time I was in Peking; and, of course, they would not send their children to the Indian school.

To my surprise, Katharine showed no sign of missing the joys of Western civilization: television, movies, and Coca-Cola. (I must admit though that on each of our trips to Hong Kong the first order of business was to have a hamburger with the works at the Hilton.) The truth is that in many ways she led a more regular family life in Peking than she did in Toronto.

For one thing, the three of us were always together in Peking, but in Toronto I was rarely able to have dinner with Katharine and Regina because of the peculiar hours of a morning newspaper. We shopped together, went on walks in the Western Hills just outside Peking, ice-skated on the Summer Palace lake, picnicked at the Ming Tombs. Every weekend there was a family outing. There was even a school car pool, with the Yugoslavian First Secretary, a Japanese trade official and I, taking turns driving our children to the French school every day.

Katharine also managed to have a few pets. In the spring we bought cicadas imprisoned in tiny bamboo cages. They were sold on the streets by peasants who had bicycled into the city from the communes during the night—probably the last free enterprisers in China. Goldfish were labelled bourgeois by the Red Guards during the early stages of the Cultural Revolution, and there were none for sale in Peking. Canton, however, had escaped this silly ban and had several goldfish shops. I bought two for Katharine and took them with me by plane all the way from Canton to Peking (1,200 miles) in a water-filled plastic bag.

Family life in Peking could be remarkably humdrum, and, for some people, exceedingly boring. Because of the virtual isolation in which we all lived, where there was nothing to distract us from ourselves, there were only major personal problems. Men who occasionally drank too much in their own countries became near-alcoholics in China; high-strung women ended up as neurotics; husbands who had previously only glanced sideways at other women became galloping libertines. It was hardly surprising that a number of marriages either broke up or barely survived the pressures of Peking.

Embassies tried to relieve the tedium by organizing sports, but few of the diplomats were interested in volleyball or tennis. The British, French and Russians invited everyone to a movie once a month, but the films usually were old and the only persons who attended with any enthusiasm were the Africans and Asians. (When I felt depressed I would go to a Russian film. Most of them weren't very good, but the Russian translator was what attracted me. He not only translated the dialogue into English, but felt impelled to tell you what was going on: "Now he holds her to his breast and he is saying with tender voice that he is loving her.")

On one occasion the French Embassy organized a car rally, offering a case of champagne as first prize. Of course nearly everyone who had a car entered, and there was great excitement. To make the rally challenging, the French had the course follow a route into parts of the suburbs which foreigners almost never visited. All went well with the contestants,

[33]

and everybody had a good time at the party at the French Embassy after the rally. Only one group was unhappy: the Chinese police department.

At every busy intersection a Chinese policeman sits in a little yellow kiosk where he controls the traffic lights. He also has a telephone, and calls ahead to the next kiosk if a foreigner's car passes him and seems headed toward the outskirts of the city where travel is not permitted. By the end of the rally, with thirty-two cars zooming up to and around the forbidden zone, the policemen were completely frazzled. And angry. They complained to the Foreign Ministry which in turn informed the French Embassy that Peking's first foreign car rally was also its last.

Inevitably, foreigners fell back on prosaic forms of entertainment: cocktail parties and dinner parties. Here is one writer's description of a dinner party in Peking:

Perhaps the conversation was less varied than the (dinner) course, for guests and hosts had seen one another nearly every day for an intolerable number of years and each topic that arose was seized upon desperately only to be exhausted and followed by a formidable silence. . . . They wore their evening clothes a little uneasily as though they wore them from a sense of duty to their country rather than as a comfortable change from day dress. They had come to the party because they had nothing else in the world to do, but when the moment came that they could decently take their leave they would go with a sigh of relief. They were bored to death with one another.

The description was written by Somerset Maugham in 1922; it would be just as accurate today. Most of the dinner parties were deadly dull, and I sympathized with the rather fat Mauritanian lady who after dinner would settle into a comfortable chair, wrap her voluminous robes around herself and gently snore while coffee and liqueurs were served.

[34]

The grandest table and the worst food were offered by the Egyptian Ambassador; his Chinese cook must have hated him. But the appointments were a thing of beauty: thick silver candelabra, dishes and crystal encrusted with gold, heavy gold-plated silver cutlery. All of these things had come from the palace of King Farouk.

The gayest dinners were given by the Finnish, Norwegian and Danish Ambassadors, all of whom were happily invested with an infectious sense of good humour. Formal dinners given by the East Europeans were remarkable for long silences and heavy sighs, as well as for the host's earnest speech which always began, "Dear comrades and friends . . ."

National Day receptions were more tolerable, partly because they were usually cocktail parties and one could ride a conversational bicycle around the room, and partly because there was the chance one of the Chinese leaders might attend. Invitations to the receptions of countries very friendly with China were always in demand, particularly among the ladies, because the handsome and debonair Premier Chou En-lai usually made a point of attending. It must have been humiliating to the Russian Ambassador that Chou En-lai would arrive punctually at the reception given by the tiny Tanzanian Embassy (even the chauffeur was in the official receiving line), but would not attend the Soviet Embassy's National Day party.

I made a point of always attending the Hungarian National Day reception because of my liking for spiced sausages, which weren't available anywhere else in Peking. Before the rise of the Communist party, the Hungarian Ambassador had once been a butcher; before his National Day he worked for several weeks in the Embassy basement preparing the many pounds of various sausages that would be served. As a diplomat, he was a great sausage-maker.

[35]

Alas, the topics of conversation were the same at both the receptions and the dinners: Chinese politics, which bored the women; and shopping, which bored the men.

There were ten stores set aside for foreigners in Peking. The two embassy districts in the east of the city, San Li Tun and Wychiadallo, each had a small shop that sold mostly tinned and baked goods. The Chinese who worked in these stores were unusually tough characters who never smiled at customers and spent much of their time trying to surpass each other in rudeness. They were forever putting up posters saying DOWN WITH REVISIONIST DOGS; and during political campaigns, one had to be agile to catch purchases and change they would fling across the counter.

Five other stores for foreigners were in Peking's downtown shopping area. These sold meats and vegetables, furs, tailored clothes and manufactured goods, jewellery and newly made "art" objects, and antiques. Lui Li Chang, a small street in the southwestern part of the city, had three shops. One sold temple rubbings and copies of burial figures, another had a large collection of old scrolls and fans (before the Cultural Revolution there were six scroll shops alone) and the third had a large collection of antique porcelain, snuff bottles and cloisonné. Before the Cultural Revolution diplomats were able to pick up many bargains, including scrolls and antiques that now are unavailable or cannot be taken out of the country. The Swedish Ambassador, Lennart Petrie, accumulated a beautiful collection of scrolls by famous old painters during his eight years in Peking. When he was re-posted in 1969, most of his collection was put to one side by the Chinese packers who were under orders to reject any item that did not bear the official red wax seal indicating it could be exported. As was customary, a Chinese art expert examined all the unmarked pieces to determine which had to remain in China. He deemed many of the items to be too valuable to leave the country. Petrie, faced with the prospect of bequeathing his collection to his successor or trying to find a diplomat who would buy unexportable goods, made a direct appeal to the Foreign Ministry. After a suspenseful wait of several days, he was told he could take the collection with him because of the "friendly relations between China and Sweden." He was the only diplomat I knew who was given this privilege.

Prices of antiques, none older than early Ching (the Ching dynasty was 1644–1911), were quite high when I was in Peking. But shortly after I left, Washington announced it had lifted its ban on the import of Chinese antiques. Almost immediately, the antique shops in Peking were closed for three days. When they reopened, many of the better pieces had vanished and the price of every item on the shelves had been exactly tripled. The wails of the foreign community could be heard throughout Peking.

The missing pieces had been taken to the Communist shops in Hong Kong, of course, where they would await wealthy American tourists. This was especially frustrating to the diplomats, who knew that on the outskirts of Peking were several warehouses filled with exquisite pieces which they were not allowed to see or buy; and these too were destined for Hong Kong.

In all of Peking there was only one place where price standardization did not apply: the secondhand stores. Like every enterprise in China, they were state-owned but they operated on the principle of charging the seller a commission if they were able to sell the item he brought in; thus foreigners called them commission shops. They were nondescript, usually only one room filled with all sorts of used things: old clothing, ice-skates, tablecloths, bits of furniture, watches and clocks, carpets, pens, radios, shoes, vases, musical instruments. In the winter, some of the stores were heated by a single potbellied coal stove; others were not heated at all and the clerks were bundled in cotton padded jackets and hats. All the shops were in old buildings, and you had to remember to step over the five-inch ledge at the bottom of the doorway; it was probably put there to prevent sand from being blown in by Peking's gale-like winds, though a Chinese told me that in the old days superstitious people believed the ledge barred tiny evil spirits from entering the building. Nowadays, the ledges trip up many an imperialist or revisionist foreigner.

Some of the shops had dirt floors, and newcomers to China were usually startled when they first saw a clerk go about his cleaning chores with a broom and a cup of water. He would take a mouthful of water, spray it in all directions through pursed lips, and then vigorously sweep; the water kept the dust down. This didn't stop the foreigners from haunting these shops and constantly looking for new ones. To discover a commission shop that no other foreigner knew about was something like finding a crown jewel, and the location was kept as guarded as a state secret. For it was in these shops that the foreigners hoped to find a bargain antique or curio.

Sometimes they succeeded. One woman bought a white fur stole for $10, took it back to her own country and discovered to her delight that it was ermine and valued at $4,000. Mihailo Saranovic, the tall, good-humoured Yugoslavian correspondent, one day showed me a two-foot-high vase he had just bought for two yuan in a commission shop. I told him it wasn't worth even one yuan (forty cents). He laughed and said he would sell it to me at that price and tossed it across the room to me. I caught it, told him I wouldn't take it even as a gift, and threw it back to him. He put it on the floor, and cheerfully said he'd give it to a relative he didn't like. Later, when he was about to return to

[38]

Belgrade and was packing his things, a Chinese art expert pronounced the vase Ming and informed him that it could not be taken out of China. I suppose it was worth $5,000.

Other less valuable but interesting items turned up in the commission shops. Once I came across a complete but somewhat battered set of knives and forks, all bearing the imprint: United States Navy. A friend of mine bought a small brass vase and later found on it the inscription: Presented by the Hungarian Women's Federation. He solemnly presented it to the Hungarian correspondent.

The vase, like many other things, had been placed in the commission shop by the Chinese Government. This was one of the ways the government could make a profit on "bourgeois" belongings confiscated from Chinese citizens before and during the Cultural Revolution, as well as on those gifts presented to Chinese officials by other governments. Many of these things were placed in the shops expressly so that foreigners would buy them, since they were clearly beyond the ideological and financial reach of the ordinary Chinese. What Chinese, for instance, would be brave enough or wealthy enough to buy a Sonnet Frères carriage clock at $100? The price was equal to two or three months' wages; anyhow, it would probably be seized from him as soon as he got it home.

When a Swiss trade fair opened in Peking, its officials told their Chinese hosts that they had brought three gold and silver watches to present to Mao Tse-tung, Lin Piao and Chou En-lai. They apparently thought they would get to meet the country's leaders, but the Chinese officials smilingly thanked them and said *they* would make sure the watches arrived at the correct destination. They did. A few days after the Swiss left town, three gold and silver Rolex watches showed up in a commission shop.

The Chinese proclivity for turning gifts into cash resulted

in one minor diplomatic flurry. An Arab ambassador on the hunt for bargains in a commission shop was startled to find on sale a silver tea service set bearing his country's crest. He indignantly complained to the Foreign Ministry, where red-faced officials profusely apologized. The set vanished from the shop that same day.

Shopping could not keep one busy forever, though some foreigners almost achieved that goal, and a dreary lassitude permeated much of the foreign community. Most of the diplomats were fed up with China. In ordinary circumstances they would have been re-posted, but they were ordered to stay months and even years beyond their usual term because their foreign ministries were reluctant to send inexperienced men while the Cultural Revolution was still going on. Not until 1969, when it became clear that stability had returned to China, were the old China hands allowed to leave.

Some of them gave up long before that point arrived. The two-man Laotian Embassy, for instance, was virtually immobile. Its *chef de mission* was noted for his tennis game, at which he practiced all day during the spring, summer and fall; and also for his parties, when he would lock the doors to keep his guests from leaving too early, and they could escape only by climbing out of the ground-floor windows. His habit of ignoring cables from home was well known, and his Foreign Ministry once had to ask the Indian Embassy to locate him. The Laotian First Secretary was a gentle little man with a puckish sense of humour. I especially admired his feat of putting a live fish in the Russian Ambassador's private swimming pool; it took a team of Russian swimmers the better part of a day to catch the fish and eject it from the sanctified waters.

Strangely, the Chinese determination to take care of the physical comforts of the foreigners didn't help matters, since it gave them less to complain about and also left them with time on their hands. The wages of domestic help were incredibly low, by Western standards. A wash amah or baby amah could be hired for about $30 a month, a cook or driver for about $60 a month. Thus a young foreign diplomat in Peking could afford a servant and a handsome apartment with a large living room, one bedroom and kitchen for about $120 a month. East Europeans candidly admitted they lived in far greater comfort in Peking than they did at home.

Food was not a problem. There was always a good supply of vegetables and meat, and not just for foreigners. I often strolled through the Chinese markets in Peking and never noticed a shortage of food (this was also true in other cities I visited). The only rationed foods were vegetable oil (about half a pound a month per person) and rice and wheat (factory workers get about forty pounds a month, office workers twenty). Fruit was plentiful during the harvest season, and it was even possible to buy apples in Peking during the dead of winter. Foreigners who had lived in both Peking and Moscow said that the availability of food was far greater in Peking.

Buying meat could be a problem for foreigners. One of the formative forces in the development of Chinese cuisine has been the need for frugality. Most Chinese dishes are cooked very quickly, often no more than seared over a very hot flame. One or two hotly burning coals are sufficient for the job. But this also means that meats must be very thinly sliced. And, of course, if meats are very thinly sliced it doesn't usually make much difference which part of the animal they come from—again a very practical device since a poor Chinese was lucky to get any meat at all, never mind choosing a particular cut.

Even today a butcher in Peking tends to work from one end of a carcass to the other, treating it much like a loaf of bread. There are no individual cuts such as chops or ribs or

[41]

roasts or steaks. Even the smallest bones are carefully stripped of meat. I often used to watch a particularly adept butcher in the People's Market who in seconds could scrape a bone to the whiteness of a desert relic.

The Chinese do not particularly like milk, butter and cheese, but all three were available to foreigners—shipped directly from an army-run dairy farm north of Peking that had been started from a herd of Holsteins bought from Holland some years ago. Milk, unhomogenized and in half-pint bottles, was delivered daily to our apartment building by pedicart. Potatoes were also not too common in Peking. The northern Chinese prefer rice, which comes in a variety of grades, but their special favourite is noodles. Marco Polo liked Peking's noodles so much that he took the recipe home to Italy and thereby founded a nation of pasta-eaters. During winter foreigners were even able to buy tomatoes and lettuce, grown in probably the only commune in China with hothouses. It was located just beyond the western outskirts of the city and, appropriately, was called Evergreen Commune.

The Chinese also produce carbonated soft drinks—cherry, orange, banana, apple and plain soda water. Katharine preferred the apple flavour. I admit a liking for Chinese beer which I found excellent, and, like most things in China, inexpensive (ten cents a quart). It is produced in breweries built by Germans and Czechs, in some cases before the Communists came to power. A variety of wines, mostly sweet, and liquors are sold in China. The most famous is Mowtai, a fiery clear liquid distilled from rice and aged in stone bottles. It is forced on unwary foreigners when they are guests of the Chinese. The Chinese also make an adequate champagne and, naturally, Scotch. It is unbelievable.

Scotch is the stream in which all diplomats swim. It was the one vital ingredient for a successful party in Peking, which placed journalists and East Europeans at a handicap.

Scotch was available in Hong Kong and Western diplomats had cases of it sent in duty-free. The East Europeans could do the same—if they had dollars. But they were paid in their own currency, and although the Chinese gave them a preferential rate of exchange (a leftover from the days of Communist solidarity), it was no substitute for dollars. Some of the Arab and Asian diplomats made a lucrative business out of their dollar accounts in Hong Kong. One Arab sold Scotch at the equivalent of $7 a bottle in Chinese money, making his profit $5 a bottle. Others dealt in records, radios, tape recorders, cameras and record players—all imported in the diplomatic bag from duty-free Hong Kong. One diplomat unloaded two cars (both Mercedes-Benz) on East European diplomats at a great profit while I was in Peking. He was doing so well at his sideline that I suspected the CD on his license plate stood for Car Dealer instead of Corps Diplomatique.

Non-diplomats like me were allowed to import as much as we wanted when we first entered China since we were, in effect, transferring our place of residence. Thereafter, we had to pay very high duty on imported goods, with the exception of two hundred cigarets and one bottle of liquor each time we reentered China. Fortunately, the Chinese never specified the size of the bottle, so Regina and I would each bring in a two-quart bottle of Scotch after every trip to Hong Kong. Regina would also bring in for her friends some small items that were not available in Peking—stockings, cosmetics, Tampax, and birth control pills (the latter began to appear in Peking stores in early 1970, but condoms could always be purchased at about one cent each).

Some of the requests I received went beyond the necessities of life. I still have the list presented to me by an East European correspondent who asked if I could buy a "couple" of items for him in Hong Kong. The list included, among

[43]

other things, two slide projectors, three cigaret lighters, one camera, one telephoto lens and fifteen records. The total bill was slightly more than $1,000 (U.S.). He said that his diplomatic friends in an Asian consulate in Hong Kong would ship the stuff up from Hong Kong (duty-free), but they weren't willing to accept his credit, nor was he willing to pay them in advance. For that matter, he didn't even suggest he would pay me in advance.

I brought back one book for him, and said the other things were "out of stock" (his list included the discount price of each item).

Aside from the fact that I had no intention of breaking the Chinese laws in order to set him up in business, there was the complicated problem of being saddled with a huge amount of Chinese money.

It is illegal to take Chinese currency in or out of the country; it must be exchanged for Hong Kong dollars at the border. Peking, however, guards its hard currency very carefully. A foreigner leaving China is not allowed to exchange his Chinese money for more Hong Kong dollars than he had when he first entered the country. This is all officially noted on a Foreign Currency Declaration form which he must fill out when he comes into China.

If he has too much Chinese money—that is, if by exchanging it he would have more hard currency than he came into the country with—then it has to be left in a sealed envelope at the border to be picked up when he next returns to China, if he ever does. And without the Foreign Currency Declaration form, he can exchange no Chinese money at all. This happened to me once on the way to Hong Kong. I had left the official form in Peking, but after much pleading, the Chinese finally agreed to let me exchange enough money for the train ticket to Hong Kong.

The border officials also forbid anyone to bring Chinese

money into the country. One correspondent forgot about a five-yuan bill (worth about two dollars) which he had tucked in his jacket breast pocket. He crossed the border and spent a week in Hong Kong, where he had his suit cleaned. When he crossed the border back into China, the customs men searched his suitcase and found the cleaned and pressed five-yuan bill in his jacket pocket. It took two hours of explanations, lectures and warnings before the Chinese let him go on his way—still apparently unconvinced that he hadn't been trying to smuggle money into China.

One of the most important items (after whisky) to bring back from Hong Kong was Black Flag roach bomb. All the foreigners' apartments were infested with cockroaches, some of them grand-daddies two inches long. But they hadn't developed a tolerance for the imperialist Black Flag spray. Nothing else had much effect on them except, of course, force.

Regina had her first experience with cockroaches on her third day in Peking, after a pleasant dinner with the British Second Secretary, Leonard Appleyard, and his wife, Elizabeth. We were sitting in their living room drinking coffee when he slowly took off one shoe, raised it on high, and carefully advanced toward Regina. Her mouth fell open as he pounced, hammering the floor with his shoe. It was a cockroach.

"Ha!" he gloated. "Got him!"

The Chinese, of course, claimed there were no cockroaches in Peking. One day I came upon a Japanese businessman in the Hsin Chiao Hotel neatly pinning six dead cockroaches in a row on his door. As we stood there admiring his handiwork, he explained that he had been having a running feud with the Chinese staff who denied the hotel had cockroaches. I saw him again a few days later, and he told me that when he confronted the staff with the pinned specimens it was suggested that he must have brought them from Tokyo in his luggage.

The Chinese habit of treating foreigners' complaints lightly did not extend to medical care. Foreigners received as good or better medical attention than they got in their own countries. They were pushed ahead of Chinese who were probably sicker, and were given private rooms despite the shortage of space in hospitals. They were also treated by the best doctors, usually European-trained, and efforts were even made to provide "Western-style" food. A number of diplomats I knew were treated for minor ailments and had nothing but praise for the Chinese. A few of the foreign women had babies in Peking, and some even had abortions (which are legal in China). The only reservation I ever had about Chinese medical care was that it perhaps had not quite kept pace with the newer techniques developed in the West, particularly in the area of equipment.

The one real drawback to being sick in China was that you had to go to the hospital for treatment. Mind you, I am speaking as a Canadian who enjoys the luxury of having a doctor who will make house calls; I realize that in most countries, and in many parts of Canada, it is necessary to get yourself to a clinic or hospital. In Peking there were three hospitals for foreigners (they were also used by the Chinese). One, located in the western part of the city, was simply called Children's Hospital. I did not visit it because Katharine was never ill. But my predecessor, David Oancia, reported that his son received excellent care there when he had a mild attack of influenza. East Europeans used the Anti-Revisionist Hospital, the name of which they did not find amusing.

The third hospital, used by non-Communist foreigners, was located at the end of a small lane beside the Peking Academy of Art, just off the main downtown shopping street, Wang Fu Ching. It was built by the Rockefeller Foundation

[46]

before 1949 and, ironically, is now called the Anti-Imperialist Hospital. It is a curious blend of occidental and oriental architecture, looking very much like an old grey brick hospital in any American city except for the roof with its alternately concave and convex green glazed tiles and overhanging eaves. Wide banks of steps lead to the entrance, and just inside is a brick screen which by tradition is supposed to protect the building from evil spirits; in fact it effectively shields the interior from curious passers-by. In the hospital the screen was quite small, being purely ornamental, and was draped in red cloth and used as a pedestal for a large white bust of Mao Tse-tung.

In warm weather patients clad in pyjamas and bathrobes sat or milled about on the front steps chatting with friends and relatives or simply enjoying the sunshine. Inside, it was depressing to a foreigner who is used to the whiteness of his own hospital. Corridor walls are painted a dull beige, and the low wattage electric bulbs do little to lighten the gloom. Both nurses and doctors wear faded blue or tan cotton trousers and greyish medical gowns that seem in need of a good washing. Actually, the gowns are clean, but the Chinese do not use bleach. Posters of Mao and his quotations are pasted on the walls. There are also a number of pictures of Norman Bethune, the Canadian doctor who died of blood poisoning in 1939 while working for the Chinese Communists during the revolution. He was made famous in China by Mao Tse-tung's essay, "Serve the People," which is memorized and recited by almost every Chinese child. Aside from Marx, Engels, Lenin and Stalin, Norman Bethune is the most famous foreigner in China. Chinese Communists who visit Canada are astonished that most Canadians have never heard of him.

Because the hospital serves as an outpatient clinic, it has various large rooms where minor ailments are treated. The

[47]

eye clinic, for instance, consists of one very big room with twelve dentist-type chairs and an appropriate number of attending doctors. Patients wait their turn in the corridor, sitting on long wooden benches. The hospital also has a dental clinic, which works along similar lines. I had a tooth extracted there by a female dentist. She was about forty years old and very efficient. The drilling machinery was obviously old, but pretty much the same as my own dentist's equipment; and the procedure was certainly the same. A sorrowful shake of the head to indicate the tooth could not be saved, a frozen gum, a tooth pulled out. The main difference was that I had to pretend to be brave, or else be put to shame by the seven-year-old Chinese girl in the next chair who didn't murmur once as her tooth was being drilled. My bill was $1.20.

There seemed to be very few ambulances in Peking; I only saw three or four during the year and a half I was there. In late 1968 there was a serious train wreck in which a number of persons were killed or injured. The accident was not mentioned in the Chinese press and the Chinese officials refused to admit that it happened. About a month after the event though, I discovered from various sources that "probably" more than thirty people had died and that the Peking authorities had commandeered the forty or fifty taxis in the city of seven million to help the few ambulances bring the injured to hospitals.

In ordinary circumstances, though, people had to get to the hospital on their own, even if they were too sick to walk. It was common to see a Chinese being cycled to hospital wrapped in a cotton quilt and lying on the back of a rented pedicart with members of the family perched beside him. He would leave the hospital the same way, alive or dead. My saddest memory of Peking was the afternoon I saw a pedicart go by carrying a plain wooden coffin. Sitting on the edge of the cart, his thin bare legs dangling, was a little boy about twelve years old. His face was squeezed by anguish and his shoulders heaved with dry sobs. Was the body that lay beside him his mother, his father? I don't know, but on that day he was the loneliest child in China.

In Peking the dead are cremated. Afterwards, there is a sort of memorial service at which eulogies are spoken. Since the Cultural Revolution there have been no religious ceremonies connected with a death, though I would be surprised if they are not still performed in small villages in the countryside. A young cadre told me that when he was going to school in Peking a few years ago, he and other students were awakened in the middle of the night by a noise outside. Looking out of the window, they saw a traditional Chinese funeral procession passing on the street below with professional mourners dressed in white robes (the Chinese colour for mourning), wailing and beating their breasts as they followed the cortege. The cadre, who was slightly embarrassed at telling me the story, said he had never seen such a thing before or since.

There were a number of foreigners who died in China while I was there, usually sailors aboard ships docked near Shanghai or Tientsin. The Chinese would cremate the body and place the ashes in a handsome lacquered box which was presented with due ceremony to a diplomat from the embassy of the sailor's country. A courier would then take the ashes to Hong Kong to be forwarded to the dead man's relatives, or simply send them by air express out of Peking.

Two foreigners connected with the diplomatic corps died while I was in Peking; neither was cremated.

One was a young Soviet Embassy guard, a victim of encephalitis. There was a small furore over what was to be done with his body. The Russians wanted to fly it home to Moscow by Aeroflot. The Chinese health authorities said this

[49]

was impossible, that the Embassy must turn the body over to them for cremation. The Russians refused. The Chinese insisted. Finally, after two days of stubborn Russian resistance, the Chinese gave in.

The second case involved a Pakistani and it proved, as in George Orwell's *Animal Farm,* that while everyone is equal in China, some are more equal than others. The man who died was the Pakistani Ambassador's father-in-law. He was an old man who had been ill even before he made the long trip to Peking to visit his daughter. A Chinese doctor visited him almost daily at the Ambassador's residence—a concession in itself—but in the end his weakened heart failed. The Foreign Ministry very quickly made a plane available to fly the body to Canton where it was transferred to a Pakistan International Airlines plane.

The Pakistanis received other concessions. During the Cultural Revolution all the churches, temples and mosques in Peking were closed. Some, such as the Lama temple called the Palace of Eternal Harmony in the northeast section of the city, were left untouched, but most of the churches were converted into schools or warehouses. However, the Pakistani Ambassador at that time, Mohammed Ali Khan (who later became his country's Foreign Secretary and then Ambassador to Washington), requested that the Dong si Mosque, built more than four hundred years ago, be reopened for Muslim diplomats. The Foreign Ministry agreed. Until early 1972, when one Roman Catholic church was reopened, the Mosque was the only building in Peking—and probably in all of China—where regular religious services were conducted.

Among the Christian diplomats, a few of the French Catholics met informally every Sunday morning to pray together and read the Bible. No other religious observances were made except at Christmas, when a short nondenominational service was held at the British mission and mass was celebrated at the French Embassy by a French priest from Cambodia. He entered China on a one-week visitor's visa, which was granted by the Chinese without question or comment though they, of course, knew who he was and why he had applied. After midnight mass on Christmas Eve, the French Ambassador led all the faithful to his residence for hors d'oeuvres and chilled French champagne.

Christmas, incidentally, was a day very much like any other for the Chinese. It was not a holiday, nor was there any outward sign that the season of goodwill had arrived. Only the small flower shop near the diplomatic quarter got into the spirit of Christmas, albeit commercially. It laid in a stock of about twenty small potted pine trees. These were snapped up by foreigners despite the exceedingly high price (especially by Chinese standards) of fifteen dollars each. We bought one, and made our own decorations from coloured advertisements in old magazines. Regina had remembered to pack the same old red felt stockings we had used every Christmas since Katharine was born; and on Christmas Eve we hung these up on the living room radiator and played carols on the record player. Later that night, after Katharine had gone to bed, we heard the sound of carols in the cold still air outside. A group of young clerks and secretaries from the British Office was making the rounds of the foreigners' buildings. We went out on the balcony to watch and listen and saw that Chinese families in adjacent buildings were doing the same thing.

Katharine, I should add, had already had a chat with Santa Claus. The French held a Christmas party in the school for the students and their parents. It was a jolly affair with soft drinks, ice cream and cake for the children, and Scotch and champagne for the adults. The children sang songs for us and, of course, Santa Claus (an embassy cipher clerk) appeared with a big bag of gifts. The presents had been bought in Hong Kong, and obviously with care. Katharine, for instance, received a Scrabble set (in English). The only other Christmas party for children was given by those notorious nonbelievers, the Russians. It was officially called a Winter Vacation party, and all the diplomats' children were welcome. There was no Santa Claus passing around gifts, but there was a cartoon film show and enough candies, chocolates, cookies and ice cream to keep the children sick for a couple of weeks.

One last note about Christmas. Although it passed unobserved by the Chinese, so also did Mao Tse-tung's birthday, which is on December 26. No mention was ever made of it in the press. And it still is true that no city, building, bridge or even street has been named for Mao Tse-tung.

The holiday season was a brief diversion in the long winter, surely the worst time of year in Peking. It was very cold and dry, so dry that foreigners shook hands gingerly because of the inevitable strong electric shock. The same dryness meant there was almost never any snow to relieve the city's greyness. Even the people seemed drab, swaddled in blue and brown quilted and hooded coats, men indistinguishable from women because of the white gauze face masks they wore.

It was possible to go ice-skating on the lakes at the Summer Palace and at Pei Hai Park, near the old Forbidden City, but even that pleasure was short-lived; the strong dust-laden winds soon deposited a film of grit on the ice surface. A few of the hardier foreigners braved the cold weather to go on walking tours, but most resigned themselves to Peking's main social activity: the usual round of cocktail parties and dinners where one would hear the same stories from the same people. Even the Chinese waiters were the same. They were hired through the Diplomatic Service Bureau, and went on

[52]

the same cocktail-dinner party circuits as the foreigners. All of them understood English and, presumably, they noted anything interesting they overheard and reported it to their superiors. Nonetheless, they were a joy to have around because they knew their business. They would arrive half an hour before the party, check the supply of alcohol and glasses, don their little white jackets and big red Mao Tse-tung badges, and take over. Their number (one waiter per ten guests) and their fee (about four dollars each) was decided by the Service Bureau, which also ensured employment for them by forbidding amahs to serve food or drink.

The most enjoyable thing one could do during the winter in Peking was leave it. *The Globe and Mail* generously allowed the Peking correspondent and his family to spend two weeks (expenses paid) in Hong Kong every three months. These brief interludes, especially during the winter, enabled us to maintain a sense of perspective during our long stay in China.

The fourteen-day breaks meant in fact that one could spend exactly ten days in Hong Kong, since the trip there took at least two days each way. This was because there were no direct flights to Hong Kong, and it was necessary to stay overnight in Canton on the way in or out of China.

There were three flights a week from Peking to Canton by "big airplane." The nonstop trip took about four hours and fifteen minutes in either a Vickers Viscount or a Russian Ilyushin 18 (the Chinese bought Tridents from Pakistan International Airlines in 1970); most foreigners tried to avoid the Russian planes because they were noisy and often had air pressure problems. The "small airplane," an Ilyushin 14, would take up to twelve hours to make the same Canton-to-Peking trip depending on weather conditions, stopping down at Chenghsien, Wuhan, and Changsha. The Chinese were very careful with their aircraft and thought nothing of delaying a flight by two or three hours—or even cancelling it altogether—if weather conditions were not considered ideal.

Once, on a flight from Peking to Nanking by "small airplane," we stayed overnight in Tsinan (about 240 miles from Peking) because of bad weather. I was the only passenger on the plane—all but six chairs had been taken out and the space filled with cargo—but there were lots of other people aboard: a stewardess, two pilots and three young men who apparently were trainees since they crowded into the cockpit with the pilots. The stewardess had a busy time. There was quite a bit of air turbulence, and almost from the time the plane left the ground she was running back and forth to the cockpit carrying air-sick bags, presumably for the trainees. I'm still not sure whether the pilots set the plane down in Tsinan because of the foul air outside or the foul air inside.

Stewardesses on Chinese planes were about as glamorous as a bowl of steamed rice. They wore no makeup and their hair was either cropped short or worn in two braids tied at the ends with elastic bands. They had a uniform of sorts: a simple white short-sleeved cotton blouse, and dark grey cotton jacket and trousers that were, inevitably, baggy. They were a far cry from being Coffee, Tea or Me girls. They did, in fact, serve tea and orange soft drinks, but there was little real work for them to do although the planes usually were filled to capacity with cadres and military officers. At the start of the trip, they would pass out candies, chewing gum, Mao Tse-tung badges, small packages of five cigarets and, if the weather was warm, straw fans (which were taken back at the end of the flight); usually the only food served was an apple and a handful of unsalted peanuts.

The main occupation of the stewardesses seemed to be to keep the passengers entertained—in a truly proletarian way,

[54]

of course. They would stand at the front of the plane, microphones in hand, and lead all the passengers in a revolutionary sing-song. Occasionally one of the girls would sing a solo while the other did a revolutionary dance up and down the aisle. Most of the stewardesses spoke only Chinese, but if there were Russians aboard it was almost a certainty that an anti-Soviet song would be sung—in Russian. Sometimes the stewardesses would come up with a new song for the passengers to learn. A long piece of brown wrapping paper bearing the words and music of the new song would be taped to the doorway at the front of the plane, and the girls would sing each line ten or twelve times with the passengers. When everybody was finally able to struggle through the whole song without a mistake, there would be applause all round—especially from the foreign passengers who had to sit through the ordeal. All the Chinese enjoyed the sing-along sessions enormously, and quite often army officers would take over the microphone to sing a solo. From a foreigner's point of view, the best thing that could be said about the noisy concerts was that they at least helped to pass the time: there was nothing else to do but read old articles from the airplane's supply of *People's Daily,* or selections of Mao Tse-tung's works. By mid-1970, though, the fervour of the Cultural Revolution had almost disappeared—even from China Aviation Administration Corporation whose employees were considered by foreigners to be among the most militant in the country—and the "singing stewardesses" were no longer part of the Peking-Canton service.

By then, there were other changes in the lives of foreigners, caused not by the end of the Cultural Revolution but by the military preparations being made by the Chinese in case of war with the Soviet Union. In early 1970, just after we had left China, foreigners were informed that trips to the Western Hills, the Ming Tombs and the Great Wall were

[55]

no longer permitted. The effect of this blow to the morale of foreigners cannot be exaggerated; car trips to these places were almost the only diversion foreigners had at the week-end during the spring, summer and fall.

The Western Hills, or more properly, the Fragrant Hills, is a large wooded area just outside Peking that includes a few pagodas and temples, including the Temple of the Azure Clouds. The trip to the Great Wall, about forty-five miles from Peking, could be made by car on a well-paved road that passed through some small villages and the beautiful and historic Nan Kou Pass, with its steep rocky mountains and hairpin turns. Great caravans from Mongolia used the pass on the way to Peking more than a thousand years ago, and some of the villagers in the area still had camels in the early 1960's. Many foreigners, including me, liked to picnic along the way, stopping at the side of the road near a magnificent stone gateway called the Tower Which Bestrides the Road. It dates from the Mongol period (1345) and is covered with bas-relief carvings of celestial guardians and the Buddha.

But the favourite picnic spot of foreigners was the Ming Tombs, about thirty miles from Peking and just off the same road that went to the Great Wall. Thirteen of the sixteen emperors of the Ming dynasty (1368–1644) were buried in the six square miles of this lovely area with its woods and streams and high hills. The site was chosen only after great deliberation which took into account not only its natural beauty but also its harmony with the *feng shui,* a list of regu-lations for avoiding evil influences. The Chinese have re-stored only two of the tombs; the others, overgrown with weeds and gently mouldering, were open to foreigners.

The idea of using a Ming tomb as the setting for a picnic might seem peculiar. But the grounds of a single tomb could cover about a million square feet and include two or three open courtyards, ornamental gates, carved marble altars and ramps, a spirit hall seventy feet high and a tumulus or burial mound perhaps three hundred feet in diameter—the whole surrounded by a thick wall about twelve feet high. So large were these tombs that two or three groups of foreigners could have a picnic at the same tomb on the same day and not see each other.

Even in disrepair the tombs were majestic. Some indication of their original richness is given by the fact that it took four years and eight million ounces of silver before the tomb of the Emperor Wang Li was completed in 1588. But it was the tranquillity as well as the historic beauty of the tombs that attracted the foreigners. Here the sound of raucous loudspeakers was replaced by songs of birds, and it was possible to have that rarest of all things in China: privacy. So isolated were the tombs that the only Chinese one saw were the few curious peasant children from a nearby commune who would go strolling past with a great air of nonchalance; and, of course, the local security policeman who would arrive by bicycle about fifteen minutes after we parked our cars, and discreetly wait outside the walls until we left to go home.

The Chinese never gave an adequate explanation for declaring the Ming Tombs, Great Wall and Western Hills out of bounds to foreigners in 1970. It seems more than probable however, that they were expanding their missile defense system around Peking and didn't want foreigners stumbling across rockets and building materials being moved along the suburban roads. By the beginning of 1971, the installation had apparently been completed since the Chinese began to give groups of foreigners permission to visit the historic sites. The trips could be arranged only by application, though, which meant that no longer could one decide at four o'clock in the morning to drive out to see the sun rise over the Great Wall.

[57]

It was a small sacrifice; much more important was the fact that foreigners began to have a rational relationship with the Chinese. This started even before we left China, with officials going out of their way to make pleasant conversation. It was a tiny concession, but in Peking the diplomatic community was used to recognizing and measuring the importance of almost infinitesimal changes that often signalled the beginning of a fundamental shift in government policy.

There was, for instance, no announcement made that the Politburo had decided to phase out the Cultural Revolution and gradually focus the intense political campaign on Mao Tse-tung's thoughts rather than on Mao Tse-tung personally. But foreigners began to be aware that this was happening when Chinese started appearing on the streets without the previously obligatory Mao Tse-tung badge, and when foreign businessmen reported that they no longer had to sit through speeches praising Mao Tse-tung before they could start trade negotiations.

Then there were the store windows. They intrigued me, though not because of their content: Every display window in Peking was draped with red cloth or painted in red and contained nothing but statues or photographs of Mao Tse-tung. It made shopping a trial, since I couldn't read Chinese and therefore had to go inside to find out if the store was a pharmacy or a hardware shop. But what I was curious to discover was how the store proprietors would ease the Chairman out of the shop windows, if and when they were allowed to do so. They were, and they went about it in a way that would have done credit to a $100,000-a-year Madison Avenue advertising man.

The first attempts at merchandising something besides politics took place in one window of the main department store downtown and, a few blocks away, in one window of the People's Market. The new display in the department store window consisted of a large portrait of Mao Tse-tung seated at his desk and writing a note; spread below were an assortment of fountain pens, brushes, pencils and ball-point pens. The People's Market display was a little more hard-sell. It consisted of a portrait of Mao, a couple of dozen brightly enamelled alarm clocks and a sign bearing Mao's quotation about "grasping revolution and promoting production." Which was another way of saying if you want to serve the revolution well, then buy an alarm clock to make sure you get to work on time.

This was in the summer of 1969; a few months later every store window in Peking was filled with attractive displays of goods. At the same time, there were other gradual changes that cheered Peking's foreigners. Their Chinese staffs became more relaxed and more willing to do a good job, and dinner invitations to Chinese officials began to be accepted occasionally. For the diplomats and correspondents, these signs meant that China was returning to normalcy and that their work in Peking would become easier. One can only guess at what it meant to the Chinese people, who had been buffeted for three years by the crosswinds of the Cultural Revolution.

5

IT was a rather smart little parade, by Peking standards. For one thing, they were marching in step; most political demonstrators ambled along with the enthusiasm of a man on the way to see his dentist. But these were youngsters barely into their teens, the militants of new China, and each wore a red cloth arm-band signifying membership in the Red Guards. They were led by a "band," twenty-four girls wearing white cotton jackets and beating old snare drums strung around their necks with brightly coloured ribbons. They obviously had been rehearsing for this moment, and they were showing off a bit as they strode purposefully toward Tien an Men Square, their faces set into the same fierce scowls that have been captured in many photographs published in the West.

Regina and her British friend, a girl who also has long blond hair, moved over to the curb to watch. I hung back, having seen them do this before. They smiled at the passing teen-agers, who at first glanced at them out of the corners of their eyes. You could see the word pass back through the ranks: "Look at the two yellow-haired foreigners over there." Marchers nudged their friends and pointed at the two girls;

[61]

heads turned; eyes stared in open curiosity; scowls gave way to answering smiles; Regina gave a tiny wave and some of the younger children waved back. By now the parade was a mess. The marchers were out of step, bumping into each other as they looked at the foreigners, laughing at their own confusion. Then a soldier who had been marching at the rear came running up to the front shouting, "*Ee, er, san. Ee, er, san* (One, two, three. One, two three)," and glared accusingly at Regina and her friend. Soon he had them back into step and scowling at the world again. We moved along.

There was nothing particularly significant about the incident, but in a small way it typified the frequent contradiction between what the Chinese seem to be and what they actually are. On the one hand, these teen-agers were normal, curious, cheerful youngsters. On the other hand, they were members of the dreaded Red Guard who had, according to newspaper accounts, beaten, tortured and killed people, destroyed ancient temples and looted homes. Unquestionably some of them did. I have talked to foreigners who witnessed merciless beatings in Peking. And I have seen the vandalizing of historic buildings such as Peking's beautiful Yellow Temple, where the Panchen Lama stayed in 1652. The lovely bas-relief carvings that covered its base were wantonly smashed. A treasure lost to China.

But while the excesses of the Red Guard movement should be condemned, it always seemed extraordinary to me that there was so little violence—considering the vast numbers of young people involved, and the fact they had been told by Mao himself that rebellion was justified. Nobody, not even the Chinese, will ever know how many teen-agers seized the previously unimaginable opportunity to travel freely around the country. A conservative estimate might be ten million, but the figure could be double or triple that. The only obstacles to travel were lack of food—city dwellers were under orders to help feed the youngsters—and China's limited transportation system, which they were allowed to use free of charge.

(It was a short-lived concession. On August 31, 1966, Chou En-lai told a Red Guard rally that it was a "very good thing" to come to Peking to "exchange revolutionary experiences." In November, Lin Piao was extolling the virtues of "travelling on foot," and in the same month the party's Central Committee issued a circular banning the use of "train, ship and bus" to Red Guards until the spring. By March, still overwhelmed by the students, the Communist party's Central Committee had published a further circular prohibiting all Red Guard travel and free food because of "overcrowding," and loss of "production and the danger of infectious disease"; and the first of Mao's orders to return home was made.)

They must have been tremendously excited. Few had travelled beyond their own village or town, and suddenly the whole of China was theirs to explore. For the first time in their lives, they were able to escape the discipline and regimen of the tightly controlled Communist system and do what they wanted, whenever they wanted. Their elders were often envious. One Chinese shook his head in disbelief as he told me that his young cousin and two friends travelled all the way to Peking from Honan Province, about five hundred miles away, and stayed in his flat for three days before returning home; he had never been more than thirty miles outside Peking.

To some observers, though, they seemed to be "unified by a transcendent vision, so infused with a sense of virtue as to be almost beatific—politicized 'flower children' of the Cultural Revolution." * This seems a romanticized view. Undoubtedly many were idealistic, but probably just as many

---

* Robert Jay Lifton, *Revolutionary Immortality* (New York, Vintage Books).

were more interested in enjoying their newfound freedom. The Shanghai newspaper *Wen Hui Pao* eventually described some of them as "wanderers" and complained: "Instead of fighting on a battlefront (of the Cultural Revolution), they wander about school campuses, parks and streets; they spend their time in swimming pools and playing chess and cards. . . ."

The capital of China was the one city that all the teen-agers wanted to visit, partly in the hope of catching a glimpse of Mao Tse-tung, but mostly just to see with their own eyes the most famous sites of China. They toured the old Summer Palace and the Temple of Heaven and gawked at the big department stores and the high office buildings. They filled the ninety-eight-acre Tien An Men or Gate of Heavenly Peace Square, which became the site of a sort of wild-eyed jamboree with tens of thousands of them alternately singing revolutionary songs and shouting themselves hoarse when a rumour would sweep through the crowd that Mao himself was going to appear on the great gate that faces the square.

To conceive what this meant to Peking, imagine that almost one million teen-agers suddenly descended on Manhattan, hungry and almost penniless, and that the New York City police were under orders not to interfere with them in any way. That, in effect, was what happened in Peking, already an overcrowded city. Its citizens were not pleased by the dislocation. The children of distant relatives would arrive unannounced on the doorstep and have to be given some place to sleep, usually the floor; even worse, the family's meager food supply would have to be shared with them. Restaurants were always filled, and many people had to walk to work every day because the poorly serviced bus system was overloaded. Shoppers had to elbow their way through the downtown stores, and families gave up their quiet Sunday stroll through the park. Rough outdoor privies shielded by canvas walls were put up on the main streets, and during the winter public buildings such as the railway station and the post offices were virtually impassable because of the hundreds of teen-agers who had staked out a sleeping place on the floor. Correspondents with stories to file late at night would pick their way carefully through the blanket of bodies at the cable office.

Admitted my Chinese acquaintance: "They sometimes did get in the way, being from the country and not being used to the ways of a big city." His comment struck me as amusing, considering Peking's general poorness and underdevelopment. But the people of Peking and Shanghai have always considered themselves the sophisticates of China—which, indeed, they probably are.

He did not mention, of course, that the Red Guards did more than just "get in the way." They were in the "vanguard of the revolution," as the Chinese press put it, which meant that they were the tool which Mao and his supporters used to regain political power. And after hundreds of conversations I have had in Peking with Chinese, embassy personnel, and "foreign friends" who lived among the Chinese, it is difficult to escape the conclusion that only an infinitesimal number of Red Guards were actually acting under direct orders from the leadership—at least in Peking. This small hard-core group knew which political figures were the targets, and led the attacks against them. It wasn't hard to do. The city was filled with hundreds of thousands of outside teen-agers who were looking for excitement. They roamed the streets, applying shears to the heads of young people who wore their hair in the "outlandish spiral pagoda style," cutting "cowboy trousers" into shorts, and converting "rocket-style" (pointed) shoes into sandals. They could also be quickly formed into a mob; but mobs have a tendency to become uncontrollable, especially when they are sprinkled

[65]

with hooligans. As a result many people were severely beaten and some even died, though Lin Piao and Chou En-lai were repeatedly telling the Red Guards not to use physical violence. They had no real way of enforcing their orders, however, short of bringing in the army and ending the Cultural Revolution. This they eventually did, but only after the Red Guards had served their purpose.

It was also a time when old grudges were settled. People who had flaunted their superior education, associated with foreigners, worn "stylish" clothes, or acquired expensive carpets and furniture, were "informed" on by their jealous neighbours. Red Guards would swoop down on the hapless accused, heap his bourgeois belongings in the open courtyard, and subject him to a public denunciation and humiliation with the neighbours joining in. If he was lucky, the ordeal might last only a few hours and he would not be pummelled and punched. Afterwards, his little pile of personal things would sit outside in the sun and rain for a few weeks. Eventually, a government truck would come along and cart the things away to a warehouse where they would be sorted and evaluated. Later they would appear in Peking's secondhand stores, or in the antique shops open only to foreigners.

There was also a good bit of nonsense that went on.

For a while, it became all the rage to get rid of "foul" street names left over from the old days. Thus, Glorious Road was renamed Support Vietnam Road, and the Well of the Prince's Palace Road became Prevent Revisionism Road. The great Boulevard of Eternal Peace became The East Is Red Boulevard. The latter was easily the most popular name and was the new title also given to a number of restaurants and small shops. It soon became a hopeless muddle—how could you call a meeting at The East Is Red when

[66]

there were dozens of them?—and the old names quietly came back into use.

Another innovation was to have policemen direct traffic with a copy of Mao's Quotations instead of a white baton. This was suddenly stopped shortly after I arrived in Peking. But the intriguing question was: Who dared give the order to discard the *Little Red Book?* Surely only Mao himself.

Then there was the amusing case of Shin Chuang-hsiang, the night-soil collector who had been so good at his job— performing it with true proletarian dedication, whatever that may mean—that he had been singled out for praise in newspapers and had been given the title Model Night-Soil Collector. He even represented a Peking district in the National People's Congress. His star rose even higher during the Cultural Revolution, and the official press carried an article by him condemning the intellectuals who had opposed the making of a film on the life of a night-soil collector (he wrote the scenario himself). Alas, poor Shin Chuang-hsiang soon fell from grace. To the surprise of almost everyone in Peking, he was denounced as a revisionist and driven through the streets wearing a dunce cap and a placard telling his crime. He had, the Red Guards discovered, the temerity to hang on his wall a photograph of himself with the detestable Liu Shao-chi, the deposed President of the People's Republic of China, instead of a portrait of Mao Tse-tung. Presumably this "capitalist-roader" lost his job as punishment, though I suspect he would consider any new employment an improvement.

The presence of the Red Guards had an impact on Peking's foreign community, of course. Some people were afraid to leave their flats; others told me that they never felt fear at any time. Certainly, shopping expeditions downtown became an ordeal because of the crowded streets and because a foreigner on foot would be almost immediately surrounded

[67]

by a shoving mass of curious "country" teen-agers who had never seen a European. One woman, the wife of a French diplomat, was in a small flower shop and became exasperated by a group of Red Guards when one of them leaned over her shoulder to look in her purse. She glared at them, and then unbuttoned her blouse and began to take it off. The Red Guards fled.

The only serious incident occurred when an East European woman shopping in the Friendship Store was attacked by a knife-wielding young man who cut her face badly before he was subdued. The Chinese gave her the best possible care, even, it was reported, bringing in a plastic surgeon from Switzerland; and she was visited in the hospital by various Chinese officials including Foreign Minister Chen Yi, who formally apologized on behalf of the government. The Chinese also took care of the young man who committed the crime. He was swiftly dragged before a public trial—which foreigners were invited to attend—in the Workers' Stadium. While 40,000 people looked on, he was denounced and sentenced to immediate execution. Neither foreigners nor Chinese missed the point.

There were, it seems to me, two remarkable things about the Red Guard movement, aside from the political strategy that gave it birth.

The first is that there was surprisingly little damage done to the cities (I speak here only of Peking and other cities which I visited) despite the fact that thousands of Red Guards were roaming through the streets without any kind of restraint. Shops were not looted, nor were their windows smashed. Buildings were not burned (I except here the British and Soviet Missions which will be dealt with in another chapter), nor were they bombed. It is not a fair comparison, perhaps, but nothing done by the Red Guards even

[68]

approached the destruction caused by riots in Detroit in 1967 and in Watts in 1965.

There was damage done to some temples in the Peking area. Ba Da Chu or the Eight Great Sites, which are located in the hills to the west of Peking, were attacked by the Red Guards. I visited the Temple of Eternal Peace, built under the Ming in 1504, and the halls containing the statues of the Buddha and some Taoist deities were empty except for some fragments on the floor. The gilded wood statues of the eighteenth Luo Han, attributed to the famous Yuan dynasty sculptor Liu Lan, were missing from the Temple of Great Compassion. The last hall of the Three Hills Monastery was a scene of devastation. The Buddha and the eighteenth Luo Han in gilded wood had been smashed beyond recognition. We had to pick our way through the debris. We tried to find a small piece to save, but there was nothing. Some of the temples were splashed with white or black paint, and numerous slogans in Chinese, such as LONG LIVE CHAIRMAN MAO, had been painted on the walls in large Chinese characters. The famous stone animals and warrior carvings that symbolically guard the road or "sound way" to the Ming Tombs had their faces daubed with white paint but, fortunately, they were not otherwise damaged. Some of the equally famous lion heads—280 of them, each different—that grace the 800-year-old Marco Polo Bridge in the western suburbs of Peking had been replaced by 1969, but I do not know whether the originals fell to the Red Guards. Strangely, the beautiful old Summer Palace near Peking University was left virtually untouched. Only the panel paintings of the "bourgeois" court scenes had been covered with white paint; it was only whitewash, however, and it quickly faded away.

There was some mystery about what happened during the Cultural Revolution to Peking's best known treasure, the

[69]

Forbidden (or Imperial) City where the emperors lived and held court. Not until the spring of 1971, when the famous Ping-Pong diplomacy began, were foreigners permitted behind its high vermilion walls. They reported everything was in order, but long before then the Red Guards apparently had been at work.

A Swiss delegation visiting Peking in late 1966 asked to visit the Imperial City. After some delays, their guide agreed. It was a very short tour, with their guide practically running them through the ancient grounds. But they could not help noticing the damaged buildings and the great chunks of baked tile figurines strewn on the ground.

"What has happened here?" asked one of the Swiss, pointing at the tiles.

"Oh, that is nothing," said the guide lamely, "these are very old buildings and pieces sometimes fall off. They are of no value."

"Then you don't mind if I take one home as a souvenir?"

The flustered guide nodded his approval, and the Swiss happily picked up a large unmarked decoration and carried it back to his hotel. Late that night there was a knock at his door. It was the unhappy guide, accompanied by two policemen. There was, he explained, a slight mistake; the tile was the property of the People's Republic of China and could not be taken out of the country. He picked it up, said good-bye, and vanished into the night.

The tile was no doubt stuck back where it belonged. The Chinese authorities, in fact, moved to protect what they considered to be the artistic or historical treasures of China, when the Red Guard began to carry out their promise—"We tear up and smash old calendars, precious vases, United States and British records, superstitious lacquers and ancient paintings, and we put up the picture of Mao."

All the art galleries, libraries and museums were padlocked and guarded by armed soldiers. The 600-year-old observatory in Eastern Peking with its ancient iron astronomy instruments was locked and protected by barbed wire. The beautiful Temple of Heaven was left open, but the exquisitely carved marble slabs on the steps of the temple building were protected by a thick layer of plaster. At the Summer Palace the huge stone lions at the entrance were encased in wood pillars decorated with Mao's quotations (thus making them untouchable).

In Shanghai, the Museum of Natural Sciences and the Art and History Museum were still closed in early 1971. A friend of mine toured the museum in late 1966—probably the last foreigner to do so—and the corridors and rooms were filled with Red Guards armed with pencils and notebooks who were carefully itemizing all the "decadent" and "feudalistic" objects. They did not, however, touch anything; and the valuable collections of bronzes, paintings and ceramics have presumably survived.

The beautiful city of Hangchow, capital of Chekiang Province, escaped damage. In 1969 I visited all its historic sites, including the famous Fei Lai Feng cliff and the nearby caves which together have hundreds of carvings, some more than nine hundred years old. All were intact.

I have no reason to think that museums and ancient buildings in other Chinese cities were not also put under guard by local authorities who were determined to make the "four olds" campaign (destroy old ideas, culture, customs and habits) a spiritual rather than physical exercise.

The second remarkable thing about the Red Guard movement was that it blunted one of the favourite theories (and fears) about China; that the Communists had created a nation of automatons who would carry out their bidding at a finger-snap. There was, it was known, some rebellion against the system among adults, particularly intellectuals who had been educated in the West. This was proved during the Let a Hundred Flowers Bloom campaign of 1958, when the call for criticism of the government met with such an overwhelming response that the authorities quickly ended it and started a purge of the complainers.

But what was alarming, if not terrifying, was the indoctrination of children. We were shown (and still are) photographs of tiny tots wearing little army uniforms and going through bayonet drill with scaled-down wooden rifles. In nursery and primary schools they were being taught to hate Americans, to worship Mao Tse-tung, to obey without question every command, to lay down their lives for the state. They were the ultimate result of brainwashing, an easily manipulated force with which China would conquer the world.

The Cultural Revolution provided the first real opportunity to see the George Orwellian product in action. The Red Guards were, after all, the first New Generation of the Chinese Communist system. Those who were seventeen or younger had been born after the Communists came to power in 1949. Even the oldest of the Red Guards, say twenty-five, were only eight years of age when Chiang Kai-shek fled China. They too had spent their formative and adolescent years supposedly being honed to ideological perfection in the Communist educational system.

How did they react to their first real test?

First of all, it can be said that they were not one unified force marching toward a truly socialist state to the drumbeat of Mao's instructions. In fact, they frequently twisted his instructions to suit their own purposes, and ignored the direct commands from the Party's Central Committee that were endorsed by Mao. They rejected the leaders' pleas to return home, to go back to school, to stop fighting among themselves. The "civil war" among the university students was

[72]

particularly vicious and, in terms of political rectitude, extremely hypocritical.

In the spring of 1968, two years after the Cultural Revolution had started, fighting was still going on at Peking University, with each side claiming that it alone was supporting Mao and obeying his instructions. Neither was, of course. What both sides were fighting for was control of the university, and their quarrel had little to do with proletarian virtues.

Peking University was out of bounds to foreigners then, but the road to the Summer Palace wound around the southwest corner of the walled campus where some dormitories were located, and it was possible to catch a glimpse of what was going on inside. The opposing factions had occupied adjacent red brick dormitories and turned them into fortified headquarters. The entrances were guarded by groups of students wearing green and yellow construction helmets and carrying wood spears. They looked properly fierce. Most of the windows in the two five-storey buildings had been broken, and the sills were lined with rocks which were thrown at enemies who came within range on the ground below.

About fifty students stood a respectable distance away, apparently content to be spectators while the opponents in opposite buildings shook their fists at each other and shouted insults. A couple of soldiers, unarmed as usual, mingled among the crowd but did not attempt to intervene. The students had propped up mattresses on the balconies to ward off missiles. It was a wise precaution, since some of the enterprising rebels had constructed a giant slingshot from a tire tube and pieces of wood and were using it like a cannon to fire rocks from the roof of one of the dormitories. It could have been regarded as funny, except that one boy was struck on the head and died. That night the faction to which

[73]

he belonged put his body on a cart loaded with ice and pulled it to the Peking Communist party offices downtown. About two hundred students stood outside the building shouting their demands for revenge, which were ignored.

A few weeks later, on July 27–28, the student leaders were summoned to the closed section of the Imperial City for a meeting with Mao. Exactly what transpired will probably never be known, but I later heard from contacts in the university that the late-night meeting had been highly emotional. Mao did all the talking, at one point almost weeping over their betrayal of his trust, but in the main angrily accusing them of being motivated by self-interest instead of revolutionary spirit. They had given him no choice, he said as he dismissed them, but to order the army into the university.

Within a week, the universities were occupied by soldiers and worker propaganda teams, as they were called, who quickly rooted out the dissidents and restored order. To make things even clearer, Yao Wen-yuan, one of the original leaders of the Cultural Revolution, made a speech on August 25, 1968, criticizing the Red Guards for their shortcomings and ordering them to accept the leadership of the workers (the worker propaganda teams).

The independent Red Guard movement had ended, and with it went much of the myth that the Chinese had developed a mind-controlling educational process that crushed individuality and produced an army of disciplined, obedient young people. It was a myth believed by Mao, as well as by the West; before the Cultural Revolution his main concern about young people was that they knew nothing of the old days and thus lacked "revolutionary experience." It has been argued even that one of the purposes of the Cultural Revolution was to imbue China's youth with the same zeal

[74]

and self-sacrifice that had inspired Mao and the other old Communists during their revolutionary days.

Whatever the case, both Mao and the young people were disillusioned. As one former Red Guard said of his colleagues: "They thought themselves the greatest people in the world. They felt they could do anything." * Instead, they found that they had been used, and that they were to get none of the real power or glory that should have come with victory. Many of them—estimates range from five to ten million—were to be sent thousands of miles from home to "work in the socialist construction of the countryside" under the no-nonsense direction of China's rough peasants. Other more recalcitrant cases ended up in army labour camps.

Two memories stick in my mind.

I was eating lunch in the Hsin Chiao Hotel when one of the old waiters smilingly took me by the arm and drew me over to the window. Outside, standing on the back of an open stake truck with other young recruits, was the revolutionary house-boy who had joined the Red Guards and led the criticism sessions among the hotel staff. The old waiters were standing around the truck, enthusiastically waving their little red books. The revolutionary house-boy managed a weak smile and waved his red book back at them as the truck pulled away.

"He go to army now," grinned my companion with satisfaction. "We say good-bye for a long time."

The other memory (actually I saw similar scenes many times) is of a group of thirty workers marching to the railway station in Peking. Leading the group were two men carrying a framed picture of Mao; two soldiers flanked the party and a man at the rear was beating a red kettledrum.

* Lifton, op. cit.

Everybody seemed immensely pleased except three young men in the middle of the group. They were not smiling, though each carried a large red paper flower. They were young revolutionaries who had "volunteered" to settle in the countryside; the factory workers were escorting them to the railway station.

However dismayed Mao may have felt about China's young people, he had no delusions about their elders. In 1957 he said, "The class struggle between the proletariat and the bourgeoisie, the class struggle between various political forces, and the class struggle in the ideological field between the proletariat and the bourgeoisie will still be long and devious and at times may even become very acute."

What Mao meant was that the Chinese people would slip into their old ways—indeed, many of them wanted to—unless the Communist party was constantly vigilant. The Cultural Revolution was his method of re-purifying the masses and the party itself, a further step toward the molding of the "new man."

Whether it is successful in the long term will depend on how long Mao lives, and on how willing his eventual successor will be to continue the various reforms (described in another chapter) into effect. In the short term, the Communist regime has suffered at least two grievous losses.

The first is the credibility of its leadership. It will be very difficult in the future for any ordinary Chinese to accept the reliability or truthfulness of any high-ranking official other than Mao—which may have been the idea behind the Cultural Revolution. In the Soviet Union, Joseph Stalin was dead for some years before Nikita Khrushchev began his campaign of denigration. But in China, men who were the giants of Chinese life for almost two decades were reduced to political pygmies in a matter of weeks: Liu Shao-chi, Chairman of the People's Republic of China; Teng Hsiao-ping, General Secretary of the Party Central Committee; Ho Lung and Lo Jui-ching, Vice-Chairmen of the National Defense Council; Peng Chen, Politburo member and Mayor of Peking.

"When I first saw Peng Chen's name mentioned in wall posters, I couldn't believe it," a cadre in Peking told me, his voice still touched with awe. "I thought it was a mistake. He had spoken to my class when we graduated. It was a stirring speech, with many great words. Now we know these words were false, that in his heart he was a revisionist."

But who else harbours secret revisionist thoughts in the leadership today? After the sensations of the Cultural Revolution, was any Chinese startled when the finger was pointed at Lin Piao in early 1972? Would any be amazed if it were next pointed at Chou En-lai? Anything seems possible now. Even before 1966 there was no guarantee that a power struggle would not ensue after Mao's death, but the Cultural Revolution in effect limited the chances of a peaceful succession. Fears of the effect on public opinion of a top-level purge are no longer a restraint, if they ever were. Only Mao remains unassailable.

Another casualty of the Cultural Revolution was discipline, the most important single force in China and probably the greatest achievement of the Chinese Communist party. It was discipline—enforced through a complex balance of pressures and rewards exerted by party cadres—that brought organization and unity to China's hundreds of millions of people for the first time. From discipline flowed all things: the country's tremendous industrial growth, the communization of agriculture, the submersion of individuality and self-interest, the incredibly puritanical morality, the total mobilization of the population for mass campaigns (two disparate examples: the Great Leap Forward and the complete elimination of flies).

[77]

Lack of discipline was felt in industry during the Cultural Revolution but to what extent it is difficult to say since the Chinese publish no meaningful statistics. Some foreign experts estimated that overall industrial production dropped 10 to 15 percent in 1967 alone (Far Eastern Economic Review, *1969 Yearbook*), while others argued there were only minor disruptions and that workers became so enthusiastic they overtook arrears and fulfilled their annual production target two or three months ahead of schedule (Joan Robinson, *The Cultural Revolution in China,* Penguin). By the end of 1969 many of the experts were revising their estimates, the optimists downward and the pessimists upward. The consensus seemed to be that the economy weathered the storm reasonably well, all things considered, and that problems were localized rather than widespread as in a civil war. In an interview with the late Edgar Snow in 1970, Chou En-lai claimed large advances for most of the economy. He said oil production in 1970 was twenty million tons (five years earlier foreign economists estimated production at less than ten million) and that China had become the world's largest producer of cotton cloth, turning out 8,500 million meters in 1970. According to the Premier, only steel production was damaged by the Cultural Revolution, ranging between ten and eighteen million tons since 1965.

It was true, though, that the general theme of the Cultural Revolution—throw out the capitalist-roaders who had seized power—virtually guaranteed that every factory, school, hospital or other institution in China would have its own individual battle to wage. In one factory, the workers might decide that all the cadres and administrators were bourgeois; in another factory, there might be only one "rotten egg," or perhaps none. It was implicit, though, that the existing authority must be challenged and if necessary overthrown. In its place was established the Revolutionary Committee, a mixture of soldiers, workers and revolutionary cadres, which eventually set the factory in order again (though Chinese newspapers are still featuring stories about workers who failed to arrive on time or feigned illness and stayed home). The Revolutionary Committee, however, was essentially local in design and purpose; it was not meant to replace the fractured Communist party which for almost twenty years had been the propelling force in Chinese life. At the beginning of 1972, almost six years after the start of the Cultural Revolution, only slow progress was being made in restoring the party structure and authority.

The loss of national discipline was apparent in Peking and other cities I visited.

The Chinese habit of spitting, for instance, had been pretty well controlled in the cities before the Cultural Revolution. If a Chinese was seized with an irrepressible need to spit, he had to direct his fire at a spittoon. These were located in all public buildings, and were usually covered by a wooden lid with a long pole stuck in the middle for convenient removal. It looked very much like the plunger in an old-fashioned butter churner. More elegant places such as the ornate Peking Hotel had each spittoon ensconced in small wood boxes that resembled kitchen garbage cans; when you pressed a foot pedal, the lid popped open.

By the time I arrived in China, all injunctions against spitting had been forgotten. People spat in the streets, in the shops, on trains, in theaters, even on the carpeted corridors of the Hsin Chiao Hotel. Foreigners were not entirely joking when they would tell newcomers that goggles were essential equipment for bicycle riders in Peking. Actually, there was usually plenty of advance warning that a wet missile was about to be launched. The Chinese have developed spitting to a fine art over the centuries and it is an unforgettable experience to watch a dignified elderly Chinese lady

[79]

begin a throat-clearing exercise that starts from her heels and works its way slowly up through her body to culminate in one grand expectoration.

Another sign of lax discipline was the sudden recurrence of dishonesty, an almost unheard-of thing in pre-Cultural Revolution days. With foreigners, the Chinese continued to be scrupulously honest, sometimes carrying it to ludicrous lengths. When Agence France Presse correspondent Jean Vincent was expelled from Peking, he and the two tough Civil Aviation guards escorting him to the waiting plane were stopped by a young pigtailed waitress from the airport restaurant who came running across the tarmac. She presented him with a small paper bag of biscuits he had left on the restaurant table.

Foreigners can still leave their hotel rooms or apartments unlocked without the slightest fear of being robbed by a Chinese. What the Chinese do to each other is another matter. Two friends of mine, for instance, had their Chinese bicycles stolen, one from in front of the hospital and the other from in front of the main department store. Obviously, the thieves thought the bicycles belonged to a Chinese.

In 1971, Chinese newspapers were condemning "theft" and there were reports of "anarchy" in some areas.

In another incident, while I was in Peking, two men in the People's Market started fighting and bystanders joined in. While the fracas was going on, opportunistic customers made off with some merchandise and a few hundred coupons for cotton cloth. All this was revealed in an unintentionally amusing notice posted in the market—sternly demanding that the articles and coupons be returned *forthwith*.

Still another example. In May, 1968, a nationwide campaign was mounted to honor Men Ho, a soldier who had died eight months earlier when he threw himself on an exploding rocket to save his comrades. The campaign began in typical style, with mass rallies and demonstrations across China calling on everyone to emulate Men Ho's devotion to Mao. A book about him was published and a song was written extolling his virtues. But a few weeks later the campaign quietly fizzled out and nothing more was heard about Men Ho. Heroes in the revolutionary mould cannot be created on order without discipline, and there was none.

As anyone who walked in the streets of Peking could see, the Chinese people had been overcome by a monumental weariness of politics; they simply didn't care any more. Their minds had been numbed by a gigantic political overkill.

6

IT is difficult for anyone who was not in China at that time to comprehend what the Chinese had to endure mentally. Every waking hour of every day, the average citizen was pounded and assaulted by relentless waves of propaganda. At precisely 5 A.M. thousands of loudspeakers in Peking would blare slogans and revolutionary music. This would stop at 9 A.M. when everyone had gone to work. But in the factories, lunch hours and rest periods would be spent reading Mao's quotations aloud or attending criticism sessions in which one had to participate vigorously or become a target. At 5 P.M. the loudspeakers would start up again, and continue until 11 P.M. After work, there would be neighborhood political meetings, which nobody could safely avoid. Even old ladies, like ghosts stepping out of China's past, could be seen hobbling on tiny bound feet to the meetings, carrying little three-legged stools on which to sit during the long harangues.

Then there were the endless demonstrations, usually to "celebrate" a new directive from Mao or to "commemorate" the anniversary of one of his old declarations. A typical demonstration would begin at 9 P.M. with the setting off of firecrackers and the thumping of drums and clanging of cymbals. Within fifteen minutes, perhaps 50,000 men, women and children (even on bitterly cold nights) would be trudging along streets repeating slogans which a cadre would read to them from a piece of paper. By midnight the demonstration would break up, but at nine the next morning it would start again. The marchers would be mostly nonworking housewives and students (who weren't going to school anyhow). By 4 P.M. their ranks would be swelled by thousands of men and women who had finished their office and factory shifts.

There was neither enthusiasm nor distaste on their faces. If anything, they seemed indifferent and bored. Even passersby didn't bother to look at the paraders. Incredibly, pedicart drivers parked at the side of the road would sleep contentedly in their vehicles, undisturbed by the pounding drums or shouting demonstrators who were passing a yard away from them.

Equally incredible would be the description of the demonstration published the next day in the *People's Daily*. "Revolutionary workers, soldiers and lower and middle class peasants (trucked into Peking from nearby communes) joyously greeted a brilliant new directive from our beloved leader Chairman Mao Tse-tung whose ever-victorious . . ." etc.

I often wondered if the people who took part in the demonstrations were ever startled when they read such glowing accounts. Probably not. They surely were used to such things, just as the taxi drivers at the stand in front of the Hsin Chiao Hotel got used to assembling in front of a picture of Mao every morning and mouthing memorized quotations, all the while watching the traffic go by. Just as the old waiters inside the hotel got used to gathering in front of a bust of Mao after the restaurant closed and puffing through a revolutionary dance while singing, "Sailing the seas depends on the helmsman, making revolution depends on Mao Tse-tung."

. There was no refuge from the ubiquitous Mao. He was, literally, everywhere. No public building of any size was without a fifteen-foot-high white plaster statue of Mao in the lobby (there was one half-mad Bulgarian diplomat who solemnly insisted that these statues marched through the streets of Peking at the stroke of midnight every May 1). If there wasn't enough room for a full-length statue, as was the case in most restaurants, then a white plaster bust about five feet high would be installed. Needless to say, all sizes of statues and busts of Mao were available, even some five inches high which people would buy to put in their homes. In fact, these figurines were the only decorations people dared to have in their homes except, of course, large framed pictures of Mao.

During the year and a half I was in China, I never saw any other decoration (excluding family snapshots) in any private house or apartment or public building. If a family was politically suspect, then the walls of their room would be covered with pictures and posters of Mao. The same held true for their place of work. The house-boys on the fifth floor of the Hsin Chiao apparently had gotten into some sort of trouble, perhaps because a number of foreigners lived permanently on that floor. Whatever the case, they had vigorously applied the paste-pot and, by actual count, there were 324 pictures of Mao stuck to the corridor walls.

Pictures of Mao and/or his quotations could also be found on match-boxes and calendars, in taxis, pedicabs, buses, trains and planes. Trains also carried a giant photograph of Mao fixed to the front of the locomotive and banked by tiny red flags. So also did fire engines, as I discovered one

[85]

day when there was a small smoke fire in one of the foreigners' flats. It was the only time I saw firemen in action in Peking and, believe it or not, they chanted quotations as they unreeled the hose.*

But this was in early 1968, when the Cultural Revolution was still going through its final convulsions. On buses, every window but the windshield was plastered with slogans and pictures of Mao. Every square inch of every wall in Peking was postered (except the ones surrounding the Forbidden City, where Mao lived). Store windows contained nothing but statues or pictures of Mao, and the radio broadcast only revolutionary music, readings from Mao's works and some news from the *People's Daily*. A few movie houses were open, but they showed only documentaries of Mao greeting Red Guards. The Peking opera and ballet companies put on two-week performances twice a year and though the program included only revolutionary works such as *Capturing the Bandits' Stronghold,* or *The Red Detachment of Women,* it was almost impossible to get tickets because of the great demand.

The opera and ballet were two of the few diversions open to the Chinese. Cards and chess were forbidden, and sports were banned. The concrete Ping-Pong tables in Pei-hai Park were never used, though the Chinese are fanatics about the game and are able to rattle off top players' statistics as quickly as a New York Yankees' sports announcer.

Aside from the official newspapers and wall posters there was nothing for the Chinese to read but the many pamphlets and booklets that carried reprints of official Cultural Revolution documents and important editorials from the *People's*

* In an interview with the late Edgar Snow, Mao Tse-tung said the personality cult had to be intensified in order to oust his enemies, but that it would be gradually de-emphasized (a Conversation with Mao Tse-tung, *Life* magazine, April 30, 1971).

Daily. And, of course, the selected works of Mao, published in four hard-cover volumes. Everyone—men, women and children—carried a copy of the little red book of quotations. It was a matter of survival. Just as in the days of America's wild West when even peaceful citizens carried a six-shooter, every Chinese carried a copy of the little red book because he never knew when he might be called upon to draw it out and cite a quotation.

Needless to say, this created something of a strain on China's printing presses. Between 1966 and 1969, Peking printing houses alone published almost 41,000,000 volumes of Mao's *Selected Works,* more than the total number printed in the whole of China before the Cultural Revolution. Even more impressive were the figures for the little red books, which surely involved the largest single printing effort in history. During the same three-year period, more than 740,000,000 copies were printed at a cost that must have been staggering, despite China's cheap labour.

There was, by the way, a small group of foreign businessmen who shared the joy of China's publishing zeal. These were the Finns, who sold China the high-quality paper used for foreign language editions of the red book, and the Italians, who sold the heavy red plastic used for the covers.

So much has been written by so many scholars about the meaning and importance of the Thought of Mao Tse-tung, from which the quotations for the little red book are drawn, that there is no need here to delve into another analysis. But it is worth noting that the scholars' views do vary.

Robert Jay Lifton, in *Revolutionary Immortality,* sees "the man and his words fused into a powerful image" to become a kind of living divinity representing immortal revolutionary status that can be bestowed on those who accept and believe.

Stuart Schram, in an introductory essay in *Quotations*

[87]

From Mao Tse-tung (Phantom Books), also notes the "quasi-religious" aspect in the melding of Mao and his writings, but argues that the total absence of any clearly defined utopian goal and the Spartan philosophy that regards revolutionary struggle as a supreme happiness in itself, are not sufficient rewards to guarantee its survival in China or elsewhere.

R. G. Oldham, on the other hand, considers many of the quotations to be little more than homespun but useful adages that roughly parallel dictums such as "If at first you don't succeed, then try, try again," and so on. (By the beginning of 1971, the Chinese themselves were beginning to emphasize the philosophical importance of Mao's writings. Several friends of mine in China listened to lengthy and bewildering dissertations on this subject from their translators, who obviously had been tutored.)

The important thing, of course, is not so much whether Mao aspires to deification for himself and his writings during his lifetime but, rather, what will happen to the dogma after his death. The vagueness of much of his writing leaves it open to various interpretations, as was demonstrated during the Cultural Revolution. On many occasions, two factions took opposite stances while claiming ideological purity in following Mao's instructions. Only a judgment from Mao could settle the dispute, but who will have the same moral authority when he has gone?

Whoever becomes the leader of China after Mao's death, the country's god and bible for many years will probably continue to be Mao Tse-tung and his Thoughts. There seems little reason for him to fear, as some Western scholars suggest he does, that he will be posthumously criticized and downgraded as was Stalin. The reverse will probably happen. China's future leaders will probably adulate Mao Tse-tung and his writings and elevate them to heights that even

[88]

Mao never dreamed possible. Of course these same leaders, having received the Mandate of Mao's Heaven, will also interpret his writings to achieve what *they* perceive to be in the country's greatest interest. His Thoughts are ambiguous enough to keep any new leader happy, for they can be implemented to create a dictatorship with extreme repression or a socialist society with wide individual freedoms. The only thing they are incapable of is being twisted into a free enterprise framework, but it is impossible to conceive that any Chinese leader or the Chinese people themselves would seriously entertain the idea of adopting a Western form of government which, in any event, would be alien to them.

It is impossible for any foreigner, even one who is living in Peking, to tell how the Chinese really feel about Mao Tse-tung and his Thoughts. The problem is to distinguish between symbolism and reality, to separate the people from the propaganda.

I don't think any foreigner who has spent much time in China would seriously argue that anything but a minuscule proportion of the population is opposed to Mao Tse-tung. To stand amid a near-hysterical crowd of 500,000 people in Tien An Men Square when Mao appears on the rostrum is an emotional experience not quickly forgotten.

Aside from the semi-religious overtones, Mao Tse-tung is undeniably a public hero to the Chinese. Through him they have seen China rid itself of foreign domination and become a power in the world again. The cost may have been great, but so have been the rewards. The great plagues and floods that killed millions of Chinese are no more. People do not die of starvation, or see their children sold into bondage. Education is no longer unimaginable to a peasant.

From all of this it does not automatically follow that the Chinese, a highly individualistic people, accept without reservation all of Mao's writings as interpreted during the

[89]

Cultural Revolution. It is difficult to believe, for instance, that the Chinese people agree with the Communist verdict that only revolutionary art is not decadent, that pictures of flowers on stamps are bourgeois. Or that the ever-present portrait of Mao with a smooth unblemished face glowing with rosy health bears any resemblance to the man. Mao is old and sick and his teeth have been blackened from the smoke of countless Szechwan cigars. The Chinese people know this.

During the Cultural Revolution, the Chinese leaders attempted to demolish the country's rich cultural heritage. Of all the phases of the turmoil, this was the most difficult for outsiders to understand. It flew in the face of Mao's constant admonition that cadres must trust the masses. Yet in this case the masses were clearly being ignored.

The truth is that Mao does not really trust the masses, any more than do the Communist leaders of any other country. In China, though, there are special reasons to be concerned about the past. Historically, Chinese art and literature were the product of the leisure class. Almost without exception, only those who were wealthy had sufficient education or time to paint or compose music or write. Thus artistic ability became intertwined with social status. Naturally, the themes of much of this work involved either themselves and people of equal or higher rank, or had a reflective quality and concerned nature. But a painting that showed the tranquillity of a misty valley, or a play based on the romance of a palace lady, was hardly in keeping with new virtues of frugality and hard work being idealized by the Communists. Even worse, the quality of life that produced China's cultural heritage continued to be an indirect source of admiration though it was the antithesis of everything communism stood for. In order to demolish the "old society" its art would have to be demolished—at least temporarily.

[90]

In its less extreme forms, the campaign has not meant that old things should be destroyed. Instead, they should be examined and criticized for their bourgeois implications. For comparison, the official press has published and praised some excruciating poetry—usually extolling Mao—written by peasants and workers who, it is argued, are able to compose verse better than "feudal lords and princes."

The Communists' distrust of the people's ability to distinguish between art and its source includes foreign influences. If you admire the work of a European writer, they say, then you admire the capitalistic system that produced him. Thus Shakespeare and Molière were reduced to "literary squids" by the Cultural Revolutionaries.

Some of the arguments against foreign writings seemed justified. A Chinese student at the Peking Foreign Languages Institute, for instance, complained with reason that his class had to study Dickens and Shakespeare though their writings were neither relevant nor useful in learning to speak English. And I could agree with Han Suyin's observation that the Long March would be a far better subject for a play than the life of a courtier. However, it makes just as bad sense to learn English by studying translations of Mao's works, and to have schools of music, ballet and art producing nothing but crudely "realistic" propaganda.

It is consoling to believe, as I do, that the Chinese, both old and young, have too great a love for beauty to swallow such propaganda no matter how much they may agree in public.

I think of the old Chinese man, the cook of a friend of mine in Peking, who stood before a scroll for fifteen minutes smiling softly to himself and gently tracing the brush strokes of a painter who had died a hundred years ago.

And I think of the warm sunny day when my wife and daughter and I were walking around one of the small Summer Palace lakes, so far from the main buildings that we could hardly hear the slogans from the distant loudspeakers. Suddenly all three of us stopped in amazement: we could hear "The Carnival of Venice" being played. A few minutes later we passed a drifting rowboat in which were seated three young Chinese boys expertly playing the song on balalaikas. All of them wore Red Guard arm-bands.

It was the only time we heard Western music played publicly in China. It was banned (nobody mentioned that some of the most popular and frequently heard revolutionary songs were written to Russian music), and so also was the classical Chinese opera. I felt sorry for the Chinese musicians one would see at banquets; they had a repertoire of about twelve songs which they had been playing for three years. I wondered if any of the musicians, all wearing army uniforms, had been members of the Peking Symphony that performed before the Cultural Revolution. Nobody was more shocked than the resident correspondents who attended the dinner Chou En-lai gave for President and Mrs. Richard Nixon, and heard that same orchestra launch into "America the Beautiful," and a spirited version of "Turkey in the Straw."

It should be said, though, that the Chinese genuinely enjoyed the "contemporary" ballets and operas which were shown in Peking. These had been composed and staged with the active encouragement and direct help of Chiang Ching, the former Shanghai actress who is Mao's wife and a leading member of the Cultural Revolution group. Early photographs show her to be an attractive woman, and it is easy to see why Mao discarded his wife and took her to the caves of Yenan with him more than thirty years ago, though now she looks somewhat frumpy with her thick glasses and her brown army trousers, tunic and cap. She was placed in charge of all cultural matters, and was reputed to be one of the militant leftists. However, she maintained a close interest in the ballets and operas she had helped originate before the Cultural Revolution. One night while I was watching a ballet in the Heavenly Bridge theater, I saw her slip in through a side entrance and take the last seat in the third row. She watched the performance attentively, taking copious notes on a writing pad, and then left quietly just before the ballet ended.

My family and I went to the ballet whenever we could get tickets. I went to the opera only once, *The Red Lantern*, and left at the intermission; the traditional Chinese music was just too painful to my ears, though the Chinese liked the opera well enough and often whistled the melodies.

Once in a while I would go to the movies, not so much to see the films, which were routinely dull propaganda, but to enjoy the luxury of being ignored as a foreigner—once the film had started. Sometimes the evening would be instructive. During one film the figure of Wu Fa-hsien flashed across the screen. Wu Fa-hsien, who disappeared from the political scene in late 1971, was an important man in China then. He was a member of the Politburo and the head of the Chinese Air Force. But he was also a very funny-looking fellow, short, fat and resembling nothing so much as an overstuffed frog. Among the less reverent diplomats he was the butt of jokes such as "Do you know how the Chinese got rid of all the flies? Wu Fa-hsien ate them up."

Anyhow, when Wu Fa-hsien strode across the screen, the audience burst into loud laughter. The Chinese have a sense of humour too, at least under the protective shield of darkness.

Much more instructive, though, were my occasional forays into the night on pub-crawling tours with a diplomat friend who spoke and read Chinese. It was then that I saw and listened to Peking's ordinary people, night-workers, pedicart drivers, street-cleaners. We would start out at 11 P.M., wearing dark old clothes, and visit perhaps four or five of the city's many "pubs." They were in fact small cafés, usually only one small room, where one could get some cold meat, tea, beer and very strong white wine. The cafés were strictly utilitarian, with unpainted wood floors, benches and six or seven tables, each with a tin can filled with wooden chopsticks. We would usually buy a pitcher of beer and two saucers of wine, which was about all we could safely balance in our hands. Sometimes the pressure would be too low in the beer barrel, and the white-aproned girl behind the counter would vigorously set to work with a tire pump. My friend would translate the posters on the walls, which often were "sorrowful apologies" by a restaurant worker who had been impolite, or failed to show up at work on time. He would also eavesdrop on conversations around us. More often than not, the Chinese were talking about us, wondering who we were, which country we came from, evaluating the price of our clothes and so on. Sometimes there would be a discussion about the propriety of approaching us to ask if we were Albanians, but nobody worked up enough nerve or interest to do so. Eventually, their conversation would return to personal matters. Not surprisingly, the talk was much the same as one would hear in any small pub. The impending visit of a relative, the price of a pair of shoes, the car accident that had occurred last week, the recurrence of an old ailment, and, of course, the weather. I never once heard politics discussed, perhaps because we were there; but anyhow I found it somehow reassuring.

Peking also has many "first-class" restaurants, some of them world famous, such as the Meeting of All the Virtues, which specializes in Peking duck, or the Garden of the Horn of Plenty or the Orioles' Rendevzous. They usually would be divided into two sections: a large open area filled with tables where passers-by could drop in for whatever meal was being served that day; and at the back of the restaurant, or upstairs, some small rooms for private dinners. The meals would be sumptuous, with perhaps six or seven delicious dishes such as sea slugs, shark's fin or chili chicken, with peanuts. The menu would be selected a couple of days in advance by the host. He might choose certain dishes, but because the cooks were never absolutely certain which foods might be available, the host's main task was to decide how much he wanted to pay. For a private dinner anything less than two yuan (about eighty cents) per person would be unthinkable. Top price was about five yuan (about $2.15) per person, excluding drinks. This, in a city where the average monthly salary was about $35, was very expensive. And yet the restaurants were always filled. The explanation was simple. Cost of living was very low and people were able to save money, but after the experience of the Cultural Revolution few were willing to spend their money on visible luxuries. A splendid dinner could not be seen, and a full belly could not be confiscated. It was also obvious to anyone who overheard the lively conversation and frequent laughter at one of these dinners, that they also provided the Chinese with an enjoyable break from the tedium of the outside world.

I am, of course, speaking about the Chinese world. Few people in China knew anything about the *real* outside world, except what they would read in the official newspapers; and they, to use an understatement, are misleading.

Albania, for example, is the subject of constant praise because it has allied itself with Peking in opposing the Soviet Union and has emulated China's style of communism (the emulation has amusing features, incidentally, and one wonders what Chinese visitors to Tirane think when they see everywhere white plaster busts and statues of party leader Enver Hoxa and little red books of *his* quotations). Hardly a day passes without the *People's Daily* publishing a stirring article about Albania's mighty army, or its new record-breaking harvest, or its gigantic advances in medical science.

One day, while listening to my translator Mr. Chung read one of these lugubrious articles, I asked him if he knew the size of Albania's population. He replied that he didn't, and refused to hazard a guess.

"Albania has about two million people," I said, and added for effect, "which means that Peking alone has more than three times as many people."

Mr. Chung laughed loudly, which meant he was very agitated. "That is impossible," he said flatly. "I don't know how large Albania is, but it is certainly larger than *that*."

I brought out a geography book and showed him Albania's position in a population table. He stared at the figure in disbelief, and asked if he could examine the book. He quickly turned to the first page, and then a smile of satisfaction spread across his face.

"Aha, look here," he said, pointing to the printed line which read: Published in the United States.

My translator had gone to university, but his specialty had been literature and his knowledge of most foreign countries was rather slight. At that, it was far greater than the average Chinese, most of whom have only a hazy idea of the outside world. Two friends and I were walking through the Western Hills when three old Chinese workmen happened by. One of them greeted us civilly and asked if we were Albanians. I told him I was from Canada, and he politely observed that Canada indeed was a very nice country.

I asked him if he knew where Canada was.

The workman did not hesitate. "Oh, yes," he said airily, and waved his hand at the nearest hill. "It's over there." His two companions were very impressed.

The Chinese also know very little about current international events. And what they do learn from press and radio reports is very one-sided. Peking makes no secret of the fact that it believes a truly good newspaper cannot be objective if it is to serve the cause of communism. During the Cultural Revolution, Chinese journalists and editors came under fire for not having a political purpose, for trying to make their newspapers lively and interesting by publishing stories about "eggs with two yolks, snakes with two heads, and a woman turning into a man." This was condemned as "wonder-hunting."

Today the *People's Daily* is very stern. There is no good news about the United States or the Soviet Union, though there are plenty of stories about their unemployment, high taxes, food shortages, poor housing, crime, riots and the like. Indeed, if the average Chinese were to believe one-tenth of what he reads, he would be convinced that the United States and the Soviet Union are in economic chaos and tottering on the edge of ruin. But no doubt he views the reports with a skeptical eye. There is too much evidence around—Russian- and U.S.-made machinery, planes and cars that are very old but often superior to what China produces—for him to accept all the dire stories in the press.

News from outside is also carried by word of mouth. A Chinese student I met knew all about the Americans landing on the moon, though there was not one word about it in China's newspapers. Foreigners are also a source of news; no Chinese who works in an embassy or is around foreign businessmen fails to hear something about the outside world. There is also a considerable amount of traffic between Hong Kong and China. During the Chinese New Year holiday, for instance, more than 100,000 Hong Kong residents visit the mainland in a two-week period. Of course they hardly constitute a great flow of information to China's 750 million people, but news about the "outside" world does travel quickly.

At this point, it is perhaps worth noting that many foreigners are as uninformed about China as the Chinese are about other countries.

A few examples will suffice. The Italian Trade Office in Peking received a request from a Naples businessman about the potential market in China for his range of religious medallions and statuettes of the Virgin Mary. A Toronto realtor asked me about the possibility of setting up a branch office in Peking. A film company asked a Scandinavian diplomat to inquire about the availability of Chinese theaters for a tour of Ingmar Bergman films.

Even foreign ministries sometimes seem unaware of political realities. One embassy had mechanical problems with its safe and cabled home for advice. The foreign ministry cabled back that the "American Embassy" in Peking might be able to help. Another foreign ministry sent congratulations by cable to Peking on the occasion of China's National Day. But the cable was addressed to the Republic of China, which is the title Formosa has adopted, instead of the People's Republic of China. The unhappy ambassador involved spent an unpleasant hour in the Chinese Foreign Ministry apologizing for the diplomatic gaffe.

In all of Peking, the Chinese who had the most intimate knowledge of foreigners were the men and women who served them as cooks, chauffeurs, translators and amahs. Unlike the top Chinese leaders—most of whom have never stepped outside their own country—they saw the foreigners laughing, crying, fighting and drunk. They knew about their morals, the kind of food they ate, the books they read and, very important to a Chinese, the way they treated their children. I don't know how much of this information they passed along to their superiors; probably most of it. But the Chinese help I met, including those who worked for other foreigners, were kind, responsive and, in general, hard-working. They kept to themselves, offering neither comment nor opinion about anything. (I am omitting the days of demonstrations against foreigners when they would be ordered out to parade against their employers and shout and spit at them, and then would report punctually for work the next morning as though nothing had happened.)

Strangely, only among the baby amahs—the kindest of the group—was it possible to see any variance in treatment of foreigners. It was revealing to watch a group of baby amahs gossiping as they sat on the front steps of the apartment, their wards in their laps. The African babies would get a desultory pat, but the European babies were cuddled and cooed over. All the children were treated well, of course, but it was quite clear that the amans who took care of European babies considered themselves superior to their sisters. For one thing, they did not have to endure the laughter of the Chinese children who would gather outside the iron fence of the compound and point at the African babies until the Chinese policeman on sentry duty shooed them away.

Despite all the official polemics about "everlasting love," and despite all the generous aid which Peking gives African nations, the reality is that the Chinese regard black people as their inferiors—as any African who attended a Chinese school could tell you. One of them, incidentally, was refused permission to marry a Chinese fellow student although he was from a country which continuously receives lavish praise in Peking's official press. When he and the girl said they would defy the authorities and get married anyhow, she was summarily sent to Shanghai. The boy promptly went on a

[99]

hunger strike. Three weeks later, when it became obvious that he was quite prepared to starve himself to death despite the pleadings and warnings of the Chinese and his embassy, the girl magically reappeared in Peking and they were married. I would see them from time to time with their little boy in restaurants or shopping.

It is well known that the Chinese consider their own culture and civilization the finest in the world. To a large extent they are right. They also consider their skin color and the shape of their eyes as most beautiful; and about that I definitely agree. But even among themselves the Chinese have definite prejudices. For centuries a fair skin has been regarded as a sign of beauty and upper-class birth. In Hong Kong, one still sees elderly Chinese carefully shielding their faces from the rays of the sun as they cross the street. In China, where intellectuals are urged to "learn wisdom from the peasants," it is supposed to be a badge of proletarian honour to have a sunburned nose from labouring in the fields. And yet, one wonders.

I mentioned to a Chinese that I was going to Shanghai, and jokingly added that I was looking forward to the opportunity to see for myself whether the girls in Shanghai were really the prettiest in all of China.

"Very nice," he allowed, "but their skins are too dark."

The Chinese are not a uniform people, and they are aware of their physical differences. In the south they are short, dark, industrious, volatile, quick-witted and quick-moving; they speak animatedly and enthusiastically. With a good subject to discuss, three Cantonese can sound like three hundred. These are the Chinese that Westerners know. They came to Europe and America mostly from the southern province of Kwangtung and still do, with Hong Kong acting as a funnel to the West.

[100]

The northern Chinese are handsome and tall; six-foot men are common in Peking. They move slowly and deliberately, and they are not quick to anger. By reputation, the north has produced most of China's great scholars and philosophers. The southern Chinese regard the northerners as arrogant, phlegmatic, even lazy. But to a northerner, a southern Chinese is not someone to trust too far.

"They are very good tailors," was the only description a Pekingese would offer when I asked him about the people of Shanghai.

Tradition dies hard in China, despite the exhortations of cadres, despite the turmoil of the Cultural Revolution.

Family, for instance, is supposed to be unimportant in China today. Yet two politically correct translators I knew brought their mothers to Peking to see the city and to visit with their grandchildren. A third travelled more than seven hundred miles to be married in his home village because his parents insisted that the marriage be performed "before their eyes." Perhaps the *People's Daily* was talking about people like him when it warned that some backsliding families were continuing the tradition of wedding feasts.

Romance is supposed to be bourgeois, since it deflects young people from serving the state. But as soon as the turmoil of the Cultural Revolution subsided, girls began to let their hair grow long and exchanged their plain white mannish shirts for colourful cotton blouses. The cosmetic counter in the main department store was once again busy selling girls cold cream and perfumed hair shampoo, though lipstick, rouge and nail polish were still banned. And in the evening, couples would sit whispering softly under the trees in the Altar of the Sun Park—victims no doubt of what the Communists call "sugar-coated bullets."

Religious superstitions are also supposed to be dead.

[101]

killed by the Cultural Revolution. The peasants have grasped Mao Tse-tung's Thoughts and are creatively applying them to build a new socialist state; so says the *People's Daily*. Yet every spring during the Cultural Revolution, the peasants in a village thirty-five miles north of Peking carefully put the traditional "paper money" on the burial mounds of their ancestors.

But even China's leaders—who say the country must break with the past if it is to achieve a future—seem unable to break their own ties to the ancient culture and standards. For instance, Foreign Minister Chen Yi, who died in 1972, was fond of quoting from classical Chinese poetry. Then of course, there is Mao Tse-tung himself. Not only do his writings have many literary and historical allusions, but he is an above-average composer of poetry. Perhaps it is just a coincidence, but in old China, wealthy merchants, famous generals and even emperors tried their hand at writing poetry (which led to some very bad stuff being written) because in that civilized society a man's real worth was judged by his scholarship and artistic sensibility.

This obsession with culture is difficult for a non-Chinese to comprehend—who can imagine Henry Ford, Dwight D. Eisenhower or Richard Nixon forcing himself to write a sonnet in order to achieve status? It is even more difficult for a foreigner to understand Peking's determination to crush culture and yet preserve it, to understand an official policy that publicly condemns "feudal" Chinese art but also calls for hard cash to be quietly spent acquiring Chinese art treasures as they come on the market in London and Paris.

These apparent contradictions have both fascinated and confused foreign observers, especially those few journalists such as myself who lived in Peking during the Cultural Revolution. And though it sounds rather pompous to say so, most of us felt a sense of obligation because we were in Peking to interpret as well as report the contradictions that abounded during the Cultural Revolution. That our efforts were often frustrated by the Chinese Foreign Ministry's peculiar Information Department was, I suppose, just one more contradiction to add to the list.

7

I had been in China only a few days, not long enough to be blasé about demonstrations and certainly not long enough to be able to work without being distracted by a commotion outside. Later, much later, I became so inured to the constant noise that I was able to keep writing a story without noticing that a couple of thousand Chinese were marching by shouting slogans. Eventually, I even managed to sleep peacefully through the shrieks of a female cadre, whose knife-edged voice blared through loudspeakers outside every morning at five-thirty reciting quotations from Mao Tse-tung and ordering everyone to spring out of bed and work for a new socialist China.

On this particular day in May, 1968, however, my senses were not yet dulled by the incessant din, and I was out on the balcony watching a parade of shouting workers when the telephone rang. It was Jean Vincent, the Agence France Presse correspondent.

"I don't suppose you've had a call to report to the Foreign Ministry," he asked, almost tentatively.

[105]

"No," I said, "but maybe they haven't got around to calling me yet."

Jean rejected my optimism. "You would have heard by now. They want me to be there in half an hour. Look, if I don't call you within three hours, you'd better tell the French Ambassador I'm in trouble."

"Cheer up," I joked, "maybe they want to congratulate you for furthering the cause of Sino-French relations."

"Hah!" he snorted, and hung up.

Jean and the other correspondents had agreed it was only a matter of time before he was thrown out of China, not so much because his writing was critical of China, but because he was breaking the rules set up by the Information Department. It was quite permissible to report on conflict within China if your story was accurate. If, for instance, the Shanghai newspaper published a story about a young coal worker who vowed to report to work on time every day, then it could be assumed—and written by a correspondent—that the Chinese were tightening discipline in the Shanghai area and workers were not reporting to their shift on time, or perhaps not reporting in at all. Hardly sensational news, but reasonably accurate.

The only really sensational news in Peking appeared on the wall posters, which the Chinese called *Tatsebao*. Wall posters are an old tradition in China where they have been used by an individual or group to record information and, more likely, complaints. They were tightly controlled by the Communist authorities except on two occasions. In the Let a Hundred Flowers Bloom campaign in 1958, intellectuals were encouraged to criticize the system. The complaints were so vitriolic that the campaign was cut off in a matter of days, and was followed by a purge of the dissidents.

The second occasion was the Cultural Revolution, when Mao Tse-tung himself told the Chinese people to put up their own wall posters criticizing government leaders or any other persons in authority. To dramatize his order, and to make sure people understood it, he painted a wall poster of his own. It said, in usual Chinese overstatement, Bombard the Headquarters. Mao, of course, is not one of the world's exponents of free speech for the Chinese or anyone else. But the wall posters were one of the weapons he had to counter the official press and radio which were controlled by a Communist party that refused him allegiance.

What happened was unparalleled in Communist history. Every party leader, including Mao, came under attack in the wall posters. Personal as well as ideological faults were exposed and bitterly ridiculed. Secret conversations among the highest officials were displayed for the lowliest peasant to read, and bad decisions made in the past by the party hierarchy were exposed and criticized.

The few foreign journalists in Peking moved about in a kind of dream world. Correspondents who had spent weeks trying to get one scrap of information suddenly found themselves overwhelmed with live news. It was as though a man dying of thirst in the desert were suddenly thrown into a flood-swollen river and found himself gulping water while swimming for his life. Instead of leisurely examining the subtleties of a suspected shift in Chinese economic planning, the correspondents had to perform like young reporters out chasing fire engines. Every day there were new posters and new stories. There was hardly time to report what was happening, never mind analyze it. It was an exciting, exhausting and rewarding time; for, although the correspondents did not realize it in the beginning, they were covering a revolution.

All the reporters who were in Peking at that time agree that the Japanese journalists set the pace. It was, of course, easy for them to circulate almost unnoticed among the Chinese, and the similarity of the Japanese and Chinese written characters enabled them to read the wall posters. They also worked together as a team, sometimes combining their passion for gadgetry and efficiency in an amusing way. At night, when new wall posters were usually put up, one walked along the street with a flashlight, reading the wall posters into a battery-operated megaphone. Two others were in a car moving slowly along the street, one driving and the other tapping out the news with a typewriter on his lap. In the end, the Japanese ingenuity and understanding of the language made them suspect in Chinese eyes.

By early 1967 the Cultural Revolution had spread across China, and fighting had broken out between Mao's supporters and enemies. This was duly reported in wall posters and Red Guard newspapers, but hardly in an objective way. Aside from the Chinese penchant for high-flown hyperbole, the people who were pasting up wall posters or printing broad-sheets were in fact deeply involved in the struggle for power. If it was to their advantage, street fist-fights would be portrayed as pitched battles with hundreds of lives lost. A savage clash between workers and students would be described in minute detail—not because it had actually happened but because faction leaders hoped it would happen. On the other hand, fierce fighting could be pictured as a reasoned argument. It became more and more difficult for foreign journalists to decide which reports were true, though this was not a particular concern of the Russian correspondents who cheerfully put the worst interpretation on every event to buttress Moscow's ideological dispute with Peking.

Eventually, the Peking authorities clamped down. A proclamation was issued warning all foreigners that reading or reporting on wall posters would be regarded as spying. It was probably authorized by Premier Chou En-lai, the

[108]

only Chinese official likely to be much worried about the damaging publicity China was receiving in the outside world.

In any case, it was the end of a joyful era for the correspondents. They could, through one way and another, surreptitiously get information from wall posters. I did. But the question was how to write it and not be thrown into jail or out of the country. It was especially frustrating because the *Tass* and *Pravda* correspondents were busy every day writing stories about everything they knew—and a few things they didn't know—without the slightest hesitation.

To understand how this could happen is to understand the working of the Oriental mind, an art at which the Soviet Union has had considerably more practice than Western nations. Stories about China that were published by Tass and Pravda always appeared under a Moscow dateline without the author being identified. Although the Chinese knew very well that the stories were written in Peking, they officially regarded the reports as Moscow-based and therefore ignored them.

The rest of us, including other East Europeans, did not have editors who were interested in maintaining a "nonexistent" bureau in Peking.

In fact, when I arrived in Peking in April, 1968, there was considerably less pressure for sensational news. The drama of the Red Guards had been pretty well played out, and world interest in the Cultural Revolution had tapered off. Fighting was still going on in various parts of China, but it was isolated and not really significant as far as overall control of the country was concerned. Although it was not conceded by Moscow or Washington, Mao and his followers had won the revolution.

Peking then was still a tense city. At night soldiers with fixed bayonets patrolled the streets, and trucks carrying troops rumbled in and out of Peking daily. Demonstrations were going on at all hours of the day and night. Sometimes they would be pathetic little parades of perhaps seventy-five persons marching around the block to "celebrate" the founding of a revolutionary committee in a neighbourhood cottage industry. Other times, hundreds of thousands of men, women and children would suddenly be out on the streets at precisely 9 P.M.—for some unknown reason a favourite time for demonstrations to start—because a new quotation had been issued by Mao Tse-tung. Giant firecrackers would be set off and red kettledrums would be thumped mercilessly until about 1 A.M., when people would slowly drift back to their homes.

With a demonstration, one at least could go out into the streets, find out what it was about, and cable a story home. Much more frustrating were the rallies held in the giant Workers' Stadium, just a five-minute walk from my apartment. From my balcony I could see the lights of the stadium and hear 70,000 people roar their approval, but of what I would not have the slightest idea. Even if I had spoken Chinese it wouldn't have helped, since the area was cordoned off by soldiers.

Eventually, of course, I would find out. One of the diplomats would read it in a wall poster or a Red Guard newspaper and pass along the information to me. Then I would work it into a different but related story in such a way that the news would get out but I could not be accused of reading the forbidden poster. It was a kind of game, since the Chinese knew what I was doing and I knew they knew; but there was a certain amount of excitement in the playing of it. Anthony Grey, the Reuters correspondent, was under house arrest when I arrived in Peking, and in the next seven weeks the Agence France Presse man Jean Vincent was declared *persona non grata* and Keiji Samejima, the correspondent of

Nihon Keizai Shimbun, was arrested in the middle of the night.

Grey's situation was deplorable. He had been under house arrest for nine months (and was to spend another year and a half in captivity), a hostage for some Communist journalists who had been jailed in Hong Kong. But all of us believed this was an exceptional circumstance that would not be repeated, though we often speculated over what would happen to one of us if a New China News Agency correspondent defected in our native land.

Vincent's case was not particularly worrisome. Each of us took the same risk with every story we wrote.

Samejima, however, was different. At one o'clock in the morning a group of Chinese soldiers had arrived at his flat, which was just below mine. They politely knocked at the door, wakening Samejima and his wife and their four-year-old daughter. When he let them in, they carefully searched the rooms but replaced everything they disturbed—except for a pile of newspapers, notes and photographs. When they left they took these things with them, and Samejima too. He was not freed until eighteen months later, when the Chinese announced that he had confessed to spying.

At the time he vanished the only thing we could find out, indirectly, was that the Chinese said he was guilty of breaking China's laws. That shook us. We all had in our offices piles of illegal Red Guard newspapers, notes of unconfirmed rumours, and sets of photographs of various street scenes. It was harmless stuff, the sort of working information that a correspondent just naturally gathers. Did possessing it mean we were spies?

Technically, yes. But no other raids were made on any other journalist's flat though the Chinese authorities knew very well that all of us had files of what could conceivably be regarded as classified information; certainly our Chinese translators had given their supervisors a detailed accounting of that, as well as a daily list of all the people who visited us. Obviously the Foreign Ministry did not regard the rest of us as being anything more than the usual nuisances that foreign correspondents are in a totalitarian society. In fact, my contacts with members of the Information Department of the Foreign Ministry left me in no doubt that they considered us a tiresome but necessary inconvenience. Because we were allowed into Peking, Chinese correspondents were allowed into our countries. I'm sure the Information Department people would have been delighted if we all just packed up and voluntarily went home. Then their correspondents could have stayed abroad, and the Information Department could have gone about its business without having to be bothered about us. What that business would be I don't know, but it didn't have anything to do with providing information to the correspondents in Peking.

Before the Cultural Revolution, the Foreign Ministry had a strong working relationship with the foreign press corps. It was never ideal from the correspondents' point of view—they being a notoriously difficult bunch to satisfy—but nevertheless there were frequent press conferences and journalists could easily arrange trips to various parts of China as well as to communes, factories, hospitals, schools and even jails.

During the year and a half I was in China, only one press conference was called by the Department of Information (which we had taken to calling the Department of Silence). We were telephoned at our homes before noon and told to be at the Foreign Ministry at 3 P.M. for an important announcement. There was considerable excitement that afternoon as we met in the Information Department and waited for Mr. Chi. He walked into the room carrying a sheaf of papers at precisely 3 P.M.

"Gentlemen," he said crisply, "I have here a statement

[112]

from the Foreign Ministry which I will read to you. Are you prepared?"

He really didn't have to ask. Pencils were poised, ready to write the news that Mao Tse-tung had died, or that China had been invaded, or some similar earth-shaking event.

He cleared his throat importantly and began. "The Foreign Ministry of the People's Republic of China hereby informs all foreign citizens residing in China that it is strictly forbidden to have in their possession any unregistered explosive, firearms or other weapons. Such things must be registered immediately with the Foreign Ministry. The order applies to all foreign nationals, including personnel of all embassies."

We looked at each other in astonishment.

"Thank you, gentlemen, that is all," said Mr. Chi, as he got up and strode out of the room with his sheaf of papers. Thus ended, with considerable puzzlement on our side, if not Mr. Chi's, the one and only press conference I attended in Peking.

There were other, less pleasant, occasions when we were invited individually to the Foreign Ministry. These summonses usually meant bad news, and were not welcomed by the journalists. It was not easy to forget that the Reuters correspondent had been invited to the Foreign Ministry and had never reappeared. Once inside the Foreign Ministry, you knew immediately if you were in some sort of trouble. If a white-jacketed Chinese boy came into the room bearing a tray of tea, cigarets and matches, it meant the meeting would be innocuous. If, however, Mr. Chi arrived and there were no tea, cigarets and matches, then you knew you were in for an unpleasant and difficult harangue.

This deliberate protocol of politeness was a very serious matter to the Chinese, and could be carried to laughable lengths. I attended one tea-less session with Mr. Chi during which he spent fifteen minutes simulating anger, distress and, eventually, sorrow, over one of my stories in *The Globe and Mail*. He had, of course, seen the original copy of my story and knew that the offending sentence in question—an inaccurate reference to Mao Tse-tung—was due either to faulty cable transmission or to an error made by a sub-editor in Toronto. I made the unnecessary explanation to Mr. Chi, who nodded thoughtfully.

"We understand this, but nevertheless we hold that you are responsible for the actions of your newspaper," he said seriously. Then he suddenly smiled and made an inconsequential comment about the weather in Peking. As if by signal, the door opened and the Chinese boy entered bearing the friendly tea, cigarets and matches. We chatted pleasantly over our tea for the next fifteen minutes and then I was politely ushered out. All very Chinese.

Also very Chinese was the Information Department's method of dealing with requests to visit the cities of Tientsin and Canton. These were the only two cities to which journalists could travel during my first fifteen months in China. Tientsin, about fifty miles away, could be visited for one day. Canton could be visited during the spring and fall trade fairs. The journalist would apply to the Foreign Ministry for permission to visit Tientsin for, say, one week and Canton for three weeks. Back would come the telephone reply: you may visit Tientsin for one day and Canton for four days. The journalist would then go to the Public Security Office and fill out a travel visa form. Under the printed section, How long do you wish to stay in destination? the journalist would carefully write: Tientsin one day, Canton four days.

I often wondered what would have happened if I wrote: Tientsin three days, Canton two weeks.

I learned very quickly that the last place to ask for information was at the Information Department. Except on

one occasion—when I was allowed to tour a factory in Peking
—every request in fifteen months for statistics or interviews
or trips to cities other than Tientsin and Canton, or visits to
schools or hospitals or other institutions was turned down.
At least I assume they were turned down. In fact, I had no
response at all from the Information Department—which I
suppose entitled the Chinese to say they had never refused
any of my requests.

At first it was frustrating. Even a simple request for information about Peking's subway was ignored. Curiously,
the subway was never even mentioned in Chinese newspapers
during the whole time I was in Peking, though certainly
every resident could hardly avoid seeing the great construction taking place along the route of Peking's old city walls
which had been torn down. The subway had still not been
opened officially at the end of 1971, but 60,000 Chinese a day
were taking the fifteen-mile ride from downtown to the
northwestern outskirts of Peking. These were specially arranged excursions, at two cents per person.

After a time, though, frustration gave way to amusement,
and on dull days I would entertain myself by writing impossible requests to the Foreign Ministry. One splendid
afternoon, I sent a letter to the Information Department asking for permission to visit any one of three places: Inner
Mongolia and the border areas where fighting between the
Chinese and Russians was taking place; Sinkiang, reputedly
the site of Chinese nuclear installations; and Tibet, which
no foreign correspondent had visited in about ten years.

There was no reply.

Only once did the Information Department answer one of
my queries. I was writing a story about Lin Piao, then the
number-two man in the country, and found some discrepan-
cies in the biographical data I had accumulated. Two his-
tories had different dates for his birth, and there were

conflicting reports about whether he had been wounded during the Korean War. I wrote a letter to the Information Department explaining my problem and asking if the information I had could be verified. An hour after I had dropped the letter off at the Foreign Ministry, the telephone rang. Such swift action startled me.

"This is the Information Department of the Foreign Ministry," said a voice which I recognized as belonging to Mr. Chi. "We have received your letter. Are you prepared for the reply?"

"Very good," I said, and grabbed a pencil. "Go ahead."

"Vice-chairman Lin Piao is the closest comrade in arms of Chairman Mao Tse-tung. Anyone who slanders Vice-chairman Lin Piao will have to bear the serious consequences."

There was a silence on the line.

"Yes," I prompted, "and the information I asked for?"

"I will repeat," said Mr. Chi. "Vice-chairman Lin Piao is the closest comrade in arms of Chairman Mao Tse-tung. Anyone who slanders Vice-chairman Lin Piao will have to bear the serious consequences."

"That's all?" I asked, incredulous.

"That is all."

The seeming perversity of the Information Department was, I am sure, due in large part to the fact that the Foreign Ministry was under severe attack during the Cultural Revolution. People in every department, including the Information section, were prime targets. All of them had superior education, many having attended school abroad. Probably only a few were not the sons and daughters of once wealthy parents. By the very nature of their work they were constantly exposed to "bourgeois" thinking because of their contact with foreigners and their constant reading of foreign publications. Their every action and word was open to minute inspection by political zealots. To give the slightest unapproved concession, or even to show untoward friendliness toward a journalist, would probably have been sufficient cause for instant self-criticism sessions. Even worse, they could be sent off to work in a paddy field for six months or longer for reeducation. One could hardly blame the Foreign Ministry people for avoiding journalists.

For official news, I had to rely on the *Hsinhua* (New China News Agency) bulletin, a set of stories translated into English and delivered to my door every afternoon by motorcycle, plus the following newspapers, all printed in Chinese: the *People's Daily*, a national newspaper printed simultaneously across the country; *Wenhuibao*, a Shanghai daily; the local *Peking Daily* and *Kwangming*, a newspaper designed for intellectuals. There were also two English language magazines, *China Reconstructs*, and *China Pictorial*, and an important Chinese language theoretical journal, *Red Flag*, which was published sporadically.

The Shanghai and Peking newspapers were the most valuable, because they were written for a relatively sophisticated audience in China's two major cities and thus offered some insights into political movements still in the experimental stage. *People's Daily* was meant to be read by everyone in China, since it was authorized by the top leaders of the country and therefore the final word on all matters. Important articles, however, were picked up by *Hsinhua* on the day of publication and sent around the world by teletype. Thus, a journalist in Hong Kong or Paris or London or Bonn could read a Hsinhua story at precisely the same moment as the Peking journalists.

The slight advantage of being able to read the local papers didn't last long. Four months after I arrived in Peking, delivery suddenly stopped and we were informed that they, like the wall posters and Red Guard newspapers, were forbidden. We were left with *Hsinhua*, the *People's Daily* and the occasional issue of *Red Flag* (whose important articles were also transmitted by *Hsinhua*).

At that, I felt fortunate to be getting Hsinhua. It at least provided English text of a number of significant stories daily (it took my translator, poor Mr. Chung, a full day to translate one article; he really was a teacher of Chinese literature in high school and was sent to me because at one time he had studied English), and it was useful reference material. Besides, *Hsinhua's* literal translations and unintentional humour also frequently enlivened the day.

They had, for instance, learned that fig leaves were connected somehow with shame. And so, a speech by President Richard Nixon would often be described as "nothing more than a fig leaf hiding the ugly tool of imperialism." Alas, the British were the only other people in Peking who understood English well enough to enjoy this marvellous metaphor.

But there was one *Hsinhua* article that had the whole foreign community smiling for a month. It was a delightful tale about a young girl who had been given a new job on the commune: castrating pigs. She went about her work diligently, since she was "in the vanguard of the great socialist revolution in the countryside." At first the poor girl was looked down at by other people on the commune who had the peculiar idea that this wasn't fit work for a woman. This troubled the sensitive young lady, but she read Mao Tsetung's quotations every night and found new strength in his words. As a result, she redoubled her efforts and soon she was the best pig castrator on the whole commune. When the story ended, she had won the respect and affection of the "old and wise peasants." The story didn't mention what the young men on the commune thought about it all.

I should add that a number of us, having been exposed to the Chinese sense of humour, suspected that some of these wonderful translations were done by defiant intellectuals

To the north of Peking, in a setting of tranquil beauty, are the tombs of thirteen of the sixteen Ming Emperors. The tombs, built between 1400 and 1700, have been left to ruin, but their original magnificence is evident even in their state of disrepair. The Chinese ignored the many splendid acres and Peking's foreign community enjoyed visiting the tombs on weekends.

The old Summer Palace, built in the early 1700's, was destroyed in 1860 by English and French troops during the Tai Ping revolution and still lies in ruins. The Summer Palace erected near Peking University in its place is a favorite haunt of Chinese and foreigners for walks, picnics, and for views of the countryside and (above) the lovely tiled roofs of the Palace buildings.

Regina, Katharine, and a friend pause on the Avenue of the Animals, part of the Sacred Way leading to the Ming Tombs. The camel, like other figures and other streets, was daubed with revolutionary slogans by Red Guards.

An afternoon of boating on the Summer Palace lake provided respite from the political pressures of life in Peking. In the winter skaters replaced boats on the lake until the vicious north wind covered its surface with a layer of grit.

Weekend excursions to the Great Wall 45 miles from Peking were permitted to foreigners. Once the scene of border fights with the Northern Barbarians, these had shifted to the Sino-Soviet border to which no foreigners could obtain a pass.

In one of the curious paradoxes of modern Chinese history, Dr. Sun Yat-sen is regarded with great respect by both Communists and Nationalists. Dr. Sun's tomb in the outskirts of Peking was constructed of blue tiles and white bricks by the Nationalists to represent the colors of their flag.

Shanghai, always a center of revolution, was one of the worst places in China for a foreigner to get in trouble. The hostile attitude of Shanghaiese was perhaps explained by the fact that before the Communists took over, the foreign-dominated port marked its park (foreground), "No dogs or Chinese allowed."

During the Cultural Revolution, China's ancient artistic treasures were threatened by the Red Guards and all the art galleries, libraries, and museums were padlocked and guarded by armed soldiers. The beautiful Temple of Heaven (left) was left open, but the exquisitely carved marble slabs on the steps of the temple building inside the courtyard were protected by a thick layer of plaster.

Children, particularly in the countryside, are taught that work as well as school is necessary for the education of the true Communist youth. Whether or not they believed it, the youngsters at Evergreen Commune (above) enjoyed harvesting grain for the benefit of visiting foreigners.

Foreigners were housed in special compounds more luxurious than those of their Chinese neighbors and typical of the special treatment foreigners received in China. This view from the front balcony of our apartment shows the fence surrounding our compound.

Many children from non-Communist countries attended school at the French Cultural Center, run like a one-room schoolhouse with all age levels combined. Within a month the children from Mali, Guinea, Bulgaria, France, Canada, Japan, Algeria, the Congo, and Cambodia were happily chattering in French while they played tag in the school's back yard. Below, Katharine with some of her classmates.

Although foreigners sometimes found themselves in the crossfire between Mao Tse-tung's supporters and enemies, the ordinary Chinese usually regarded pale-skinned "round-eyes" with friendly curiosity. Above, some young people smile down at me from a bridge in the Summer Palace.

Peking Airport was the ideal place for foreigners, including my daughter Katharine, to get a close look at Chinese leaders welcoming foreign dignitaries. She even got into a North Vietnamese reception line to meet Premier Chou En-lai, seen below talking to his protocol chief Han Ssu.

October 1st is National Day, a holiday across the country and the time for a parade involving up to a million people crossing the huge Tien an Men Square. During the Cultural Revolution Mao Tse-tung's personality cult reached near hysterical proportions. Above, soldiers carry a white statue of Mao Tse-tung in a march accompanied by hundreds of red flags.

Workmen wait for their morning recitation from the ubiquitous little red book of quotations from the thought of Mao Tse-tung. Every Chinese man, woman and child carried a copy as a matter of survival. He never knew when he might be called upon to draw it out to cite a quotation.

Everyone wanted to be on the march and beat a drum during the Cultural Revolution, including this group of young boys. Regina and Katharine, standing on the curb in front of the Friendship Store for foreigners in Peking, soon grew accustomed to the daily demonstrations.

In every public place in China, busts of Mao Tse-tung occupied prominent positions—at least until the end of the Cultural Revolution. Typically, the practical Chinese made the busts and statues of plaster rather than bronze or marble.

"Sailing the seas depends on the helmsman, making revolution depends on Mao Tse-tung," was the popular quote from the little red book which inspired this float at the National Day celebrations. Mao's ship is escorted by hundreds of marchers carrying billowing blue silk sheets representing waves.

Poster art also boomed during the Cultural Revolution. We saw this young painter carefully transforming a miniature of Mao into a billboard-size painting in a Peking park. Work and political education are the virtues on which the People's Republic of China was founded and received renewed attention during the Cultural Revolution when many huge posters depicted these values represented by muscular, aggressive workers armed with Mao's little red book.

During the Cultural Revolution, politics superseded work. Day and night propaganda blared from loudspeakers and we could view demonstrations such as this one daily from our apartment window.

who daringly added their own touch to the messages inside the Communist fortune cookies.

Although the cutting off of local Chinese newspapers and the prohibition against reading wall posters irritated foreigners, the two moves were part of the restoration of discipline that signalled the end of the Cultural Revolution. This tightening-up process was being exerted on the Chinese masses as well. By the middle of 1969, wall posters were not being put up at all in Peking unless approved by the Communist authorities, and local newspapers were very circumspect in reporting the news. What was happening, of course, was not that the leaders were imposing new censorship strictures, but that they were simply reimposing the old rules that had been set aside during the Cultural Revolution.

This meant that the diplomats and journalists began to rely more and more on each other for information about China. Cocktail parties—and there seemed to be one every day in Peking—were the favourite birthplace of gossip and rumours. The Albanians, Tanzanians and Zambians, all good friends of China, would drop little bonbons about the tremendous achievements they had seen in a factory or commune in some distant province. The East Europeans, always morose, would mutter darkly about a new peasants' uprising that had been ruthlessly crushed by Mao's forces. The French would chuckle about the latest illicit romance in the diplomatic corps. The Scandinavians would cheerfully spread rumors about a Kremlin plot to overthrow Alexei Kosygin. The straight-faced British would make poor puns which foreigners either didn't understand or would accept as fact. The Indians would deliver undecipherable and endless dissertations on the intricacies of Chinese Communist methodology.

Occasionally, a scrap of information would surface which a journalist could tuck away and, after gathering corroborating evidence from other sources, eventually use in a story. The most sensational news, however, would usually come from an East European diplomat and therefore had to be discounted. The Russians and their allies were always trying to plant rumours with the Western journalists, since a damaging story about the Chinese in West European or American newspapers would be a hundred times more effective than a thousand similar stories from Tass and Pravda.

My most effective sources were a handful of diplomats who were serious students of Chinese affairs or had genuine contacts among the Chinese, and also a very small group of "foreign friends" with whom I had infrequent but extremely valuable contact. These were people who had been hired by the Chinese to teach or work in government institutions. Because most of them are still in China—and a few are unable to return to their own countries—I do not feel free to describe them and their work, or how we would meet. I should add, though, that these people did not give me "secret" information in the spying sense; in fact, most of them were basically sympathetic to the Chinese. What they did give me were their personal observations of how the Cultural Revolution reforms were being carried out, and the reaction of the Chinese to them.

Among the journalists there was very little pooling of information. The East Europeans pretty well kept to themselves, with only the Yugoslavian and Rumanian correspondents being really successful at straddling the ideological barrier. The Rumanian correspondent, incidentally, had the distinction of never having one of his stories about the Cultural Revolution appear in a Rumanian newspaper, though he cabled an article home every day (Bucharest and Peking were and are on very friendly terms).

Sometimes all the journalists would have a social evening together. But these were rare occasions, usually to welcome a newcomer or to say farewell to a departing journalist. Strangely, there was no great feeling of camaraderie despite the fact there were only sixteen of us in Peking. (In Washington, incidentally, the press corps numbers more than 1,000.) The combination of politics, competition and Peking's pressurized atmosphere was not fertile ground for friendships.

One correspondent who did become a good friend was the West German, Hans Bargmann, a tall, red-faced and corpulent man who had spent four years in China. During that time he had acquired a genuine liking and understanding of the Chinese people, and his advice to me on political matters was always sound. He also had acquired a fund of funny stories, mostly raunchy, which he could reel off nonstop for hours. Most important for him, though, he had also acquired a wife in Peking—a tall, pretty girl named Jette who was a secretary in the Danish Embassy. They had been married in a Chinese civil ceremony for—as Jette often reminded Hans—a total cost of twenty-five cents, and lived in the Hsin Chiao Hotel in downtown Peking. Their two rooms were not ideal, cold in the winter and steaming in the summer. In addition, their quarters were on the south side of the hotel, five floors above the construction site of the "nonexistent" subway; the noise from trucks and building machinery went on all day and night and conversations with the Bargmanns were more often shouted than spoken. All the furniture was Chinese and well-worn, having been in the hotel since it was built in the early 1950's. On the walls were pictures of Mao Tse-tung which the Bargmanns did not dare take down. But in a corner of one room, like a pure symbol of capitalism, stood a huge Kelvinator refrigerator which they had imported from Hong Kong.

Despite the Spartan furnishings of the Hsin Chiao Hotel and the noise and the general filth of the corridors, there were certain advantages to living there. For one thing, the hotel was centrally located, just a ten-minute walk from Tien An Men Square, the Peking Communist headquarters and the main shopping areas. Any demonstrations or unusual activity—such as the sudden appearance of Mao downtown— took place practically on your doorstep; and the twenty-four-hour cable office was also within walking distance. San Li Tun, the area where I lived, was about six miles away—a fact that I had reason to regret on many late winter nights when my battered Volkswagen refused to start and the taxis had stopped running. Then I'd bundle myself up in an overcoat and Chinese fur helmet and pedal through the deserted streets to the cable office. It was very healthful.

Another advantage to living in the Hsin Chiao was that it was the hotel where most foreign visitors stayed. The grandiose Peking Hotel, located on the main street, the Boulevard of Eternal Peace, was reserved for visiting Chinese officials and important "foreign friends." But nobody in those two groups would talk to journalists anyhow. To the Hsin Chiao, however, came foreign businessmen, minor political delegations, African gymnastic teams, and all sorts of people who had been given the rare opportunity of visiting China during the Cultural Revolution. And they *would* talk. Indeed, after two or three weeks of the Hsin Chiao with nothing to do and nowhere to go, they were desperate to talk to anyone. Sometimes they would have nothing much to tell you, but other times you would learn that the Chinese were negotiating for the purchase of several million dollars' worth of steel or fertilizer, or that a Swedish engineer had arrived to supervise the installation of his company's hydroelectric generators that would supply electricity to the whole city.

The Chinese were often surprisingly unconcerned about letting you know who was staying at the hotel. When I heard that members of the Canadian Wheat Board had arrived in

Peking, I went to the Hsin Chiao and asked at the reception desk if there were any Canadians staying at the hotel. Putting this question took about fifteen minutes, because of my broken Chinese and the desk boy's broken English. Finally, with the help of two other desk clerks, I made myself understood. There were congratulatory smiles all around as they reached into a drawer and handed me *all* the guest registry cards to look through. I found the names and room numbers of the Canadians, and a number of other people too.

The Chinese, on the other hand, could sometimes be as communicative as the Great Wall. The fourth floor of the hotel, for instance, was out of bounds. The Chinese never said this, and the elevator operator would let you off at that floor if you asked. But two soldiers would be waiting in the corridor to take you courteously but firmly back to the waiting elevator. We later discovered, after they had been released, that the Gordon family had been installed on that floor. Eric Gordon had worked for the Chinese and had decided to return to Britain. He and his family vanished after getting a Hong Kong visa from the British Office in Peking. Actually, they were stopped from leaving when the Chinese found some notes on China written on the back of Mao pictures that Gordon was trying to smuggle out. The Foreign Ministry refused to give British diplomats any information about the Gordon family. It turned out they were under guard for two years in the Hsin Chiao Hotel, where journalists and diplomats often would have dinner or lunch.

The fact that the Gordons could be hidden right under the nose of Peking's foreign community was not surprising. The Chinese have absolute confidence in their security system, and with good reason. It is absolutely impossible, for instance, for a European to wander unnoticed in Peking. In some of the suburbs, where foreigners are rarely seen, it is very difficult even to walk along the street without being accompanied by thirty or forty youngsters eager to see if you really do have blue eyes and if hair really does grow on your arms. In addition, every area of Peking has its own street committee which supervises and controls all activity in the neighbourhood. A stranger is immediately noticed and watched. What he does is carefully recorded, along with his car license number. If he takes a forbidden photograph—and this, depending on the sensitivity of the local cadre, might include a picture of Chinese children—he will be suddenly surrounded by a mob of Chinese demanding the film. If he refuses, he will be hustled off to the nearest police station where his film will be confiscated and where he will receive an hour-long lecture on his crime of provoking the masses. He might even be ordered—like an erring schoolboy —to write an apology. Most foreigners caught in this predicament would write a noncommittal note saying they had not intended to offend the masses, but if the masses had indeed been offended, then it was regrettable. The alternative would be to sit for a further three or four hours in the police station listening to lectures.

I know of only one case where a foreigner was actually followed by Chinese security police. For the last two weeks of his posting in Peking, this junior diplomat was trailed everywhere he went. It wasn't done subtly. Two plain-clothed Chinese in a 1963 Ford (a very conspicuous car in Peking) would drive twenty yards behind the diplomat's car during all hours of the day and night. When he parked to go into a store or restaurant, they would park a short distance away and wait for him. The diplomat, who had attended university in Peking some years earlier, wasn't worried by the attention; he would usually wave to them every morning (they ignored his greeting).

[124]

"You have to understand the Chinese," he explained. "You see, they are being far too obvious. They want me and everybody else to know that I am under surveillance. It can only mean one of two things: I have annoyed them in some way and this is their way of letting me know unofficially; or they are warning me and my Chinese friends not to meet. In either case, they are clearly intent on avoiding a formal diplomatic incident with my country (which was friendly with Peking), so there is nothing to be worried about."

This same diplomat, by the way, was convinced that the Chinese had bugged all the foreigners' apartments as well as the embassies. It may have been true of the embassies (one French diplomat evidently thought so; whenever we talked in his office he always put his thick fur hat over the telephone) but I couldn't believe the Chinese would think it worth the effort—or would have sufficient translators—to eavesdrop on the foreigners' flats. The most exciting thing they'd probably hear would be the details of a new love affair; and the Chinese, unlike the Russians, have never shown any interest in using sex to blackmail diplomats or correspondents.

All of us, however, thought it likely that certain telephones were tapped. Some ambassadors were certain of it, and used the telephone to get across a point to the Chinese indirectly. By prearrangement, one would call the other and sound off about a particular problem. The system usually worked, they said. I remained pretty skeptical about telephone tapping until my Shanghai experience. I was staying at the Peace Hotel and decided to call Regina in Peking. I put in the long distance telephone order at the main desk, and went up to my room to await the call. It came about half an hour later, but Regina and I had been talking for only a minute when the telephone operator cut in on our conversation.

[125]

"Will you please speak more slowly and clearly?" she said.

"I can hear just fine," said Regina, but there was no response. The problem, of course, was that our slurred and rapid conversation could not be followed by the operator or whoever was listening in.

But Shanghai, I should add, was probably the most politically sensitive city in China during the Cultural Revolution.

8

SHANGHAI is the largest and most famous city in China. Even its name, which in Chinese means "above the sea," has a special significance in the English language. But the days when sailors were shanghaied have ended (in Shanghai anyhow) along with Shanghai's title as the most corrupt city in the world. Gone now are the notorious gin mills, opium dens, gambling houses and the prostitutes renowned for their beauty and number. Gone too are the swashbuckling adventurers and the insular foreign community which gained a foothold in 1842 during the Opium War when the city surrendered to Vice Admiral Sir William Parker. English, French and American consuls followed in the wake of his fleet and after the Treaty of Nanking claimed special territories and privileges for their fellow countrymen who were soon to settle in Shanghai. Thus began the infamous concessions, which were to be a source of humiliation to the Chinese for more than one hundred years.

(The last "imperialistic" remnant fell in 1967 when Red Guards stormed the British Consulate and physically ejected its diplomats. The large brick mansion stood at the juncture

of the Huang-pu and Soo Chow rivers, and site of the first
concession which was created by the British in 1843. When
I was in Shanghai in late 1969, bamboo matting had been
wired to the iron fence around the grounds and foreigners
were forbidden entry; the Chinese were apparently using
the building for municipal offices.)

Over the years, the foreigners became more numerous and
soon established factories and banks and business houses as
Shanghai developed into a thriving port. Impressive buildings, skyscrapers in their day, sprang up along the Bund, the
wide street facing the Huang-pu River. They give Shanghai
the flavour of a Western city, but they also serve as a permanent reminder that foreigners once controlled Shanghai. Not
that the Chinese, who have almost a masochistic tendency to
cherish old grievances, would ever forget this past. No visitor
(not even President Nixon) can escape being told by his guide
that the park along the Huang-pu once bore the sign, NO
CHINESE OR DOGS ALLOWED.

Perhaps the long foreign domination is one of the reasons
that Shanghai has been a center of turmoil for many years.
It was here that the Chinese Communist party was founded
on July 1, 1921. And it was here, four years later, that some
demonstrating students were killed by foreign police in the
May 30th incident. This led to armed uprisings in Shanghai
and other cities until, in 1927, the revolution was crushed
by Chiang Kai-shek. The defeated Communists fled to the
countryside and formed the Red Army; eventually they returned.

It was also in Shanghai that Mao Tse-tung planned and
mounted the Cultural Revolution, and many of its extreme
ideas and experiments found a welcome there. A Shanghai
cadre told me this was because the city was a large industrial
area and its high worker population was politically sophisticated. But it is also true that the Shanghaiese have always

[128]

been a freewheeling, volatile and independent-minded people. Even Mao and other leaders in Peking had trouble keeping Shanghai's ten million people in line during the Cultural Revolution. At times, the city was far to the left of the official line, but Peking seemed reluctant to impose its own authority except on matters of national urgency.

Because of this semiautonomy, Shanghai was not a good place for a foreigner to get into trouble, especially a nondiplomat. The foreigner who accidentally took a picture in the wrong place, or did or said something suspicious, was likely to find himself clapped into jail before he had a chance to turn around. And in those days it was very unlikely that Peking would intervene. A handful of British who had lived in Shanghai for many years were arrested for no apparent reason during the Cultural Revolution, and it wasn't until 1970, when tempers began to subside and Peking got full control back, that they were released.

Foreign seamen seemed to get into difficulties more often than anyone, though their captains gave them plenty of advance warning of what to expect in Shanghai. Sometimes it was because they knowingly took dangerous risks, such as recording the position of navigational buoys or noting the registration numbers of ships. Those who were caught by the Chinese, arrested and eventually released, explained that they kept such records as a hobby. One British sailor, though, Peter Crouch, admitted in London that he had taken notes at the request of the British Navy; a few days later he retracted his statement.

Other seamen got into trouble through boredom. It was a difficult life for a sailor in port, and there were few sights sadder than a group of Italian sailors meekly drinking beer in the ornate dining room of the Peace Hotel, once one of the liveliest spots in the wicked city of Shanghai. Now the only entertainment for sailors is to drink or to read the

Thoughts of Mao Tse-tung, displayed everywhere. Most of them prefer to drink, and this led to problems during the Cultural Revolution. If they were drunk enough, and frustrated enough, they would take revenge on the Chinese by ripping up pictures of Mao or throwing his books into the Huang-pu River. The Chinese didn't regard such acts as pranks.

One Western sailor, who had been drinking and thinking a great deal (a dangerous combination in China), bought a plaster bust of Mao Tse-tung and happily trundled it back to his ship. He placed it in a strategic place in his cabin and peppered it with a pellet gun until it fell into pieces. In the morning, frightened at his beery bravado, he carefully picked up all the pieces and deposited them with the ship's garbage. Unfortunately, the pieces were recognized by the Chinese who arrived to pick up the garbage and within an hour police and soldiers were conducting an investigation. The ship's officer, being a sensible and reasonable man, decided that the Chinese were also sensible and reasonable and therefore would understand and forgive one more of the many drunken sailors they must have seen in port. He told them the truth. The Chinese promptly locked the sailor up, and his ship had to leave without him. He was detained in Shanghai for many long weeks, faithfully reading Mao's quotations every day and admitting the error of his ways.

This particular sailor was from a friendly country, but his embassy in Peking had little success in easing his situation. His case was not sufficiently important for Peking to get into a hassle with Shanghai.

I myself had a slight but irritating brush with Shanghai officialdom.

In mid-1969, the Foreign Ministry had finally agreed to let me travel to Shanghai, Nanking and Hangchow to visit factories, communes, schools or whatever else was permissible. In Nanking and Hangchow, I was met by pleasant guides who quickly arranged tours. In Shanghai, a tall, hawk-nosed man named Mr. Lo met me at the railway station and led me to a waiting taxi.

"Welcome to Shanghai," he said. "Have you decided what you would like to do while you are here?"

I told him that I had indeed decided, and gave him the ritualistic request for a visit to a factory, commune or school.

"Ah, I am afraid that is not possible," he said. "You must have the approval of the Shanghai Revolutionary Committee, but tomorrow is Saturday and the offices are closed. Perhaps we can inquire on Monday."

"But how can that be?" I spluttered. "The Foreign Ministry visa says that I must leave Shanghai on Sunday. You knew I was coming and what I wanted to see. And anyhow, today is only Friday. Why can't we see the Revolutionary Committee today?"

"Very regrettable," he said. "The Revolutionary Committee is busy this afternoon and cannot see you. We knew you were coming, of course, but we did not know what you would want to visit and therefore no arrangements were made. Very regrettable."

"This is silly," I said as the car stopped in front of the hotel. "What do you suggest I do in Shanghai today, tomorrow and Sunday?"

"I think a visit to the Shanghai Friendship Store for foreigners would be very interesting," he said in the elevator. We found my room, and Mr. Lo settled himself into a chair and lighted a cigaret.

"Well, Mr. McCullough, what would you like to do in Shanghai?"

"How about a visit to a museum?"

"The museums are closed for renovations at the moment."

"Can we go for a boat trip along the Huang-pu River?"

[131]

"That area is out of bounds for foreigners."

"Can I see some of the temples and other historic areas of Shanghai?"

"They also are closed for renovations."

"How about going to a movie?"

"There is nothing playing at the moment."

"All right," I said desperately, "why don't the two of us go for a walk in one of Shanghai's parks?"

"Impossible, they are too crowded."

Mr. Lo lighted another cigaret, and we sat in silence for a few minutes while he blew out clouds of smoke.

"Well, Mr. McCullough, have you decided what you would like to do in Shanghai?"

"I think I have been seized by an irresistible urge to visit the Shanghai Friendship Store," I said.

"Excellent." He smiled. He stubbed out his cigaret, shook hands with me, and said good-bye.

Mr. Lo, I should tell you, was not the most disagreeable Chinese I met. That title goes to a certain Mr. Hsu, who worked for the China Travel Service in Canton. Mr. Hsu was a short, pock-faced man who had more arrogance than a Ming emperor and was marvellously adept at offending foreigners. If you were in a hurry, Mr. Hsu would barely be able to put one foot in front of the other. If you wanted to dawdle, Mr. Hsu would be seized with a sense of great urgency, sometimes even pulling you along by the sleeve. To every request his reply was "not possible"; to every situation his response was a quotation from Mao Tse-tung. It got ridiculous. One sunny afternoon I remarked that the sky was beautiful. Mr. Hsu immediately chanted: "Our great leader Chairman Mao has written, 'Where do correct ideas come from? Do they drop from the skies? Are they innate in the mind? No. They come from social practise, and from it alone . . .' " etc., etc.

Mr. Hsu was a terrible pain in the neck. Even worse, he nearly always was the guide assigned to me in Canton.

At first I tried to be pleasant with him, but that only seemed to make him angry. I would greet him at the Canton airport like a long-lost friend, tell him how well he looked and how glad I was to see him again. He would sulk for a bit, and then read aloud such tracts as the 1966 Circular of the Central Committee all the way from the airport to the hotel. Finally, I declared war on Mr. Hsu, which is to say that I became as childish as he was.

Whenever he found that something was "not possible" to do, I would recite Mao Tse-tung's dictum: "Serve the people." Every time we passed a shop selling goldfish, I would remind him that the people of Peking had wisely forbidden the sale of such bourgeois things. It didn't improve his disposition, but it certainly improved mine. When he began to read a political tract, I would interrupt with a discourse about the Fenian Rebellion or some other obscure bit of Canadian history. He would retaliate by reading more loudly. On one half-hour ride from the hotel we spent the whole trip making speeches at the same time. After that rather noisy episode we had an unspoken truce. In fact, it was so unspoken that only the most necessary conversation passed between us. The last time I saw him was in the lobby of the Canton hotel, just as I was leaving China for the last time.

"I understand you are returning to your home in Canada," he said. "Do you think you will ever return to China?"

I told him that I would like to see China again someday, but that it seemed unlikely.

"That is a pity," he said. It was the first time I had seen him smile.

Even without Mr. Hsu, Canton could be a dreary place. Winter was a terrible time. Canton is in a semitropical latitude but January and February are damp and cold. The Tung Fong or East Wind Hotel—called the Goat Town Hotel before the Cultural Revolution—is like a deserted warehouse then. Its six hundred rooms are usually empty, except for six or seven diplomats, journalists or businessmen who happen to be passing through. On one bleak January day I was the only person registered in the hotel. It was lonely.

The staff, which lives in the hotel, is impossible to find in the "off-season." Room service is nonexistent, and the unheated hotel is bone-chillingly cold. The handful of foreigners sit at the same table in the hotel restaurant and eat dinner wearing overcoats and fur hats. Experienced travellers staying overnight in Canton in the winter always take along a bottle of whisky and a hot water bottle: the whisky for inner warmth and the hot water bottle, which could be filled with the hot water tea flask in the room, for outer warmth.

Summer in the Tung Fong Hotel would be very hot and humid, but at least endurable. The only problem was mosquitoes, but a can of spray repellent brought along from Hong Kong would keep them off. The rooms, incidentally, had hooks on the ceiling over the beds for mosquito nets. On my first trip into Canton I asked for one. "Not necessary," said the desk clerk, "we have no mosquitoes in Canton." The next morning I showed him a sampling of the various red welts raised by mosquitoes and he blandly said, "They must have come from Hong Kong." I later got off the elevator by mistake on the fourth floor where the staff lived and discovered that *their* beds were protected by mosquito nets.

The Tung Fong also had some permanent guests: two Pakistanis and their families. I met one of them while having breakfast at the hotel on a January morning. He had come in to buy two bottles of orange soda pop, and I couldn't help noticing him, partly because he and I were the only persons in the huge dining room, and partly because of his strange appearance. He wore wool mittens and a heavy over-coat that came down well below his knees, almost hiding his red-striped pyjama trousers. His feet were bare except for thin sandals. His thick fur hat came down to his·eyebrows, and a scarf was wrapped around his face so that only his eyes showed. He saw that I was staring at him and came over to the table.

"English?" he asked, his voice muffled by the scarf.

"No, Canadian."

He put the two bottles under one arm, unwound the scarf and stuck out his hand. "Allow me to introduce my-self," he grandly announced in a British accent. "I am the director of the Pakistan International Airlines office in Can-ton. If I can be of any service do not hesitate to call upon me in my office here. And please forgive my unorthodox dress; I find it very difficult to adjust to the cold weather here."

Business was not booming, he told me sadly, and he asked if I had seen PIA's billboard down the street. I had indeed: it was the only advertising billboard in the whole of China. It didn't inspire much traffic, though, since the Chinese were not allowed to travel outside the country except on official business. A few of them used the airline to go to Albania, and incoming flights carried Pakistanis emigrating to Hong Kong. Being one of the three foreign airlines with landing rights in China (Air France goes to Shanghai, and Aeroflot to Peking) is more a matter of prestige than profit.

Life in Canton was boring for the PIA director and his assistant. Not only had they little work to do, but they and their families had no outside entertainment other than occasional walks around the hotel where they lived. Their

[135]

wives cooked on little iron stoves on the balconies outside their rooms. Their children amused themselves by playing badminton in the hotel corridors. They did not go to school, partly because they were not welcome and partly because the Pakistanis did not want their children exposed to the massive propaganda of the Chinese school system.

Their only breaks in the dull routine were the annual month-long trade fairs held in Canton in April and October. These were also enjoyed by the correspondents in Peking who, if they could get the Foreign Ministry's permission, gladly travelled the 1,000 miles to Canton for a chance to write some news.

There was, first of all, the business of the fair itself. Buyers and sellers from around the world (excluding Americans) would haggle with tough Chinese traders in a seven-storey cream brick building which contained displays of agricultural and manufactured products. Many of the items were exhibited for prestige reasons: a digital computer that played the song, "The East Is Red," and a heavy unstylish Red Banner limousine priced at $14,000. Anyhow, they were not marketable abroad. Other goods, such as walnuts or clay chinaware, might be available but only in limited supply and with unfirm delivery dates. This would be an irritation to the foreign businessmen, but to the journalists it would be interesting information for a story on how various facets of the Chinese economy were faring. At the spring 1969 fair, for instance, foreigners found they could not purchase pharmaceuticals. This confirmed reports that China was putting new demands on its drug industry, building up a stockpile in case of war with the Soviet Union and also distributing pharmaceuticals throughout the countryside as part of its "barefoot doctor" campaign to provide medical care to peasants.

The big business news was provided by foreign sellers, who would negotiate sales of steel, fertilizer, and even complete factories, worth millions of dollars. Some of the smaller sales also produced interesting stories—such as the Canadian who sold British Columbia jade to the Chinese, and the German who sold four of the largest Mercedes-Benz limousines, all bulletproof.

Best of all, though, was the fact that journalists were able to share the entertainment provided for the businessmen. This meant that we were able to join tours to factories and communes, a privilege I received only once during a year and a half in Peking. It wasn't much of a treat for the businessmen, of course, nor were the evening amusements provided by the Chinese. These included a color movie of the Ninth Congress of the Communist party, and some performances of revolutionary ballets and operas. But some of the fine Chinese restaurants were open to foreigners, including the delightful boat restaurant in the Pearl River where one could sit on the upper deck and watch junks lazily sail past—all the while shelling a great plate of steamed prawns and dipping them in a rich garlic sauce.

Businessmen had a difficult time in Canton, especially during the heated days of the Cultural Revolution. Often they had to sit through hour-long readings of the works of Mao Tse-tung before business discussions would begin. And the negotiations more often than not would be placed in charge of a young revolutionary who was politically correct but who didn't have the slightest idea of prices or even of the products he was supposed to be selling. In addition the foreigners would have to wear Mao Tse-tung badges and spend at least an hour touring the "propaganda floor" of the fair, which consisted of nothing but displays of badges and books of Mao's works and giant-sized pictures of the Chairman. It was a tribute to their desire for profit that most of them managed to endure it all with a smile—while they were with the Chinese.

Very few foreign businessmen got into trouble at the fair, though some seemed to court disaster deliberately. One Westerner I knew took photographs in Canton and sold them to Hong Kong newspapers and magazines. Another businessman, equipped with a puckish sense of humour, decided to bring in a tape recording of "The Stars and Stripes Forever" to entertain his associates. He had a harrowing few minutes at the border when Chinese customs men asked him to play the tape. They listened to the song and then asked him what it was. They seemed satisfied when he explained it was a Dutch folk song. He was allowed to go on his way, but he didn't play the tape in Canton.

Sometimes a newcomer to the trade fair would get into difficulty because he was unfamiliar with the ways of the Chinese.

One businessman, a novice in China, had been carrying on an innocent but joking banter with a hotel waitress at every meal. Then one day he playfully tugged at one of her long braids. The girl gave a horrified squeal and ran to the kitchen. Within seconds, the startled man was surrounded by ten angry shouting waiters and the accusing girl. Then he was hustled off to the trade fair's revolutionary committee where an army officer gave him a severe lecture on the crime of molesting Chinese girls and ordered him to leave China immediately. An hour later he was on the train to Hong Kong, frightened but still marvelling at the thought he had apparently propositioned a Chinese girl.

That, of course, was one of the worst offenses a foreigner could commit, as well as one of the most useless; for a foreigner to enjoy sex these days in China, it is necessary to have a good memory. Even if she were interested, no Chinese girl would dare become involved with a foreigner. Nonetheless hope springs eternal, as anyone could see by looking at the hotel's lost and found department. This rather obvious display of Chinese honesty consisted of an old walnut china cabinet located in the dining room. On the shelves behind its unlocked glass doors were assorted odds and ends lost by hotel visitors: ball-point pens, two playing cards, a few combs, an upper plate of false teeth, some coins and a dusty package of prophylactics.

Many of the foreigners had been doing business with the Chinese for years and were old hands at the game. They had been through various political phases in China and could be just as patient, or as stubborn, as their hosts. One international trading firm, for instance, had been involved with the Chinese long before the Communists came to power in 1949. In fact, the company once had considerable holdings in China. After the revolutionary dust had settled, they found they no longer were property-owners but instead had a very fat bank account in Canton. It wasn't of too much value, since the Chinese forbade the company to take the money out of China, though its representatives were permitted to draw upon the account for expenses during their visits to Canton. As a result the company's agents attended every trade fair in great numbers, living in suites of rooms, dining royally at every meal, ordering Chinese champagne by the bucketful, and magnanimously entertaining other businessmen. As one of their officials said to me, "We could attend Canton fairs for the next fifty years and still not spend all the money the Chinese owe us."

The frustrations of dealing with the Chinese led foreigners to devise their own innocent amusements. Some of the French played soccer on a nearby field every morning; others played poker long into the night. And during Oktoberfest, a group of nostalgic Germans invaded the hotel kitchen one night with a suitcase of German peas and cooked up a mighty caldron of pea soup. The soup-eating and beer-drinking ended in the small hours of the morning when they conducted a noisy parade through the hotel corridors.

The Chinese apparently regarded the episode as a pardonable foreign idiosyncrasy, and said nothing to the Germans. In fact, the Chinese tried to be accommodating hosts during the trade fairs, though visitors could not help but be aware of the strains of the Cultural Revolution with its overtones of xenophobia.

Two weeks before the fair was to open, Canton authorities would warn the public that they should treat foreigners politely at all times, but also that they should be watchful for spies. It was assumed, with good reason, that the foreigners would report everything they had seen while in Canton. So posters were scraped from walls on the main streets, extra loads of vegetables and meat were made available in the markets, brightly coloured bolts of cloth were put on display in downtown store windows, and unauthorized political demonstrations were banned in the areas of the hotels and fair building.

Despite their morbid fixation about spies, the Chinese seemed determined to avoid trouble with foreigners. The one exception was the Japanese, whom the Chinese traditionally regard as physical, cultural and intellectual inferiors. Yet the humiliating truth is that Japan not only successfully invaded China—and ruled with a very harsh hand—but also emerged from the defeat of the Second World War as the industrial and technological leader of Asia. This has been a bitter pill for the proud Chinese to swallow—especially because Japan has allied itself with the United States—and the Japanese businessmen at the Canton fair bore the brunt of China's anger and frustration. Individually, they became

[140]

the means by which China could reach toward an unattainable national goal: the humbling of Japan.

The Chinese considered the matter a personal and private quarrel between China and Japan. All the Japanese were separated from other foreign businessmen. They were housed in a different hotel, where they ate and also attended political meetings under Chinese direction. It was only at the fair itself that outsiders caught a glimpse of how the Chinese forced the Japanese to lose face. Sometimes twenty or thirty of them, all wearing large Mao Tse-tung badges, would be seated in the middle of an exhibition hall studiously reading Mao's little red book of quotations while other foreigners looked on. Occasionally, a group of Japanese would be rounded up to parade outside the fair building in support of one of Mao's instructions. They were, of course, also very vulnerable to charges of spying and it was almost inevitable that one or two would be put under arrest for a few days at every fair.

I always thought it remarkable that the Japanese, to whom a personal affront is supposedly cataclysmic, would keep coming back to China to suffer indignities. Traditional values are apparently not priceless.

9

ALMOST the first question asked of a foreign correspondent who has been in Peking is, Did they censor your stories? Naturally, most Westerners automatically assume that the Communist regime would not let journalists write freely about China. Some of this belief has been altered by the experiences of the team of newsmen who accompanied President Nixon to Peking, and especially by that arch-conservative William F. Buckley who tried desperately to find nothing good to say about what he saw in China. Being a guest of the Chinese, as the Washington press crew was, is somewhat different from being a barely tolerated lodger, as most of the resident correspondents are.

Nevertheless, it is true that the Chinese exercised no censorship over the journalists who lived in Peking. We did not have to submit articles in advance to the Information Department of the Foreign Ministry. As in London or Washington, a journalist simply took his story to the cable office and presented it at the "Foreign Telegram" counter. The clerk, usually a pigtailed girl who could not read English, looked at the copy to make sure all the letters were clear and counted the number of words—pausing occasionally over a long word and holding up two fingers to inquire if it was one or two words. The number of words and the time the cable was sent were registered in the correspondent's cable charge book; and that was the end of that. Of course all the cables, whether stories or personal messages, eventually ended up in the hands of the Information Department.

Other stories, usually long background or feature pieces, were sent out by mail (eleven days from Peking to Toronto). These also went out of China unchanged and unhindered. The only problem I had at the post office was when I would accidentally paste a stamp on upside down. If it was a portrait of Mao, the post office would refuse to accept the letter.

This does not mean that the mail was not opened and read by the Chinese. I knew two diplomats who insisted it was. One showed me a letter he had received from an elderly aunt who lived in an English village. On the back were a couple of pencilled Chinese symbols and some artistic doodlings. The other diplomat told me that during a cocktail party a Foreign Ministry acquaintance had solicitously inquired about the health of his mother. But the diplomat had not told anyone about the letter he had received from his father saying that his mother had suffered a mild heart attack.

I always assumed that my mail was opened, and in letters to the Toronto office I would sometimes make a point of complaining in strong terms about a particular problem I might be having with Chinese officialdom. Whether by accident or not, the problem often would be resolved soon after the letter was mailed.

The only overt form of censorship involved photographs. Before the Cultural Revolution, pictures and negatives could be sent freely in the mail; in fact, the two *Globe and Mail* correspondents who preceded me usually sent undeveloped rolls of film to Toronto in order to save time. The

[144]

Chinese did not even see the photographs until they were published in Canada. By the time I had arrived, though, the Chinese had indeed recognized the wisdom of the old Chinese saw, "One picture is worth a thousand words," and all photographs had to be developed in Peking and examined by (of all people) the Customs Department. I should add that not one picture of many hundreds I sent to Toronto was ever turned down.

Although there was no formal censorship, all the correspondents were conscious of certain restraints. The Chinese did not impede the flow of stories out of Peking—at least while I was there—but the journalists were held accountable for every word that was published abroad under their names. The West German correspondent, for instance, was called to the Foreign Ministry for a lecture about one of his stories that had referred to Vice-chairman Lin Piao as the crown prince of China. The bourgeois implications of the phrase were too offensive for the Foreign Ministry to ignore. It was a more-in-sorrow-than-anger lecture, however, because the Chinese knew the phrase had been inserted by an editor in Bonn.

As one might expect, the most sensitive subject to write about was Mao Tse-tung, and especially his state of health. If Mao had not appeared in public for two months one could say so in a story: it was a fact. But to go on from there to conclude that this probably meant that he was ill, would certainly result in a stiff dressing-down from the Foreign Ministry.

These unspoken ground rules were stifling to a Westerner, whose normal concern was usually only the law of libel and slander. But the greatest problem a correspondent faced in Peking was himself. By being lazy or overly cautious, he could impose a self-censorship more rigorous than any the Chinese might set.

[145]

This raises the question of whether Peking or Hong Kong is the best place from which to report on China. I could present a persuasive argument on either side, but it seems obvious that to have good coverage of China a newspaper should publish reports from both Hong Kong and Peking.

Hong Kong is a lively listening post to China. With diplomats, businessmen and refugees constantly crossing the border, the city fairly seethes with rumours and stories of what is happening in China. The difficulty is to sift fact from fiction. Then there is the main China-watching factory, the offices of the American Consulate, where a large staff produces voluminous research reports, many of which are made available to journalists and academics. To be dependent solely on that source of information, though, carries obvious risks. The Hong Kong-based journalists are well aware of these drawbacks, and most of them exercise judgment and responsibility.

Most of them also admit the drawbacks of writing about a country which they are not allowed to visit. After all, one can read many descriptions of a camel, but there are no substitutes for the understanding that comes from seeing the creature with one's own eyes. Or, in the words of Derek Davies, editor of the *Far Eastern Economic Review:* "There isn't a journalist in Hong Kong who wouldn't give his right arm to get into China."

Of course, many journalists (and academics too) are getting into China now, and without having to trade any of their limbs for the privilege. The end of the Cultural Revolution will mean a gradual easing of restrictions on foreign visitors, and it rather pleases me that Canada is partly responsible for causing the change to happen so quickly.

Canada's offer to establish diplomatic relations presented Peking's leaders with a range of opportunities that forced them to look outward.

[146]

There were, first of all, obvious implications concerning the United States. In April, 1968, before Pierre Trudeau had been elected Prime Minister, I met Chinese officials in Peking and we discussed the Canadian political situation. I said I was confident that he would be Canada's next leader, and that he would press for diplomatic recognition of China. The Chinese were politely skeptical.

"I do not think that is possible," said one of them, shaking his head. "However Mr. Trudeau may feel, Canada's economic ties with the United States make it impossible for the Canadian Government to take a decision that would injure the position of Washington's ally, Chiang Kai-shek."

When Trudeau was elected, however, his government did just that. After the summer of 1968, when the foreign policy review ordered by Trudeau had been completed, Ottawa approached Peking through third parties to ask whether a formal Canadian initiative would be received favourably. For Prime Minister Trudeau's advisors, it must have seemed a relatively simple matter. If the Chinese said no, then the idea of recognition could be quietly dropped. If the Chinese said yes, then negotiations could be completed reasonably quickly—since the Canadians had already decided to give way on the only really contentious issue, the so-called Two Chinas policy. Nobody, least of all Prime Minister Trudeau, could have guessed that the Sino-Canadian talks would drag on for more than a year and a half.

Many of the reasons for the long delay can only be guessed at, and for the most part are probably not important anyhow. What is interesting, though, is the possibility that Canada may have unwittingly played a role in *almost* bringing American and Chinese diplomats together for a meeting three years before the arrival in Peking of Presidential advisor Henry Kissinger.

The peculiar sequence of events that took place in the

last two months of 1968 and the first two months of 1969 probably began with Canada's bid to recognize China. The offer necessarily implied that Ottawa was willing to break off relations with Formosa; there was no point in suggesting negotiations otherwise, since both China and Formosa were adamant in their opposition to two Chinas.

This must have opened intriguing possibilities to Peking's leaders, who undoubtedly believed that Washington had prompted the Canadian move, or at least had approved of it. On the latter point they were probably correct; White House spokesmen were surprisingly mild when asked by jounralists to comment on Ottawa's approach to Peking. In any case, the important thing is that Peking probably *assumed* that the United States was using Canada to make a placatory gesture and decided, in time-honoured Chinese fashion, to respond in kind.

It was a strangely unsubtle gesture—in fact, it amounted to a public declaration of intent—that left no room for misinterpretation.

What Peking proposed, in a statement issued by the Foreign Ministry on November 26, 1968, was that the Sino-American talks in Warsaw be reopened on February 20, 1969, at which time "the new U.S. President [Richard Nixon] will have been in office for a month and the U.S. side will probably be able to make up its mind." (*Peking Review,* November 29, 1968.) The statement also suggested two items for the meeting's agenda: the withdrawal of American troops and military installations from Formosa; and, for the first time, an agreement on peaceful coexistence.

The Chinese proposal startled the United States and the rest of the world. In Peking, diplomats noted that on the previous day the Chinese newspapers had reprinted Mao Tse-tung's 1949 speech calling for trade with non-socialist

[148]

countries and for flexibility in peace talks.* They also recalled that the Chinese and Americans had not met for ten months and that their last scheduled meeting on May 29, 1968, was cancelled by Peking with the explanation that there was "nothing to discuss."

Clearly the Chinese now had something they wanted to discuss and all the evidence was pointing to peace and trade.

December passed by without incident, but January proved to be a fateful month. President Richard Nixon, speaking at his first Presidential news conference on January 27, said: "Until some changes occur on their side . . . I see no immediate prospect of any change in our policy [toward China]." Whether his words were the result of reflex rather than reflection—he perhaps being nervous at facing the press —Mr. Nixon had blundered.

There is some evidence that he had merely expressed himself badly, that even then he was far from being intransigent. In *Pacific Community* (October, 1970, Tokyo, Jiji Press), James C. Thomson, Jr., tells this story: "In the first three months of his administration, Richard Nixon met at the White House with a handful of senior specialists in East Asian studies from the university community. The subject was China policy; and one after another, the professors urged the President to take new steps toward normalization of relations with Peking. The last scholar to speak, a staunch conservative, took quite a different view, however, pressing the old familiar case for containment and isolation. When he had finished speaking, the President—heretofore noncommittal—is said to have commented, 'You know, Professor, *I* used to think that way too. But it seems to me that times have changed.' "

* Report to the Second Plenary Session of the Seventh Central Committee of the Communist party of China, March 5, 1949.

[149]

His statement seemed a clear rebuff to Peking's call for a meeting. The Chinese leaders, however, are expert in the use of colourful rhetoric, and they probably were prepared to regard Mr. Nixon's comments as verbal fencing—at least until they could test his real intentions toward China. And for that, the means were at hand.

Three days before Mr. Nixon's press conference, a diplomat named Liao Ho-shu had left the Chinese Embassy in The Hague and asked the Netherlands Government for political asylum. He was the acting chargé d'affaires of the embassy. In fact, as was later discovered, he was only the titular head of the mission; a young "revolutionary" from Peking had been sent to The Hague and was actually in charge of the embassy, which was one of the reasons Liao Ho-shu had defected. (A prominent American Sinologist who is noted for his pro-Formosa views told me that he had interviewed Liao in Washington and that "the man was obviously a minor diplomat, who knew very little about what was going on.")

In Peking the Dutch Chargé d'Affaires was summoned to the Chinese Foreign Ministry. He steeled himself for a table-pounding session. Dutch relations with the Chinese were somewhat cool anyhow, and it seemed a certainty that the Chinese would accuse his country of plotting the defection and would demand that the diplomat be turned over to the Chinese Embassy immediately. To his astonishment, the meeting was remarkably restrained. There were no accusations against the Netherlands Government and the request for the return of the Chinese diplomat was made in a perfunctory way, almost as an afterthought.

Only on one point were the Chinese emphatic: they did not want the defector handed over to the Americans. Clearly, with the Sino-American talks less than a month away, the message was meant for the United States Government as well as the Netherlands Government. The Dutch Chargé d'Affaires hurried back to his office and sent an urgent cable to his Foreign Ministry.

What happened after that is a mystery. It is inconceivable that the Dutch, who were anxious to improve their relations with China, would simply reject the Chinese request out of hand, or not tell the United States Ambassador about it. One can only assume that Washington had full knowledge of all the circumstances, but nevertheless pressured the Dutch into giving up the Chinese diplomat.

The obvious question is why?

Why was Liao Ho-shu not left in Dutch hands at least until the Americans had met with the Chinese in Warsaw? It would have meant a wait of less than three weeks. If it was vitally important that the Central Intelligence Agency interrogate the defector immediately, then why was it not done quietly in Holland? Surely the Dutch authorities would have been willing to cooperate. And if he could be questioned only in the United States—an idea that is difficult to accept—then why was he not spirited away to Washington without public fanfare?

One can also wonder if it was annoyance with the Americans that caused the Dutch Government to wash its hands of the whole affair publicly by announcing to the press on February 2, eighteen days before the United States-China talks were to open, that Liao Ho-shu was going to the United States (*The Globe and Mail,* Associated Press, February 3, 1969). The same news report from The Hague had "informed sources," which would only have been United States Embassy officials, saying that the Rumanian Embassy had "played a part in the defection." This rubbed more salt in China's wounded pride, because Peking had been proclaiming its great friendship with Bucharest. Other news reports around the world speculated that Liao Ho-shu was in charge of the Chinese spy network in Europe and that he would eventually go to Formosa.

Peking's reaction was understandable. Considering Mr. Nixon's comments at his press conference and the subsequent American behaviour over the defector, both of which placed the Chinese in a humiliating position, it seemed obvious that Washington had no interest in reducing tension between the two countries. On February 19, the day before the talks were to begin in Warsaw, the Chinese cancelled the meeting and accused the United States and Dutch Governments of conspiring to persuade Liao Ho-shu to "betray" his country. Significantly, though, the Chinese merely said "the present anti-Chinese atmosphere" made the talks "very unsuitable," * thus leaving the door open to future talks.

What would have happened if the meeting had been held?

State Department officials later said their side would have raised the possibility of an agreement on peaceful coexistence (which the Chinese had also proposed) and also would have offered to discuss postal and telecommunication problems and the exchange of reporters, scholars and scientists. The Chinese, for their part, would probably have wanted to discuss trade matters and, perhaps, an eventual solution to the Vietnam and Formosa problems.

A year later, on January 20, 1970, the Chinese and Americans finally did meet in Warsaw. But by then the propitious moment for talks had long passed. Peking's leaders were apparently divided on the idea of approaching the United States, and Washington's actions had played into the hands of those who argued that the Americans could not be trusted. A few months later, the fall of Prince Norodom Sihanouk and the widening of the Vietnam War in Cambodia and Laos gave Peking the opportunity to pose as godfather to

* *The Globe and Mail,* Associated Press and *The New York Times,* February 19, 1969.

Indo-China's revolutionaries; it was a role that increased China's status as an important power in Southeast Asia, but reduced the possibility of an immediate approach to the United States.

The Liao Ho-shu incident deeply disappointed Pakistani, Norwegian and Rumanian diplomats in Peking who had been working hard to convince the Chinese that Washington's thinking toward China was changing. Just as disappointed were their embassies in Washington which had been trying to persuade the White House that the Chinese feared the Soviet Union and wanted at least the beginning of a rapprochement with the United States.

Their motives were based on national self-interest, not altruism. All of them would gain if the Pacific area were stabilized and if China struck a balance between the Soviet Union and the United States. And all were absolutely certain that the United States and China were no threat to each other's national security.

Despite the setback, they continued their efforts through 1969 and 1970. One ambassador in Peking even went to Washington for talks with Henry Kissinger.

For geographical and political reasons, Pakistan finally became the most important intermediary in these convoluted diplomatic talks. At one point, the Pakistanis even flew Chinese messages directly from Karachi to California to avoid the possibility that word about Kissinger's proposed Peking trip might leak out. They not only kept the secret, but also carefully stage-managed Kissinger's eventual flight from Pakistan to China so that American journalists on the scene were not aware of what was happening. While Kissinger was in Peking, for instance, Pakistani helicopters were busy flying back and forth to the resort in Pakistan where Kissinger was supposedly recovering from a stomach ailment. One can only wonder if Pakistan's great help to Washington during those

[153]

delicate negotiations was one of the reasons for President Nixon's surprising outburst against India during the Bangladesh crisis.

Despite all the secrecy about Kissinger's trip, incidentally, there was one clue that might have led to the biggest news break of the year if it had been followed up by an enterprising journalist. When the official itinerary of Kissinger's visit to India and Pakistan was announced, a sharp-eyed reader might have noticed that he was staying in Pakistan longer than in India and wondered why. Considering the tense relations between India and Pakistan, a United States Government official simply would not spend more time in one country than the other—unless he had an extraordinary reason.

I didn't even notice the discrepancy, and if I had I'm certain I would never have come up with the answer: Peking.

But to return to the early days of February, 1969. During all the furore over the defection of Liao Ho-shu, Ottawa had been excitedly awaiting the beginning of negotiations with Peking on diplomatic recognition. In fact, the Chinese and Canadians were scheduled to meet in Stockholm on February 21, one day after the Chinese and Americans were supposed to have met in Warsaw. At this point, though, it must have been painfully clear to China's leaders that they had seriously overestimated Washington's influence, if any, in the Canadian decision. They probably felt something like the girl who accepted an invitation to a party from two brothers and then arrived to find that the handsome brother she really had her eye on had decided to stay home.

The establishment of diplomatic relations with Canada would be an important step into the world community, but a whole new set of calculations was necessary if China was to get maximum benefit. There was little time for such deliberations in Peking. In February there were still economic and political problems to be resolved, and plans were also going forward for the important Ninth Congress of the Chinese Communist party which was to be held on April 1. New ventures in foreign policy would have to wait until at least then. In addition, small but bloody clashes broke out along the Sino-Soviet border and the Russians began to drop broad hints that it might be necessary to use massive force to teach China a lesson.

In Stockholm the talks went along in desultory fashion, with the Chinese saying they were interested in recognition but refusing to engage in the bargaining process that would achieve it. After the Ninth Congress, however, there were signs that Peking's leaders had arrived at some foreign policy conclusions. At the end of May, ambassadorial posts that had been vacant since 1967 began to be filled with new appointments, and the sudden cordiality of Chinese Foreign Ministry officials startled foreign diplomats in Peking. Travel permits to various cities were given to diplomats and correspondents for the first time in years, and even the Sino-Soviet border tensions abated after September when Premier Chou En-lai and Premier Alexei Kosygin met in Peking and apparently agreed to disagree peacefully.

That same summer of 1969 the Chinese began to suggest to diplomats that they no longer viewed the United Nations as a concoction of the devil. The message was also delivered to the Canadians in Stockholm, causing Canadian External Affairs Minister Mitchell Sharp to tell reporters in New York in September that Peking had indicated an interest in joining the United Nations.

What Mr. Sharp meant, of course, was that in Stockholm the Chinese were pressing the Canadians for a commitment to vote for China's admission to the United Nations. Hand in hand with this was Peking's stubborn insistence that Canada publicly accept China's sovereignty over Formosa as part of the price of diplomatic recognition. It was an important point to Peking. Italy, Belgium and Austria had expressed varying degrees of interest in recognizing China, and whatever formula Ottawa and Peking agreed upon would also be applied in diplomatic negotiations with other countries. Eventually, as the months rolled by and the voting day in the United Nations came closer, Peking decided to accept a proposal made earlier by the Canadian negotiators: that Formosa not be mentioned in the formal agreement that China and Canada would sign, but that Peking could add a codicil stating its ownership of Formosa and that Canada could add a further note stating its notice of China's claim without comment.

The date was October 12, 1970, some twenty months after the talks had begun in Stockholm. Perhaps the long and tedious negotiations were inevitable, given the preliminary confusion about Canada's purpose and the seeming lack of firm direction in China's foreign policy. But it is also possible that the long delay was partly due to miscalculations by Peking and Ottawa.

Once the Chinese realized that Washington was not behind Ottawa's decision to recognize Peking, it would have been logical for them to reason that Prime Minister Pierre Trudeau had taken the step because of strong public opinion in Canada. Nothing could have been further from the truth.

If anything, there was a monumental disinterest among nearly all Canadians on the subject of diplomatic relations with China. In favour of recognition were some newspapers (including *The Globe and Mail*), the academic community generally and the numerically unimportant New Democratic Party. Opposed were most Canadian-Chinese, various right-wing politicians and private individuals, and many ethnic groups whose countries were dominated by the Soviet Union

[156]

—to them communism was communism, whether it was the Peking or Moscow brand.

Trudeau could make no political yards by including recognition of China as part of his election campaign. He already had the support of the liberal academics and intellectuals, and there was no point in alienating the large blocks of ethnics who lived in the western provinces where his Liberal Party was traditionally weak. In addition, there were some Liberal Members of Parliament who strongly disapproved of formal ties with Peking.

One of these was Toronto lawyer Perry Ryan. Even after the election, which Trudeau won with ease, Ryan remained unalterably opposed to recognition of China as well as to the Government's proposed reduction of forces to the North Atlantic Treaty Organization. To him, there was no thaw in the cold war. In January, 1969, a month before Sino-Canadian negotiations were to open, I spent a couple of hours with him in his hotel room in Hong Kong, discussing China and sipping Canadian Club whisky. He had just come from Formosa, which he had visited during a "fact-finding" mission assigned to him as a member of the House of Commons Committee on External Affairs. While I listened to him talk, I became increasingly impressed by his naiveté and by the effectiveness of the Formosan public relations machine.

He extolled the democracy of the Nationalist regime, and seemed quite surprised when I said political criticism of Chiang Kai-shek could result in a jail term in Formosa. I mentioned the discontent of native Taiwanese, but he assured me that this was Communist propaganda; his hosts had introduced him to a Taiwanese who had assured him that everyone was happy. He even suggested that only the Americans prevented the Formosans from recovering China.

As I prepared to leave, he proudly showed me a special program the Formosans had printed for his visit. It was more like a magazine, printed on expensive glossy paper with the cover showing in colour the crossed flags of Canada and Nationalist China. The first page had a large studio portrait of Ryan and, under it, his biography. His itinerary was printed on the remaining pages. Altogether it was a handsome and expensive production for a minor Canadian politician.

Unfortunately for the Formosans, Ryan had little influence on government policy. In fact, his inability to sway the government's position on China and other issues with which he disagreed eventually led him to cross the Commons floor and joined the Conservative Party.

It was doubtful, however, that anyone could have persuaded Trudeau to change his mind about recognizing China; for Trudeau, the internationalist and academic, it was a personal commitment made long before he had any political aspirations. Not generally known, too, is the fact that the Canadian Cabinet under Prime Minister Lester Pearson, Trudeau's predecessor, had already agreed to recognize Peking. The decision was not implemented because Pearson was about to announce his retirement and felt it would be unfair to saddle a new leader with a foreign policy initiative he might not favor. Trudeau, then Justice Minister, was a member of the Cabinet but the new party leader (who would automatically become prime minister) would have to be elected at a national convention. At that point Trudeau had not even decided to run for the leadership.

Trudeau's interest, perhaps even fascination, in the Far East and China stretched back many years. In 1949, during the last days of the struggle for control of China, he managed to slip across the border at Hong Kong and work his way as far north as Shanghai just before the city fell to the Communists.

In 1960 he visited China again, this time with a group of French Canadians and later co-authored with Jacques Herbert a slim and cheerful chronicle of their travels entitled *Two Innocents in Red China* (Oxford University Press).

The book's preamble noted the ineptitude of having Western policy toward China "improvised in the backrooms of Washington and Rome on the basis of information gathered in Hong Kong and Tokyo by agencies that clip and collate various items from Chinese newspapers."

Still later, the authors commented: "We keep thinking of the automobile industry of Canada, which in 1965 refused orders from China even though its workers in Windsor were unemployed. We keep thinking of the market lost—in deference to the feeling of the [U.S.] State Department—to the profit of the Polish, Czech, Russian and German factories, whose cars you see everywhere in China."

It should have surprised nobody that Trudeau would move to have his country establish diplomatic relations with China.

Another factor, albeit a minor one, that may have contributed to the prolongation of negotiations in Stockholm was Ottawa's insistence that all Canadian diplomats and personnel posted to Peking be given a permanent exit visa in advance by the Chinese Foreign Ministry. This request was turned aside by the Chinese, who said the Canadians would receive the same privileges as all other diplomats in Peking.

On this point, and perhaps on others as well, Ottawa was acting on the advice of the British Foreign Office. Long before the talks began in Stockholm, the Canadians had several consultations with the British. Ottawa was not seeking London's opinion about recognition, though the British apparently seized the opening to say that they thought it foolish to approach Peking at that time (1968) because extremists in the Chinese leadership would interpret the move as indirect approval of China's barbarous behaviour toward the diplomats, especially the British, during the Cultural Revolution.

London was justifiably outraged at the treatment its people received from the Chinese. I shared that feeling, as would anyone who lived among the British diplomats trapped in Peking. I admired their great courage and, besides, liked them personally; they were very kind to me and my family. For these reasons, perhaps, I am somewhat prejudiced in my belief that their sorry situation in Peking might have been eased—and that the twenty-seven-month ordeal of Reuters correspondent Anthony Grey might have been shortened—except for the British Government's dismaying lack of political perception.

10

WHEN we first arrived in Peking, no people were as kind to us as the British. Even, in fact, from the time that Regina and Katharine and I stepped off the plane at the airport. Through a mixup in our cable from Hong Kong, our translator failed to meet us when the plane landed at 11 P.M. In most cities of the world, it wouldn't have mattered. But at Peking Airport, there are no buses into the city and there are no taxis. There isn't even an official Chinese who speaks English.

But there were two British couriers, bringing diplomatic bags from Hong Kong to Peking. The men were tall and grey-haired, seemingly cast from the same mould. And in a way, that was so: both were retired officers from Her Majesty's Navy who had taken on the job of diplomatic courier. We had noticed them in Shanghai—where we had spent an hour between planes on the way to Peking—because they had sat themselves down in the airport restaurant and sternly demanded *and got* fish and chips, bread and butter, and tea with milk and sugar.

We liked their style.

[161]

But there we were at Peking Airport, virtually stranded and with Katharine practically asleep on her feet. I told the two Britishers who we were, and explained our problem.

"Not to worry," said one of them. "We're being met by a little English station wagon, but we'll all squeeze in somehow."

We did. Regina sat in the front seat, with Katharine asleep in her lap, the Chinese driver weaving his way through the dark countryside. The couriers and I perched on the diplomatic bags in the back of the station wagon.

That was our first experience with the British in China. But there were other things to remember, like the British diplomat's wife who arrived on our third day in Peking carrying a big cardboard carton filled with boxes of corn flakes, mayonnaise, peanut butter and other things unavailable in Peking that she thought a child would like. And the invitation from the British Chargé d'Affaires, Sir Donald Hopson, to consider ourselves "part of the family" and use the mission's swimming pool whenever we wanted to. Then there were the other wives of British diplomats who took Regina on shopping tours to show her where all the stores were.

These may seem like small gestures, but they were very important to newcomers in what then was a very alien country. And they were made by people who could have been forgiven if they had been more concerned with their own problems. For at that time, the spring of 1968, the British were trapped in Peking and had no idea when, if ever, the Chinese would let them return to England. They were hostages in two separate battles: one among the Chinese themselves; and another between Great Britain and China. There was nothing at all they could do while they waited for their futures to be settled, except try to keep up their spirits and

[162]

ask themselves how Britain and China became involved in a confrontation that was, after all, completely illogical.

Militarily, Britain was no threat to China. In fact, because of financial problems, Britain was withdrawing armed forces from the Pacific, thus breaking at least part of the military encirclement China had loudly complained about for years. Economically, China was benefitting from its association with Britain. In 1965, the year before the Cultural Revolution began, Chinese exports to Britain were $83.2 million while imports were $72.3 million. The total balance of trade in Chnia's favour for the three years before the Cultural Revolution was $44.3 million.

Beyond that, Britain was one of the first Western countries to recognize the new Communist government (along with Finland, Norway, Denmark, Sweden and Switzerland in January, 1950) after it came to power in 1949, though there may have been some resentment that Britain, unlike the others, established an office with a chargé d'affaires rather than a full embassy with an ambassador.

Despite all these things, no other foreigners in Peking, not even the Russians, were treated as harshly as the British during the Cultural Revolution. Ironically, it was the Russians, not the British, who crossed China's border in July, 1967, and destroyed Chinese patrol routes. But is was the British, not the Russians, who a few days later had their mission in Peking burned to the ground.

The real reason for Britain's difficulties with China was, of course, Hong Kong.

And yet Hong Kong was Peking's most important source of income: in 1965 the Chinese exported $406.3 million worth of goods to Hong Kong, most of it eventually being re-exported to other countries, while importing $12.5 million from the colony. Why should Peking tamper with—and

[163]

perhaps destroy—a badly needed source of hard currency? The greater part of the colony, the New Territories, would anyhow revert to China in 1997 when Britain's ninety-nine-year lease for the area expired.

Admittedly, Hong Kong was and is a constant source of embarrassment to Peking. It sits there, a piece of China occupied almost solely by Chinese—to whom China promised protection in its constitution—that is governed as a colony (under imperialism) and even worse is thriving (under capitalism). Besides that, Hong Kong harbours Taiwanese agents, the Jesuit Intelligence service and the American Consulate, a huge intelligence plant that has about two hundred full-time employees and acts as a telescope on China—interviewing refugees, gathering printed material from the mainland ($1.50 for a smuggled Canton newspaper; higher prices for papers from cities farther north), listening to Chinese radio broadcasts and collating information. It has, for instance, biographical files on 30,000 Chinese Communist officials.

Even before the Cultural Revolution, the Russians were having great propaganda fun tweaking Peking's nose over Hong Kong as they argued that *their* brand of communism was the most faithful to Marx and Lenin.

In December, 1962, Khrushchev made a speech to the Supreme Soviet reminding the world that European colonialism still existed off the coast of China. Two years later a Russian delegate spoke before a twenty-four-nation UN special committee on colonialism and used Hong Kong as an example of an area that should be restored to the country from which it had been seized. That same year Pravda accused China of collaborating with British and United States money interests in Hong Kong to exploit the working people and, in a strange turnabout, described the colony as a "major center of slanderous propaganda and subversive activity conducted by *Peking* against the Soviet Union." Tass added its voice a few months later, saying that China, if it wanted to, could in a few months correct the sorry situation in Hong Kong where millions of Chinese were languishing under colonial oppression.

Peking chose to ignore these frustrating accusations. Only occasionally, as though to keep the record straight, would the Chinese comment publicly on Hong Kong before the Cultural Revolution. This usually took the form of protests against the colony being used as a "rest and recreation" center by United States servicemen, "the invaders of Vietnam." Sometimes there would be a detailed accounting of the number and types of United States naval ships and planes entering and leaving Hong Kong; and also a listing of the technical equipment and supplies bought by the Americans and shipped to Vietnam. All of which indicated that the Chinese were no slouches at the intelligence business. But Hong Kong is a depot for intelligence agents of almost all kinds (the Soviet Union has been trying unsuccessfully for years to install a "trade office" in Hong Kong).

A veteran diplomat stationed in Hong Kong assured me that I should expect my telephone in any of the large hotels to be tapped by the British, the Americans, the Chinese—or maybe all three. And he swore that the Chinese Communists in Hong Kong trailed all journalists and diplomats from Peking.

In any case, it is obvious that neither the activities of agents nor the embarrasment of having a colony on its doorstep outweighs the advantage to China of maintaining a source of hard currency worth about $500 million a year (including Communist commercial interests). For regardless of treaties and conventions, the colony exists only at the behest of China. If Peking cut off supplies of water and food to the colony, it would soon expire. And Peking has done neither.

[165]

The cause of the riots in Hong Kong—which led directly to the burning of the British Office in Peking and the beating of its diplomats—can probably be traced to the impetus of the Cultural Revolution movement rather than to any kind of coordinated plan concocted by Peking's leaders.

By the beginning of 1967 the storm of revolution was sweeping across China; it was inevitable that the waves would splash over Hong Kong.

In China there was absolute confusion. Charges of treason were levelled against the Chinese leadership, but among the general population nobody was certain exactly which leaders were the traitors. "Bombard the headquarters," ordered Mao Tse-tung, inviting the masses to assault the party's Central Committee, that previously unchallenged bastion of authority. And the party's hundreds of thousands of cadres and millions of members charged to the attack—but not always in the right direction, it seems. It was not a time for the faint-hearted; cadres had to attack or be attacked. By word and deed, party members had to go further and further to prove their loyalty, all the while being pressed by the actions of the rampaging Red Guards who cared not one whit for discipline, tradition or the party.

For a long time the Communists in Hong Kong merely looked across the border. Then they began to copy their elder brothers, perhaps on orders from that troubled south China city, Canton. A few minor labour disputes in the early months of 1967 produced gatherings of Communists who shouted slogans and waved their red books of Mao's quotations—just as the Communists in China were doing—and made a series of "just demands" in arrogant and abusive language. Then on May 11, fighting broke out over another labour dispute, this time in a plastic flower factory near North Kowloon. This was followed by a demonstration during which hundreds of Communists marched on Government

[166]

House and pasted "big character posters" on the gates—just as was being done in Peking.

The campaign that followed, organized by the Communist banks, trade unions, schools and business organizations, had as its maximum goal the winning of political and economic concessions that would leave the Hong Kong Communist leaders in effective but unofficial control of the colony. But the demonstrations, street fighting, strikes and the inevitable terrorist cowardice of planting homemade bombs in public places only alienated the population.

Peking was not pleased. By the end of October, the Communist party organization had neither muscle nor money and its leaders were summoned to Peking. The day of reckoning had come; Peking could hardly disapprove of the Hong Kong "compatriots" who had enthusiastically followed Mao Tse-tung's slogan, "It's right to rebel," but they could and would deal with failure—ascribing it, of course, to lack of implementation of the thought of Mao Tse-tung.

In fact, Peking's response to the Communist campaign in Hong Kong was something less than wholehearted, except for verbal support. Kwangtung Province, which is adjacent to Hong Kong, suffered serious dislocation during the Cultural Revolution but nevertheless managed to continue to supply food to the colony, though it turned down requests for additional water supplies. And at the border, Chinese Army guards prevented demonstrators from crossing into British territory. The substance of Peking's financial support was indicated by the fact that in September, 1967, the Hong Kong party chiefs were telling strikers to find jobs because there wasn't enough in the till for strike pay to be continued.

By January, 1968, Hong Kong's homemade Cultural Revolution had completely disintegrated and the local Communists were back at their most important task for the mainland: earning United States dollars.

This probably was exactly what Peking wished they had been doing for the previous seven months. The revolutionaries' campaign had accomplished nothing, but lost a great deal. It had failed to take into account Mao's dictum: "The revolutionary war is a war of the masses; it can be waged only by mobilizing the masses and relying on them." Not only had the Hong Kong Communists failed to mobilize the masses, but they also alienated them with vicious terrorism and economic hardship (the low income levels of Hong Kong society, which the Communists should have been cultivating, felt the financial bite more than any other group when the consumer price index rose 12 percent in the five trouble months, May–September, 1967).

When the Hong Kong miniature Cultural Revolution developed, some observers began to detect overtones of racism, though one could just as convincingly argue—as the leaders in China would—that it was a simple case of imperialism versus socialism. What can be said is that a surprising latent bitterness toward the British bobbed to the surface. To find its cause, one must probably look far beyond Hong Kong and the events of 1967—perhaps back more than one hundred years to the days when the British military might was used to further commercial interests in China—including the sale of opium which the Emperor had ordered banned.

The idea that the Communist leaders of modern China should still be smarting over the humiliations that feudal China received at the hands of the British stretches the imagination. And yet . . .

At the end of 1968, when many of Britain's most serious problems with China had been resolved, two British diplomats in Peking met with officials in the Chinese Foreign Ministry to discuss the case of Anthony Grey, the Reuters corespondent who had been under house arrest in Peking since July, 1967.

During the interview, as the British pressed their right of consular access to Grey, one of the Chinese suddenly slammed the desk with his fist and shouted emotionally: "It's about time you British realized that the days when England could sail her gunboats on China's rivers are gone forever."

How much of this anglophobia was responsible for the persecution of the British diplomats will probably never be known. Nor will it ever be known whether the violence against them resulted mainly from a miscalculation by China's leaders. Among Peking's diplomats, most of whom had gone through the grim days when the British Office was besieged and sacked, opinion was evenly divided. Some believed that everything went according to plan, that the firing of the Office simply could not have occurred without the approval of one or more of the top leaders, Chou En-lai, Lin Piao, Chen Po-ta, Chiang Ching or Mao Tse-tung himself; others argued that the decision was made on a relatively minor level, that Chou En-lai himself saw the flames from the Imperial City and ordered out the army and fire departments.

The latter argument has some basis in fact.

For three weeks in August, the Foreign Ministry was in the hands of a violent Red Guard group, known as the May 16 Detachment, which had stormed into the Ministry offices, injuring soldiers on sentry duty and destroying and seizing secret files. These extremists, who enjoyed the support of some leading members of the inner Cultural Revolution Group, reportedly even installed as Foreign Minister the former Chinese Chargé d'Affaires in Indonesia, Yao Teng-shan.

In the midst of this turmoil, on August 20, British Chargé d'Affaires Donald Hopson was summoned to the Foreign

Ministry to receive a protest. He and his First Secretary, Raymond Whitney, arrived at the Ministry but could not enter the massive gates because of hundreds of Red Guards milling about. While they debated what to do, a Chinese stuck his head in the car window.

"Are you from the British Office?" he whispered. They said they were.

"I'll meet you in the International Club in ten minutes," he said. "I'm from the Foreign Ministry."

The British diplomats drove around the corner to the International Club, a rather fancy name for a Victorian-style grey brick residence which houses a restaurant, billiard tables and bowling alley for the use of foreigners. There they received the official protest note from the People's Republic of China. It set a forty-eight-hour deadline for various demands to be met by the Hong Kong authorities "otherwise the British Government must be held responsible for all the consequences arising therefrom." (This is a set phrase used by Chinese officials to express disapproval; I even heard it directed at me on a couple of occasions by the Information Department; a variation of it, which uses the words "serious consequences," is considered a grave warning.)

Hopson rejected the note and at 10:45 the next evening, exactly forty-eight hours after the expiry of the "ultimatum," the British Office was surrounded by demonstrators. But was it intended that the demonstration that night should become a violent attack? Probably not.

A few days later, on September 3, an order was issued forbidding Red Guards to enter foreign embassies. And on September 5, the former Chargé d'Affaires Yao Teng-shan and two radical members of the Cultural Revolution Group, Wang Li and Lin Chieh, were removed from their positions. Two more members of the same group, Chi Pen-yu and Kuang Feng, were also ousted five months later and were specifically accused of being responsible for the attacks during the summer on foreign missions in Peking, and also of plotting against Chou En-lai and Chiang Ching. The leaders of the Foreign Ministry coup—presumably the same men who directed the British Office attack—had been punished.*

Much later, a Chinese in Peking told me: "The people of Peking are not proud of what happened to the British Office that night. A country of seven hundred million people does not prove its greatness by attacking twenty-two foreigners, whatever their nationality."

Whether or not the Chinese regretted the events of that night, and whether or not the burning took the country's leaders by surprise (which they would never state publicly then since it would be an admission that the Red Guards were indeed uncontrolled), the fact is that a group of diplomats who were supposed to be under the protection of the Chinese Government had been beaten and humiliated and a foreign mission had been sacked. Indeed it was fortunate that some of the British diplomats were not trapped in the smoke-filled corridors and burned to death. At that, most of them suffered violence at the hands of the Red Guards. The men were punched and kicked and spat upon; hands tore at their genitals.

The few young girls who worked as secretaries were also badly treated. They were chased into the street by the howling mob. Red Guards clutched at the girls' hair, shoved their hands into their blouses and under their skirts and tore away parts of their clothing. It is easy to imagine the girls' terror as they struggled through the crowd trying to get away from people who seemed to have gone mad.

* In June, 1970, Chinese workmen quietly began to reconstruct the burned-out office, and in 1971 Chou En-lai apologized to the British Chargé d'Affaires for the 1967 incident and explained it had been caused by "bad elements" who had since been "corrected."

One of the girls managed to get across the street to the closed iron gates of the Albanian Embassy. The mob closed around the girl again while Albanian diplomats stood inside the gates and laughed.

Another girl, more fortunate, managed to get directly across the street to the Finnish Embassy where she was quickly pulled inside and the gates slammed shut in the face of the Red Guards. The girl was almost incoherent with fright. The Finns promptly fed her a double Scotch and some of the ladies undressed her and put her under a hot shower. As she stood under the shower, still crying and trembling uncontrollably, great hanks of her hair were washed to the floor.

It should be noted, though, that the Chinese soldiers on duty did try to stop the Red Guards from molesting the diplomats though they were badly outnumbered and were for the most part unsuccessful. One diplomat was saved by a soldier who pushed him into a small guard room in front of the Office to escape the mob.

The behaviour that night of the Albanians, surely the most unlovable people in the world, was not too surprising. But what was astonishing was the behaviour of some of the other diplomats.

One Western ambassador in Peking was in his residence playing bridge when the attack on the British Office occurred. An excited aide telephoned the news to him, only to receive a lecture on the neutrality of his country. The ambassador ordered him to call all members of the embassy and tell them they were on no account to become involved in the "British affair." Then he returned to his bridge game. The attitude of some other diplomats ranged from indifference to hostility; the wife of one diplomat from a Commonwealth country later told a British diplomat that "the British Office was at fault and deserved what it got." The

[172]

woman, apparently, had just as deep a well of bitterness to draw from as did the Chinese.

Other diplomats rallied around the British, notably the Scandinavians—who had nothing to gain and much to lose since they had been treated civilly by the Chinese. There were many individual acts of bravery, most of which cannot be described even today because these gay and principled people, from ambassadors to clerks, did certain things which their governments could not possibly approve, then, or now.

Generally, diplomats whose countries' relations with the Chinese were more or less on an even keel tried to ignore what had happened while those embassies which also were having troubles with the Chinese were sympathetic and helpful. Among this latter group were the Russians, and it is doubtful that Anglo-Soviet relations had been as genuinely warm in the last fifty years as they were in Peking in 1967–68. Soviet diplomats in Peking will never forget (or so they frequently said) the occasion when Chargé d'Affaires Sir Donald Hopson and other British diplomats linked arms with the Russians at the airport to hold off Red Guards who were trying to harass Soviet women and children leaving Peking.

In those days Hopson personified British courage and correctness, admirable qualities especially during a siege. He was determined to "put up a good show."

At National Day receptions in Peking, for instance, the Chinese guest of honour would usually make a speech and throw a few handfuls of insults at one of the countries with which China was quarrelling at the moment, at which point the offended diplomats would rise from their chairs and walk out the door. The Russians, in fact, usually sat near the exit so they could leave with a minimum of effort. Not Sir Donald.

When the denunciation of his country began, Sir Donald would shake hands with each of the diplomats at his table

and unhurriedly make his way to the table of the host ambassador who was seated beside the standing speaker. There,
to the ambassador's discomfort, he would apologize for having to leave the reception early and gravely shake the ambassador's hand. Then he would slowly walk out of the room.
It infuriated the Chinese.

Sir Donald was a classic example of the right man in the
right job at the right time. What the British needed in
Peking then was not a suave statesman but a tough disciplined soldier. That was what they had in Sir Donald, a
former war hero who faithfully did calisthenics every day.
Privately he was relaxed and affable. He was proud of his
baritone voice and had an extensive repertoire of songs,
many of them with bawdy lyrics. He also liked barrack-room
jokes, which he told very well. That side of him, though, was
reserved mostly for his peers—other ambassadors, that is.

With his own staff he seemed reserved and aloof. He would
appear at the tiny British Office swimming pool—located beside the burned-out Office—nod hello at his junior diplomats
and then lie in the sun on the opposite side, away from
everyone else. An officer among his subordinates.

It was this attitude, it seemed to me, which kept the
British from buckling under the Chinese pressure. He ran
the Office as though it were a besieged garrison, which indeed it was.

On the day after the fire, for instance, Sir Donald insisted
that his staff report for duty, though of course the Office was
nothing but a blackened shell. Sir Donald, who just a few
hours earlier had been seen with his clothing ripped and
blood streaming down his face, was there to greet them. On
his orders, they assembled wearing casual sports clothes and,
despite their bruises, played tennis and swam as though nothing had happened.

He also ordered his staff back to the firing line.

[174]

Young British diplomats, some of them just in their twenties, were sent into the streets in pairs at night to read wall posters. It was dangerous business for any foreigner; for these young men, who had been beaten by screaming Red Guards, it was terrifying. But they did it.

It could be argued that Sir Donald was unnecessarily harsh and demanding; for no one could have foreseen what was to happen in the months ahead. Perhaps he was just reacting instinctively, as a well-trained officer is supposed to.

The British, including Sir Donald, thought that they would be recalled to London after the burning. Some of them even felt certain that diplomatic relations would be broken by the British Government and that the Office would be closed. Junior officers, who were due to be recalled anyhow, packed most of their belongings in wooden crates (the Chinese refused to send packers). But these crates stood untouched for almost a year in the foreigners' compound. The British finally gave up and unpacked the crates; vases and other breakable objects, incidentally, had been bundled protectively in the remains of secret files that, months earlier, had been hurriedly pushed through the Office paper-shredding machine.

Sir Donald himself had been due to finish his Peking posting in 1967. In fact, a farewell dinner had been given in his honour by other heads of missions, and a sterling silver tray—the useless gift which departing ambassadors receive from their colleagues in Peking—had been formally presented. But Sir Donald, and most of the other members of the Office, were not to leave Peking until almost a year later. The Chinese refused to issue exit visas.

In the months that followed, with the British wondering if they would *ever* be allowed to go home, the Office morale could have been expected to disintegrate. The long period of uncertainty, with dreary week after dreary week slowly passing by, was far harder to take than the beatings on the night of the fire, or the humiliation of being frog-marched up and down the foreigners' compound by Red Guards. It was especially difficult for diplomats whose wives and children had left before the exit embargo; they did not know if they would see each other again.

During the worst period of the early days, the British morale was highest. Like a good officer, Sir Donald kept his men busy. He pushed them into working hard—though there was precious little work that could be done because normal avenues of information had been cut off and the Office files had been almost completely destroyed.

There was a great deal of personal courage displayed. It would have been understandable, for instance, if the girls had refused to do anything more than work during the day and lock themselves in their flats at night. But even those attacked on the night of the fire would put on their smart miniskirts and bicycle downtown alone to go shopping.

Operation Effigy was another example of the British spirit. Chinese demonstrators had strung up a straw effigy of Prime Minister Harold Wilson at the entrance gate to the British Office grounds. Strangely, the British regarded this as much an outrage as the burning of the Office, and they decided that a blow should be struck for England (though not for Harold Wilson, whose handling of the Sino-Anglo dispute had angered many of them). And so began Operation Effigy, whose goal was to remove Mr. Wilson's proxy. Logistically, the problem was how to get out to the front gates, cut down the effigy and carry it away without being stopped by the Chinese security guards who patrolled the entrance. This project engaged the attention of most of the staff of the Office for several days. Finally an operational plan was worked out.

One dark night, a car suddenly backed out of the long

[176]

driveway and skidded to a stop beside the effigy. A diplomat leaned halfway out of the car window and snipped the wire holding the effigy. The car then sped back up the driveway. All that the startled guards saw was Mr. Wilson's straw head sticking out of the window of the car vanishing around the corner of the darkened Office. The British were disappointed that the Chinese Foreign Ministry ignored the incident.

Another small blow was struck by Noeleen Smyth, the petite Irish nurse who operated the British dispensary in a small office adjoining her flat. After Red Guards had invaded the British flats and splashed the characters DOWN WITH BRITISH IMERIALISM in white paint on her front door, Noeleen promptly pasted a large paper Union Jack on top. It bore the words: I'M BACKING BRITAIN.

These small but important (to the British) counterattacks were carried out in the early days of the troubles. The morale problems for the British really began when the Chinese simply left them to their own devices, refusing to allow them to leave China but otherwise ignoring them. There was increasing discontent with London's efforts—or lack of efforts—to get them home.

Some of this discontent was focused on Sir Donald, who accepted responsibility for his superiors' orders—even though he privately may not have agreed with them.

One evening, in the spring of 1968, I attended a showing of *The Bridge Over the River Kwai,* in the British Office. I suppose almost everyone there had seen the film years before, but most of us had forgotten how well Sir Alec Guinness played the role of a dedicated and brave officer who could not be bowed by the Japanese but whose stern principles were somehow misdirected as he tried to prove to the enemy the superiority of the British soldier. Sir Donald sat near the front of the room, not speaking, not turning his head once,

[177]

although he must have heard the whispered conversations at the back of the room as his staff compared the fictional and real British Army officers.

As time passed and London seemed content to do nothing, the diplomats became increasingly nervous and depressed. One senior man did almost nothing but search for Chinese snuff bottles for his collection and sun himself beside the swimming pool. But he was an exceptional case. The British men and women bore their situation resolutely and only rarely expressed their frustration to an outsider. Yet they had good cause to complain publicly and privately about their Government's handling of the affair.

11

FRENCH Ambassador Lucien Paie knew Foreign Minister Chen Yi quite well. The worldly Chen Yi, who liked wearing sunglasses and was fond of Philip Morris cigarets and good wine, was a frequent dinner guest at the Ambassador's residence. But that was before the Cultural Revolution. Now Chen Yi himself was in trouble with the Red Guards who accused him of bourgeois leanings; nor did the tough old soldier endear himself to them when he angrily lectured their leaders at Peking Airport for their behaviour toward departing foreign diplomats.

It was at the airport, on a different occasion, that the French Ambassador managed to speak privately to Chen Yi for the first time since the Anglo-Sino troubles had begun. He described his distress at the treatment the British diplomats were receiving and asked if the Foreign Minister could intercede on their behalf.

"Great Britain is quite unimportant in world affairs," replied Chen Yi brusquely, as he turned his back on the French Ambassador and walked away.

Peking's leaders had recognized that the British Government was dealing with China from a position of self-imposed weakness, and they were prepared to take advantage of that fact. Further evidence of this was the attitude of Peking after the British Office fire. London made a formal protest to the Chinese. The reply in effect approved of the action of the Chinese "masses" and dared the British to do something about it. The question was: What was the British Government prepared to do? The answer soon became obvious: Nothing. Not only had the Chinese twisted the British lion's tail, but there was no reason for them to let go.

In the weeks that followed, as British diplomats in Peking were followed and bullied and harassed, London's formal protests were treated with disdain by Peking. London's undeclared but obvious policy was to sit out the storm quietly and wait for better times. Peking's radical leaders were probably amused when Foreign Secretary George Brown sent a cable to Foreign Minister Chen Yi asking if it were possible for the two of them to meet to discuss ways of improving Sino-Anglo relations. The message was ignored; it was clear to the Chinese that London would do nothing to prevent them from setting their own timetable for dealing with the British diplomats.

It should be noted, too, that in a separate move the Foreign Office encouraged the British press to mute its voice on the treatment being received by Anthony Grey and the British diplomats. This advice was based on the theory that publicity would not only arouse public opinion and push the Government into an awkward position on the Chinese question, but that it would also offend Peking and perhaps worsen the position of the British.

Another reason for London's "sit it out" policy—as it was explained by British officials—was that if diplomatic relations were broken off the British had no guarantee that their diplomats would be allowed to leave, that they would then be left completely unprotected in Peking. Even if this didn't happen, withdrawal of the mission would mean that Anthony Grey and other non-diplomat British nationals in China would be deserted.

None of this reasoning took into account other related factors.

The British experience with the Chinese, in fact, was that only firmness and, where possible, retaliation, had much effect. At one point, for instance, the Chinese attempted to tamper with the diplomatic pouch being carried to Peking by a British courier. London promptly told Peking that if it happened again, Chinese diplomatic pouches sent into Britain would receive the same treatment. There was no further trouble. Again, when the Chinese police trailed British diplomats and denied them the same rights as other diplomats to visit the Ming Tombs and the Great Wall, London immediately limited the travel of Chinese diplomats in London and had British bobbies follow them ostentatiously. Peking saw the light: the Chinese police disappeared and British diplomats were able to join their colleagues for picnics at the Ming Tombs and the Great Wall.

During this period, incidentally, the British diplomats amused themselves—and buoyed their morale—by playing games with the Chinese security police. They worked out infinite variations to the simple business of taking the five-minute trip from the foreigners' compound of Wychiadallo to the British Office—to the consternation of the Chinese police. Sometimes three diplomats would travel halfway to the Office in a car, closely followed by two Chinese policemen in another car. Then two of the diplomats would get out and each walk a different direction to the Office while the third diplomat would proceed alone in the car—leaving the Chinese in a dilemma about whom to shadow. Other times a pair of diplomats would set forth on bicycles and then separate at

[181]

a crossroads, each taking a different route to the Office. It was mild entertainment, though, and did little to abate the increasing nervousness of the British. Some of the women became so intimidated by the constant presence of the police that they gave up their shopping outside the compound.

India and the Soviet Union, unlike Britain, understood the Chinese very well. When the Indian or Russian Embassies in Peking were attacked, the Peking Embassies in New Delhi or Moscow received the same treatment, with sometimes a few extra licks thrown in for good measure. And although relations between China and these two countries remained at basement level, the Indians and Russians in Peking were never besieged the way the British were, and they received at least a chilly respect from the Chinese.

As a weapon for the British, of course, retaliation had its limitations. The Foreign Office could not order the Chinese Office in London to be burned to the ground nor, unlike the Indians and Russians, could it organize a "spontaneous" demonstration at the Chinese Office or have London's East End toughs attack Chinese diplomats.

It is interesting that Peking keenly felt the lack of such initiative and accordingly ordered its London diplomats to rush into the street armed with axes and, of all things, baseball bats, to attack British policemen patrolling outside. Photographs of the ensuing melee were used by the Chinese to show how *their* diplomats were being beaten by the fascist British. It was a marvellous example of Oriental logic, something like the old Chinese custom of attaching a lovely name like River of Gold to a small smelly creek (there actually is such a creek with such a name in Peking) because what something is *said* to be is far more important than what it really *is*.

An unrelated but somewhat similar example was the "spontaneous" demonstration of grief displayed by Peking's citizens when Ho Chi-minh died in 1969. For about an hour one sunny afternoon, I stood across the street from the North Vietnamese Embassy and watched truckloads of Chinese arriving to pay their respects. Around the corner, they would be organized into a single line and moved along to the residence. Just before they entered, each person would be given a white paper flower from two large cardboard boxes. After this had gone on for some time, and several hundred Chinese had filed into the residence while more were still arriving, I began to have visions of the Embassy walls bursting and thousands of white flowers tumbling out like popcorn. Every time a box of flowers would be emptied, a fresh box would arrive. I walked around to the back of the Embassy, where the "mourners" were filing out and returning to their trucks. But by the rear door of the building, four Chinese were standing guard beside a big cardboard box, and ordering each person to drop in his flower as he left. When the box was filled, it was carried around to the front of the Embassy to be ready for the next truckload of arrivals.

As a propaganda device, the bat-swinging episode in London was silly: the crude attempt to portray the British police as "fascist oppressors" could convince only the Chinese who were hardly in need of convincing. But the incident, which took place shortly after the British Office in Peking was sacked, presented an important insight into Chinese thinking. It showed that Peking—perhaps because of pressure from the moderates in the leadership—had decided that it must somehow justify to the world its actions against the British in China. That the method chosen was unsophisticated and unsuccessful—at least in Western eyes—was of far less significance than the fact that the Chinese felt it necessary to do anything at all.

Perhaps Peking's leaders were worried about the reaction of the African and Asian countries they were trying to influence or, more likely, about the reaction of international

Communist parties outside the Soviet Bloc who were being asked to choose between the Russian and Chinese brands of communism.

As it happened, Peking had little to fear.

The ambassadors in Peking who tried to organize a strong petition of protest were stymied by the doyen of the diplomatic corps, the United Arab Republic Ambassador. He suddenly fell sick when they asked him to exercise his responsibility and circulate a petition. The Danish Ambassador went ahead anyhow, writing the protest and collecting the signatures. The UAR Ambassador suddenly recovered and demanded his right by protocol to deliver the petition. He took one look at it, though, and announced that he couldn't possibly present a protest framed in such strong language. Then he proceeded to water it down until it was so innocuous that the dissenting ambassadors angrily refused to have anything to do with it.

Meanwhile, the British Foreign Office did not consider that the Chinese-inspired fracas in London might mean Peking was sensitive to world opinion. Instead of putting Peking into the glare of publicity, the Foreign Office continued its policy of press restraint and relied on the conventional diplomatic formula of dignified protest notes. This method of attack can be successful only if there is a credible threat that diplomatic relations will be cut off if the protest notes go unheeded, but London was clearly not prepared to take this serious step. The Chinese were aware of this, and thus the British were in a position of trying to bluff an opponent who had already seen their cards.

About one year later, in the summer of 1968, the Foreign Office decided to reverse its policy of silence. Considering the circumstances, which had changed considerably over the previous twelve months, it seemed to be an inept and perhaps even dangerous move.

When public pressure might have helped—in the latter months of 1967, just after the British Office in Peking had been sacked—London had adopted an official posture of stoic calm while its diplomats in Peking were beaten, persecuted, humiliated, separated from their families and denied the right to return home. Then, in July, 1968, when the first of the British diplomats had received an exit visa and when even the Russian diplomats in Peking were privately conceding that normalcy was returning to China, London decided to lash out at the Chinese. It was a case of doing the right thing at the wrong time.

Consider the sequence of events. In the last week of July, 1968, the Chinese Foreign Ministry suddenly summoned two British diplomats who, to their astonishment, were greeted with smiles and given three exit visas. After a year of waiting, they were elated. But was this just a momentary aberration in the Chinese Foreign Ministry, or would there be more exit visas? And, most important, would diplomats be allowed to leave China; the first three permits had been for a clerk, and a guard and his wife.

Five days later, the British Office received another call to report to the Foreign Ministry. This time there were four exit visas, and one of them was for the British Commercial Secretary, Theo Peters. This was the signal the British had hoped for; the logjam had been broken. But a month before this happened, the British Foreign Office had decided on a "new initiative," i.e., to try to apply pressure on the Chinese through publicity. Now, with British diplomats and staff being released, the question was whether to go ahead with the planned policy change.

The logical decision, one would have thought, would have been to postpone the "initiative" as long as the British staff was continuing to receive exit visas. After all, the whole purpose of the policy change was to secure their release. If this already was happening, then why launch a campaign that might lend support to anti-British elements in the Foreign Ministry and perhaps jeopardize the chances of the remaining diplomats to return home? There was plenty of time to go ahead with the campaign—if the flow of exit visas dried up.

The British Foreign Office apparently considered this option but—with curious reasoning and belated determination—rejected it. Thus, when the first of the British diplomats to leave Peking, Commercial Secretary Theo Peters, arrived in London, he called a press conference and lambasted the Chinese. In Peking, other ambassadors shook their heads in bewilderment and began predicting that the rest of the Britishers would never get home. In fact, the exit visas continued to be issued, usually at intervals of one week to ten days. But this does not alter the fact that London had embarked on a needlessly reckless course that did not take into account China's political realities, and that the British diplomats were being released despite rather than because of London's new policy.

In addition, the "initiative" may well have had other repercussions.

Looking at the question on another level, it undoubtedly was in Britain's interest to do all it could to strengthen the hand of Chinese leaders such as Premier Chou En-lai and Foreign Minister Chen Yi, who London believed were doing their best to restore balance to Chinese foreign relations. What was the effect on their position when Peters and other released diplomats broke their customary diplomatic silence to denounce China publicly, when a minor British attaché stepped across the border and then—rather childishly, albeit dramatically—turned and spat toward China and the Chinese frontier guards? And all of this to a blare of publicity from the British press, which was reflected in newspapers around the world.

It must have been difficult for the Chinese moderates to argue that the release of the British diplomats was doing China's image much good. And it must have been easy for the Cultural Revolution radicals to argue that, as they had said all along, the counsel of the moderates was wrong on this issue and, more importantly, wrong on other issues as well.

Whatever wider implications London's maneuvers might have had within the Chinese leadership, there was still another person to be considered: Reuters correspondent Anthony Grey—and he did not have even the meager protection of diplomatic status. Grey was placed under house arrest in July, 1967, in direct retaliation for the arrest in Hong Kong of a group of Chinese Communist journalists during the riots there that summer.

I did not meet him; he already had been confined to his house for eight months when I arrived in Peking. Strangely, though, both my arrival and departure in China were connected with him.

I had been in Peking only four days, not long enough for the correspondent's accreditation to be transferred from my predecessor, David Oancia, when Sir Donald Hopson and his Second Secretary, John Weston, were permitted to visit Grey for the first time. They were allowed twenty minutes, but stretched it out to twenty-five minutes and that same afternoon called a press conference for the correspondents.

It was a very low-key affair. We met in Sir Donald's apartment (his official residence had been converted into offices after the British Mission had been sacked), and Sir Donald and Weston politely poured us sherry and passed around cigarets while we spent about five minutes discussing the

[187]

weather. Then Sir Donald read a prepared statement which described briefly the state of Grey's health and the general subject of their conversation. We asked Sir Donald a number of questions, some of them leading, but his answers were quite cool, almost detached. Someone asked for an opinion about Grey's mental state after his long period of confinement, and the reply was: "I think he is doing quite well really, under the circumstances." The answer was flat, unemotional.

We correspondents left Sir Donald's flat as a group, discussing Grey as we walked down the stairs from the third floor. The consensus was that Grey was apparently bearing up remarkably well, despite the sorry conditions in which he found himself. The one jarring note was delivered by Weston, who had walked down the stairs with us. We had just begun to say good-bye to him when his face suddenly contorted and he clenched his hands in anger. "Jesus, what a bloody savage thing this is!" he shouted, and quickly turned and strode away.

At the time, we put this outburst down to Weston's attachment to Grey. They had been very friendly in the brief two months between the time Grey had arrived and had been put under house arrest; and during the few weeks Grey's phone had been left connected after his arrest, Weston had called him daily and they had played chess on the telephone. What we did not realize at the time was that the British Foreign Office was following a policy of deflecting attention from the plight of Grey as well as its diplomats in the hope this would help them. As a result, the reports that Oancia and the other correspondents wrote about the Grey interview reflected the account given by Sir Donald: complete but unemotional information. And the British press, which is expert in taking a one-paragraph story and bouncing it up in the air like a balloon for weeks on end, quickly allowed the Grey case to slip into obscurity once again—still acting on the advice of the British Foreign Office.

A year and a half after that interview I was preparing to leave Peking. My successor, Norman Webster, had arrived and had received his accreditation; there was little left for me to do except arrange a cocktail party to introduce him to the diplomats and other correspondents. My family and I were to leave on Saturday, and the party was held on Friday at 5 P.M. But that same morning, the last of the Hong Kong Communist journalists had been freed from jail in Hong Kong; naturally, most of the sixty guests at the party were talking about Grey's expected release. The British arrived late led by Chargé d'Affaires John Denson. They were quickly surrounded by diplomats and journalists who were told that despite numerous telephone calls to the Chinese Foreign Ministry, no answer had been given to inquiries about Grey.

It was just about then that Mr. Chi, an assistant deputy head of the Foreign Ministry's Information Department, arrived at my flat with another Chinese from the same department. To say that we—all of us—were surprised to see them would be an understatement. I had sent invitations to the Information Department as a matter of courtesy, but I hadn't expected the invitations to be accepted. No member of the Foreign Ministry had attended a correspondent's cocktail party since shortly after the Cultural Revolution began.

Denson knew Chi very well. Chi, who spoke excellent English, had acted as translator when Denson met with the deputy director of the Information Department to discuss Grey's case. Denson and his staff, spying Chi as soon as he entered the room, immediately homed in on him.

"What about Anthony Grey, Mr. Chi?" asked Denson. "When are you going to allow him to leave his house?"

"But Mr. Denson," protested Chi with a broad smile, "the

[189]

Chinese Government has made it very clear that when the Chinese correspondent is released from prison in Hong Kong, then Mr. Grey will be free to leave his house."

"That we know," said Denson, his face reddening, "but the Chinese correspondent was freed this morning. Surely the Chinese Foreign Ministry has been notified by now. I've been trying to reach your people all day to find out what is going to happen to Grey."

"But Mr. Denson, today is a holiday at the Foreign Ministry and nobody is working," said Chi.

Denson, now exasperated and angry, almost shouted, "All right, then, Mr. Chi, when will the Foreign Ministry be working and when will Grey get out?"

Chi's smile grew broader, and he paused to sip a glass of orange soda. "If the Chinese correspondent has indeed been released, then I expect our colleagues in Hong Kong will inform us early tomorrow morning and then Mr. Grey will, of course, be free to leave his house whenever he likes."

At this Denson swung away from Chi, muttered an apology to me about having to leave early and rushed back to the British Office to send a radio message to London that Grey would be out of house arrest the next morning, October 4. Other diplomats and correspondents also quickly filed out to send word to their own offices, and the party soon broke up.

Even today, I don't know whether or not Chi came to the party for the express purpose of telling the British that Grey would be released the next day. But one thing is certain: Chi knew very well that the British would be at the party, and he had come prepared to give them the official word about Grey.

Grey in fact was released the next morning, but by then my wife and daughter and I were flying between Peking and Shanghai, on our way out of China.

All the correspondents had strong feelings about Grey. It was easy to imagine ourselves in his position, for he was the victim of circumstance. He had done nothing wrong, as the Chinese admitted. His only error was in being in the wrong place in the wrong time; and even that mistake was almost corrected.

According to one British diplomat who was in Peking at the time of Grey's arrest, the British Office had foreseen the possibility that Grey might be picked up in retaliation for the imprisonment of the Hong Kong Communist journalists. The British diplomats advised Grey to apply for an exit visa and get out of China. Grey followed their advice. He asked the Foreign Ministry for an exit visa. Then, as he was preparing to leave, he received a cable from Reuters telling him to stay on in Peking a while longer. A few days later Reuters cabled again to say that it might be wise for him to leave, after all. By then it was too late: the Foreign Ministry had cancelled his exit visa, and soon he was under house arrest.

Reuters' miscalculation cost Grey twenty-seven months of his life.

For me, personally, the most frustrating thing was that I could do nothing to help Grey. During the eighteen months I was in Peking, I made a point of dialling his telephone number two or three times a week, but the line was always busy—even on the day before he was released. And whenever I drove past his house I would beep a dot-dot-dot-dash on the car horn in hopes that he would recognize the V for victory signal and know that people outside remembered him. I wonder if he ever heard it.

From time to time I would also write stories about the British situation in Peking, and mention Grey and the fact that he had been under house arrest for many months. But the stories had little effect in Britain where the press was

[191]

deliberately downplaying news about the country's diplomats in China.

In any case, as well I knew, the resolution to Grey's situation rested in London. The British Government could do one of two things to try to secure his release: It could generate publicity about him to pressure or embarrass the Chinese into releasing him; or it could order the Hong Kong Government to free the Communist journalists.

In the early stages of Grey's detention, publicity might have helped him as well as the British diplomats in Peking. Certainly, it could not have made their situation any worse. But the real answer to Grey's freedom was to release the Hong Kong prisoners.

This was not possible at the time of Grey's arrest, nor for some months afterward. Hong Kong was still in a state of turmoil. To have shown any sign of weakness would only have encouraged the Hong Kong Communists to increase the level of rioting and bombing. But by the summer of 1968 it was clear that the miniature Cultural Revolution had failed, that it was opposed by the vast majority of the Hong Kong Chinese, and that even Peking was fed up with the colony's Communists. The Chinese Government was intent on restoring the status quo in the colony with one exception, Anthony Grey, who represented their way of saving face. This was recognized in London, but the British Foreign Office bowed to the wishes of the Hong Kong Government.

The attitude of the Hong Kong authorities was quite clear, and I heard it expressed many times in conversations with Europeans living there. One hot evening I sat on the balcony of a high apartment building overlooking beautiful Hong Kong bay and listened to a young English woman.

"We should never release any of those damn Communists," she said. "They tried to destroy us. They tried to kill women and children. If we let them out, they'll just start all over again. They have to learn a lesson and the only way to do it is to be tough. They received a fair trial in a British court and they were found guilty. Now they must serve out their sentences, just like any one else would have to. It's too bad about Tony Grey, but the lives of the millions of people in Hong Kong are a lot more important. Why should we satisfy the Chinese leaders?"

Her impassioned argument ignored the political reality, of course. The fact was that the Hong Kong revolution was finished. Whether or not the Communist journalists were released made no difference whatsoever, except to Grey. If Peking wanted to stage a riot the next day in Hong Kong, then a riot would be staged—regardless of whether the Communists stayed in or out of the colony's prison. What she was really talking about, whether she realized it or not, was a question of the *British* in Hong Kong saving face. Yet one wonders who really would have lost face if the Communists had been freed and if, on Grey's release, the British Foreign Office had publicly explained its action and roundly denounced the Chinese for their treatment of Grey.

But the British in London left the question of Grey's fate to the British in Hong Kong, and they couldn't have cared less about him. Reuters, which did care about Grey, also behaved strangely.

In June, 1968, when Grey had already spent a year under house arrest and his future looked extremely bleak, I had lunch in Hong Kong with a member of the Reuters organization. We talked about Grey and about China and about Hong Kong. Finally, he confided that he was feeling very pleased with himself. He had, he said, just pulled off an excellent business deal. He had just sold Reuters' economic service to the Bank of China. The Bank of China, which occupies a

[193]

large building in downtown Hong Kong just opposite the Hilton Hotel, is the heart of the mainland's financial enterprises in the colony and, reputedly, also is the center of the network of Communist organizations.

Reuters could apparently see nothing wrong in selling its services to the very people who were keeping a Reuters correspondent locked up in Peking.

12

ONE curious aspect of the quarrel between Britain and China was the effect it had on the Russian diplomats in Peking. Journalists who were stationed in Peking many years ago have noted the feeling among foreigners that "it's all of us against all of them," but the feeling became a fact during the Cultural Revolution. (The feeling was well described by Frederick Nossal in *Dateline—Peking,* Longmans, and by Jacques Marcuse in *The Peking Papers,* Arthur Barker, Ltd.) This was especially true of the Russians and the British, and the bond transcended political differences—at least on the Soviet side.

It is doubtful that the British were even aware of it, but the Russians made clear to me that they felt a particular debt of gratitude toward the British. This was because Sir Donald Hopson had led his staff out to Peking Airport in 1967 to help the Russian diplomats defend their departing wives and children against attacks by several hundred Red Guards. In so doing, Sir Donald not only ignored the possibility of involving his country in another political incident with China, but he also rejected the Chinese Foreign Ministry's indirect

[195]

warning that foreign diplomats should not go to Peking Airport because they would be involving themselves in a Sino-Soviet affair (this message was circulated by an ambassador whose country was friendly to China).

This personal debt was intensified by the fact that the Russian diplomats, no doubt acting under orders from Moscow, had not lifted a finger to help the British when they were besieged by the Chinese. By the beginning of 1970, however, the Russian affection and admiration for the British had once again been replaced by deep distrust and, even worse, bitter dislike. The story of how it happened is in some ways amusing.

Starting in mid-1968, the Chinese began to issue exit visas to the British diplomats and one by one the Englishmen who in some cases had literally stood side by side with the Russians against the Red Guards, began to leave Peking. By the end of the year they had all returned home while the Russians, of course, remained. The new British diplomats had not endured the Cultural Revolution and felt no special bond with the Russians.

This in itself would not have bothered the Soviet diplomats; they were not treated as bosom companions by Western diplomats in any part of the world. But two things in particular about the "newcomers" annoyed the Russians.

The first, strangely, was that the British replacements didn't have sufficient respect for their predecessors—at least in Russian eyes. The British, in fact, did admire the men and women who went before them, and they had great pride in the way the British Office conducted itself during the troubles. But it is very un-English to show one's feelings in public, or to pat oneself on the back. Thus when among strangers, the new British diplomats would use a small joke or understatement to turn aside compliments about their predecessors. Their attitude puzzled and offended the literal-minded Russians.

On one occasion a young British diplomat and his wife invited a group of people, including a Russian, to an outdoor barbecue by the British pool. Just a few yards away were the charred remains of the sacked British Office. The party was going well, with everyone hungrily eating weiners and drinking Chinese beer, when the hostess suddenly noticed she was running out of charcoal.

"Oh, it's all right, there's lots of charcoal over there," she laughed, and pointed at the burned-out office. "The last time we had a barbecue we had to use charcoal from the ruins. Just think, we probably were eating hot dogs cooked from what was left of Sir Donald's ambassadorial desk."

The Russian was so disgusted that he didn't eat anything else that night.

What really upset the Soviet Embassy, though, was the British film show. Every two weeks, the British Office received a new movie in the diplomatic bag from Hong Kong. It was shown every Tuesday night to anyone in the foreign community who wanted to see it. Attendance was always good despite the small screen (bed-sheets were tacked on each side of it when the film was wide-screen) and despite the mostly poor quality of the films; it was one of the few entertainments the foreigners had in Peking.

In any case, the British had nothing to do with the choice of films. They were shipped to Hong Kong by the British Army for the amusement of soldiers posted there, and then sent on to the British Office. In addition, only British films were shown because of the high cost of securing the distribution rights to American or foreign films. Whenever a good movie did come along, two or three British diplomats would usually organize dinner parties and then take their guests back to the Office for a special showing. And that was what happened on the disastrous night that the film *Morgan* was shown.

Afterwards, when the British Chargé d'Affaires held a postmortem on what happened, it turned out that only one of the British diplomats had seen the movie before. And it hadn't occurred to him that the dark comedy about a schizophrenic young London Marxist would have any political overtones. He realized it that night, though, and like his co-hosts, slid deeper into his chair as the film flashed across the screen. The Russians and other East Europeans watched in stony silence as the movie showed photographs of Marx and an ape hanging side by side on a wall, and a scene of the young hero dancing madly around the hallowed grave of Marx.

As the film progressed, the senior Russian diplomat considered whether he should walk out in protest; all the other East Bloc diplomats were watching for the signal which he, by protocol, had to give. He decided to stay, but left immediately after the film without waiting for the customary nightcap—and was followed by other East Europeans. His colleagues later criticized him for his decision.

The whole thing sounds as silly now as it did then, but it was a very serious matter in Peking. I talked about it several times to Russian diplomats but was unable to persuade them that the British had not shown the film with malice aforethought.

"Of course it is natural that you as a Canadian would try to defend the British," said one Russian, "but there is no question in our minds that the British knew this was a dirty film and deliberately invited us and our colleagues in order to humiliate the Soviet Union and all Communist countries."

I had a slightly different—and unintentionally funny—

opinion from a Yugoslavian diplomat. The Yugoslavians of course consider themselves outside the Russian camp, but the emotional ties between the two countries remain very strong.

"I do not know if the British showed the film on purpose," he said, "but the Russians certainly should have walked out. Believe me, I would have if the movie had shown a picture of Tito and an ape on the wall instead of Marx and an ape."

All of which perhaps tells something of the state of communism in Eastern Europe, for the Russians would certainly have left the film in protest if it had shown a picture of Brezhnev instead of Marx beside an ape.

The seriousness, or pettiness, of the incident was illustrated by the fact that both the Soviet Embassy and the British Office held separate meetings to decide what to do. After some discussion, the Russian Chargé d'Affaires ruled against filing a formal protest with the British; while across the city, the British Chargé d'Affaires ruled against sending an informal apology to the Russians. (The Arab missions were not so hesitant about protests. They made formal representations to complain to the British about the film *Judith* starring Sophia Loren, and *Lawrence of Arabia,* starring Peter O'Toole; they said *Judith* was pro-Israel and *Lawrence* was anti-Arab.)

These were but minor matters. The one thing which sharply re-drew the line between the Russians and all other non-East Bloc diplomats in Peking was Czechoslovakia. After August, 1968, things could never be the same.

In Peking, diplomats and correspondents excitedly listened to the BBC and Voice of America broadcasts every day to follow the Czech resistance to Moscow's demands. Some of the Poles, Hungarians, Rumanians and Yugoslavians—far more idealistic than the East Germans and Bulgarians—were outspoken in their defense of Dubcek's reforms. To these

[199]

East Europeans, all Communists themselves, the Czechoslovakian program was a logical development in the evolution of communism.

I asked a Hungarian diplomat what he really thought of Czechoslovakia's attempts at liberalization. He looked around with an elaborate display of caution and whispered: "Great!" A few weeks later, after Russian, Polish, Bulgarian, East German and Hungarian soldiers had invaded Prague, he was loudly defending Moscow's action. In a quiet corner at a cocktail party, I gently inquired: "And how does it feel now to be the representative of a successful invading army?"

He turned on me angrily, and said: "Look, my friend, don't expect me to feel sorry for the Czechs. When we Hungarians were having our own problems in 1956 [the Hungarian uprising], we found Czechoslovakian tanks strung along the border with their guns pointed at us."

Some Soviet-Bloc diplomats were so shocked by the Russian action that they unwisely were critical in public. On the day of the invasion, one Pole went to see a Western friend and wept openly as he talked about Czechoslovakia. One by one, all of these diplomats were recalled home within two months and I later learned that some of them had lost their jobs in the Foreign Ministry.

The acting Czechoslovakian Chargé d'Affaires, who actually was a first secretary, was also recalled. It was inevitable. When I first heard of the Soviet intervention, I drove over to the Czechoslovakian Embassy to see if I could talk to him. Nobody answered the doorbell and the Embassy seemed deserted. I tried the door; it was open so I walked inside. There was no one in the large foyer, but I could hear a voice from one of the upstairs rooms. Suddenly, there was a roar of approval and a few minutes later people began coming down the stairs, led by the acting Chargé d'Affaires.

It was a strange sight. There were men, women (including one who was pregnant) and children coming down the steps. Some of the women and children were in bathing suits (the Czechs had an outdoor swimming pool); some of the men were in shorts, others were in business suits. Not only was every Czech at the meeting, but it had been called in a hurry.

"I am sorry," said the Chargé d'Affaires, "but we just heard the news from Prague and decided to call a meeting to discuss what to do. As you see, we felt it important that every Czech here be present."

He was wearing old trousers, sandals and a short-sleeved sports shirt. He looked tired and his eyes were red-rimmed; he had been up all night listening to the radio for news and waiting for a message from his Foreign Ministry.

"But there was no message," he added. "We had only our Government's protest note to the Soviet Union and the other Warsaw Pact countries denying they had been asked to occupy our country, and asking that they leave.

"We never expected this," he said wearily, rubbing his forehead. "We just never thought this would happen. Our military attaché even went on home leave. He's somewhere between Peking and Moscow; he probably doesn't even know what has happened."

A girl came in carrying two sheets of paper. The Chargé d'Affaires gave them to me.

"There are about seventy of us in the Embassy," he said, "and all of us have voted approval of these statements. Now they will be sent to all the embassies in Peking so that everyone will know where we stand."

I looked at the mimeographed statements, one on each page. The first was a copy of the Czechoslovakian Government's protest note. It had been hastily translated into English and there were typing and grammatical errors. The

[201]

second page contained the Embassy's statement. It was beautiful and courageous. It was also sadly futile, and everyone in the Embassy must have known it.

It read: "All members of the Embassy of the Czechoslovakian Socialist Republic in Peking fully support the just position of the Czechoslovakian Government and condemn the illegal invasion and occupation of their motherland."

The next day the Chinese Government broke its silence on the situation when Premier Chou En-lai made a speech at the Rumanian National Day reception condemning the Soviet Union and its four Warsaw Pact allies for their "surprise attack" on Czechoslovakia. Representatives of the four countries and of Mongolia immediately walked out, but the Czechoslovakian Chargé d'Affaires stayed.

A few days later, at a North Vietnamese National Day reception, Chou En-lai again lashed the Soviet Union verbally, and once again the Poles, Hungarians, Bulgarians, East Germans and Mongolians walked out with the Russian Chargé d'Affaires while the Czechs remained seated along with the Rumanians and Yugoslavians. Then, when the Chinese Premier denounced the Czech "revisionists" for capitulating "to the bayonets of the Russian revisionists," the Czechoslovakian Chargé d'Affaires also walked out.

There wasn't much the Russian Chargé d'Affaires could do about the Rumanians, whose government was trying to pursue an independent foreign policy, but he decided he wasn't going to tolerate impudence from the Czechoslovakian Chargé d'Affaires whose country, after all, had been occupied by the Soviet Army. In blunt terms the Czech was told that he had to leave diplomatic receptions with the other East European diplomats if the Soviet Union was insulted.

He didn't refuse; he simply stopped attending receptions at which a Chinese official was likely to speak, making the excuse that he was ill. Whether he really was sick didn't much

[202]

matter, for a few weeks later a new Czechoslovakian Chargé d'Affaires arrived from Prague and he was sent home. I often wondered what happened to him.

Meanwhile the Czechoslovakian affair was having an effect on Sino-Yugoslavian relations.

Yugoslavia had never really been on friendly terms with the Soviet Union since their split in the 1950's, but with Stalin's death and the ensuing moderation in Russian foreign policy, there was some optimism among Yugoslavians that the two countries could coexist peacefully. Events in Czechoslovakia proved otherwise; the Warsaw Pact countries could use the same excuse of "saving socialism" to justify invading Yugoslavia. China recognized these fears, and soon the Yugoslavians in Peking—whose Embassy walls still bore traces of Red Guard artistic efforts such as DOWN WITH YUGO-SLAVIAN REVISIONISM and HANG TITO THE DOG'S HEAD—had the unusual experience of seeing their country defended against Russia in the Chinese press.

Yugoslavia regarded both China and the Soviet Union with equal cynicism, but the Russian action could not be ignored. By the end of August, members of the Yugoslavian Embassy had been ordered to cut off all but business contact with the Soviet Embassy. This was a hardship to the Yugoslavian women and children, most of whom spoke only their own language and Russian. They no longer could go to the Soviet Embassy's swimming pool or weekly film shows.

Thus the Russians found themselves estranged from both the Yugoslavian and Rumanian diplomats. Even in the other East European embassies only the most reactionary of the diplomats could be wholeheartedly in favour of Moscow's arbitrary action against Czechoslovakia. The Western embassies also froze out the Soviet Embassy, except for formal functions, and their diplomats rarely missed an opportunity to let the Russians know how they felt.

On the first anniversary of the Czechoslovakian occupation, for instance, the Dutch Chargé d'Affaires made sure that the weekly program of recorded music held in his mission featured only Czechoslovakian music. No Russians attended.

Gradually, the Soviet diplomats retreated behind their old barricades, emerging socially only for formal dinners and receptions. They no longer expected sympathy for their country's confrontation with China, except from their East European friends. But at that time, in late 1968, the Soviet diplomats probably did not expect the confrontation to move soon from words to bullets.

Among Peking's Western diplomats, opinion was divided on the question of the armed clashes along the Sino-Soviet border in March, 1969. Some believed Peking was responsible. They argued it was an old Chinese ploy in times of internal strife to conjure up the threat of a "barbarian" invasion in order to unite the people and to make new demands for increased industrial and agricultural production.

The same argument, however, could be used against the Russians. There was discontent at home and among the peoples of the Soviet Bloc countries over Moscow's heavy-handed treatment of Czechoslovakia a few months earlier. And there was open criticism from Communist parties located in countries outside the Soviet orbit. This was especially vexing to the Russian leaders; they wanted to have a unanimous condemnation of China at the World Communist Congress which was to be held in Moscow in June.

Was this sufficient reason for the Soviet Union to inspire a "Chinese attack"? Perhaps. Certainly Moscow was the first to announce the border clash (Peking later revealed there had been a number of other incidents about which both sides had remained silent) and Russian ambassadors abroad were almost immediately at the doors of foreign ministers to explain the Soviet Union's innocence in the affair. Peking seemed to have been caught flat-footed by Moscow's well-orchestrated publicity campaign, and it took a few days for the Chinese propaganda mill to organize some sort of rebuttal.

This, in brief, took the form of a denial of Soviet charges and a repetition of Peking's familiar position on border negotiations: that because Russians had occupied certain Chinese territories for many years through "unequal treaties," Peking was willing to discuss a settlement on the border's present lines; but before that could be done, Moscow must first repudiate the "unequal treaties" foisted upon China by the imperialist Tsars.

Peking's apparently reasonable position was ignored by much of the world, which usually views China as an aggressor in any situation. Also ignored was the fact that China's inadequate supply system to the north and its military inferiority made a provocation along the Manchurian border foolhardy in the extreme. In addition, China's economy was just in the first stage of recovering from the Cultural Revolution and much of its army was fully occupied with domestic problems (indeed, these were good reasons for the Russians to create a border incident, along with the possibility it might cause dissension within the Chinese leadership).

There was still another factor to be considered.

Moscow must have been alarmed when Peking suggested to Washington that the Sino-American talks be resumed in Warsaw in February, 1969. The idea of a peace pact between the United States and China—which was what Peking had proposed—raised the frightening possibility that the world's wealthiest nation and the world's most populous nation might form an alliance against the Soviet Union. Because of American ineptness the Warsaw talks were not held, but the Chinese made it clear they were postponing the meeting, not cancelling. It would be surprising if some Kremlin hawks had not weighed the merits of a preemptive military strike

[205]

against China; in fact, East European diplomats in Peking later said their countries had been asked by Moscow to consider such a plan.

It had certain advantages. A quick thrust against military and industrial targets would set back China's economy and war potential for at least a decade; and if the attacking forces withdrew quickly to well-armed Russian defense installations along the border, there would be no danger of a protracted and debilitating land war within China. Obviously, the only reaction of the Western countries would be mild recriminations at the United Nations.

The disadvantages, which obviously won the argument, were that the Chinese had a nuclear capability and might use it against the Soviet Union; and that an open attack against China would destroy Russian influence in other parts of the world.

In Peking, meanwhile, the Russian diplomats were concerned with more prosaic matters. Two days after the border clash, trucks with loudspeakers were parked around the Embassy grounds and thousands of Chinese began to gather in the adjoining streets. The Russians, remembering the hectic days of the Cultural Revolution, prepared for the worst. Food supplies were laid in, and in the main building facing the front gate all the windows were boarded up. But the demonstrators, heavily infiltrated with soldiers, were very orderly. They marched up and down the main thoroughfare near the Embassy but they did not enter the short street that led to the main gate. Nor were they allowed to parade along the street that led to a side entrance to the Embassy; this was kept clear by Chinese police so that foreigners could go in and out freely.

I drove along there myself, and went inside the Embassy to talk to the Russians. It was very noisy because of the loudspeakers, which were operating full-blast from 9 A.M. to 10 P.M. There was little to talk about anyway. The demonstration was going on, but aside from the din nothing much was happening. Suddenly the Russian grabbed my arm.

"Look, they're coming," he said, and then added, "You are here at a historic moment; we are about to be attacked."

I peered between the cracks in the boarded window. Sure enough, they were coming. About one thousand shouting Chinese were marching down the street toward the front gate. I began to wonder if there would be much point in trying to explain to them that I was a Canadian. But when they reached the gate, they stopped abruptly, shook their fists, shouted slogans and then marched back up the street again. The performance was repeated by another thousand. And then another thousand. Finally, I saw that they were indeed performing. Stationed by the gates were Chinese photographers and movie cameramen. The whole thing was being recorded for presentation across the country and abroad.

There were a few minor incidents that captured headlines. One was accidental, and the other two were instigated by the East Europeans. A British Second Secretary was mistaken for a Russian when he tried to circulate among the demonstrators, and was turned back by a flurry of icy snowballs thrown by children. One struck him on the forehead and opened a quarter-inch cut. To his surprise, the world press reported the next day that he had been stoned by Chinese demonstrators.

The other incidents involved an East German diplomat who tried to drive through the crowd to the front gate, though the side entrance was open, and as a result had his car stopped and rocked; and two *Tass* correspondents who were shoved around by the crowd when they went out the front gate and tried to argue with the demonstrators. These were the only

[207]

incidents that occurred during seven days of demonstrations (stretched over eleven days); the Chinese did not even retaliate when Russian demonstrators broke windows and splashed paint on the Chinese Embassy in Moscow. Obviously, the Cultural Revolution days of attacks against foreign embassies had ended. In fact, there were to be no more parades around diplomatic quarters, and very few demonstrations of any kind. (My successor in Peking, Norman Webster, reported only two demonstrations from May, 1970, to February, 1971, both against United States involvement in Indo-China.)

One diplomatic incident *almost* occurred. The Soviet Chargé d'Affaires decided to give a farewell luncheon for the French Ambassador, who was soon leaving Peking for another posting. Despite the demonstration, the Russian refused to postpone the party. The invited ambassadors, convinced that the Russians were deliberately using them, were furious. If they did not go, they would affront the Governments of France and the Soviet Union. If they did go, they might have a hassle with Chinese demonstrators. And that, of course, would force their foreign ministries to make a formal protest to Peking—which would delight Moscow.

The Pakistani Ambassador, whose country had very friendly relations with China, refused to be drawn into the trap; he turned down the invitation. The other ambassadors decided to take advantage of the fact that their telephones were tapped. By prearrangement, they spent hours calling each other to discuss the diplomatic consequences if their cars were attacked by demonstrators. It worked. On the day of the luncheon, the crowds parted quietly and the ambassadors drove in and out of the Soviet Embassy grounds without incident.

The end of the demonstration—and the Ninth Congress

[208]

of the Chinese Communist party the following month (April) —seemed to mark a turning point in Sino-Soviet affairs. There were further border clashes in the spring and summer of 1969 and large movements of troops in the area,* but in September, Premier Alexei Kosygin met with Premier Chou En-lai at Peking Airport and the tension eased appreciably.

By the beginning of 1971, Peking's policy toward the Soviet Union had become reasonably clear. The Chinese would continue to regard the Russians as revisionists and neocolonialists but were willing to have normal governmental relations with the Soviet Union. A trade agreement was signed and ambassadors were exchanged; Chou En-lai even invited the new Soviet Ambassador in for a polite talk. But as the Russians themselves recognized, there was to be no ideological reconciliation. China was moving out into the world again, salving international wounds opened during the Cultural Revolution, attempting to establish diplomatic and trade relations around the world, and in general proving it could get along with countries of "differing social systems." It may have been insulting to Moscow, but the Chinese were obviously lumping the Soviet Communist regime into this latter category.

Perhaps it was where the Soviet Union belonged. One cannot judge a whole country by a group of its diplomats, but because my wife speaks Russian fluently we spent many afternoons and evenings within the walls of the Soviet Embassy in Peking—attending dinners, movies and dances,

* The 1970 survey of the Institute of Strategic Studies said that in 1969 the Soviet Union had moved 20 divisions into the area, but that its total of 28 divisions was outnumbered by the Chinese. However, the report added that China's "medium and light tanks and its limited artillery units are no match for the massive weight and capacity of the armored and artillery forces available to Soviet commanders on the border." *The New York Times,* April 12, 1970.

having picnics and barbecues, playing badminton and splashing in their swimming pool, watching Katharine and their children play together. And though the ideological differences could never really be forgotten, it was difficult to believe that the Russians' natural cultural affinity was toward the East rather than the West regardless of communism.

13

THE night was clear and bitter cold. The wind, rocketing down from Siberia, banged away at our little Volkswagen. I slowed down a bit. It was dangerous enough driving in Peking at night even without being buffeted by the wind.

We were on the road that winds around the northeast outskirts of Peking, the open commune fields on one side and the occasional darkened apartment building looming up on the other side. Regina was slouched down on the seat beside me, her shoulders hunched so that her face was buried in her coat collar. A dark mass appeared on the road ahead. I drove even slower and switched from parking lights to headlights (illegal in Peking) and saw that it was a cart loaded with bricks being pulled by three donkeys. As we swerved around the cart I caught a glimpse of a figure muffled in a goatskin coat sitting at the front of the cart. He didn't look up, probably asleep.

"I wonder what time it is," said Regina.

It took quite a while to reach the next street lamp—they were about one hundred yards apart in that section of Peking—where we stopped so that she could look at her watch in the dim light of what surely must have been a 10-watt bulb.

"It's almost two o'clock," she said. "I guess we missed Irkutsk and Omsk at least."

And what, I asked myself, am I doing spending the second hour of 1969 slowly freezing myself to death by driving through the countryside of Peking to get to a New Year's Eve party at the Russian Embassy? For that was where we were going.

We had left the French Embassy just as the annual New Year's Eve party for Western diplomats was getting into full swing. Well, perhaps that is the wrong description. The diplomats and their wives, all dressed in tuxedos and evening gowns, had spent the evening decorously dancing to waltzes and foxtrots. But the French Ambassador and his staff were busy pouring chilled champagne for their guests—the Chinese waiters had insisted on leaving at the stroke of midnight —and a junior attaché was preparing to slip a Herb Alpert record on the record player.

"Well, we promised we would go," said Regina. "Anyhow, it would be interesting to celebrate at least part of New Year's Eve in the Russian Embassy."

We had promised. Our Russian friend had said that we would be most welcome. We could join the Russians in toasting the Embassy at midnight, toasting Irkutsk at 1 A.M., Omsk at 2 A.M. and so on, as midnight arrived in various Soviet cities until finally at 6 A.M., those celebrants who were still standing could toast the Russian capital, Moscow. But of course, he added understandingly, you will want to spend New Year's Eve with the other Westerners at the French Embassy. But no, we protested, we would be delighted to come to the Soviet Embassy, and would leave the French Embassy early to do so.

So there we were, driving up Anti-Revisionist Street (formerly Sino-Soviet Friendship Street) to the great iron gates of the Russian Embassy at 2 A.M. on January 1.

It looked deserted. The main Embassy building was in darkness, and the gates were barred. The two Chinese security policemen on duty stared at us impassively, their faces partly obscured by thick fur helmets and their olive-green greatcoats flapping in the wind. They did not speak or move.

After two minutes of waiting, I announced to Regina that I was going home. But then a Russian, also wrapped in a greatcoat, appeared out of the darkness and rolled open the gates. He pointed to the road winding around the main Embassy building, smiled happily and carefully saluted as we drove by. Vodka? I wondered.

We drove along the tree-lined road, passing silent buildings but not seeing anyone. At last we came to a building with lights on and we pulled up in front of the entrance. Before the car had even stopped, our Russian friend was opening its doors; the guard at the gate must have telephoned that we were on our way.

He solemnly gave each of us a bear hug, then took us by the arm up the stairs and into the building. He took our coats and said, "Wait here for a moment, then I shall take you to the party. It is almost time for Omsk."

As he walked away, Regina turned to me with a startled look. "Do you hear what I hear?"

"If you hear Frank Sinatra singing 'Strangers in the Night,' then you hear what I hear," I said.

Our friend returned, led us down a stairway and into a large hall. Now there was a new record playing—"Hello Dolly" by Herb Alpert—and three middle-aged couples were vigorously doing the twist in the middle of the floor. Ranged along two sides of the room were long tables covered with white cloths and loaded with caviar, black bread, sausages,

[213]

and hundreds of bottles of Chinese beer and Russian wine and vodka. At one end of the room was a screen; every half hour or so a Russian film of slapstick comedy was shown. It didn't help much; the party was gloomy, and it was easy to see why. There was, to put it mildly, a shortage of women. There were about seventy men sitting around drinking steadily and seriously, but I counted only ten women—and two little boys who were lively enough despite the late hour, sliding back and forth across the almost empty dance floor.

It had been almost unanimously decided at the Embassy that the two children would be allowed to stay up late New Year's Eve. They were in Peking for only three weeks and had become the darlings of all the Russian men, many of whom had been separated from their own wives and children for almost a year. The two boys would soon be returning to Moscow, and so would most of the women there that night. They had been allowed to come to Peking for a few weeks to visit their husbands.

We stayed only an hour, despite the friendly reception given us; it was too depressing.

The plight of these men and women, caught in the Peking-Moscow ideological quarrel, has never been reported in the Soviet Union. Yet they did suffer.

The beginnings of their troubles, of course, were described fully—for political reasons.

In late January, 1967, following a fracas in Moscow involving Chinese students, the Soviet Embassy in Peking was besieged by thousands of screaming Red Guards. Outside the Embassy walls, dozens of loudspeakers blared night and day, making sleep impossible. After they had endured more than seven days of this turmoil, Moscow decided to bring home all the women and children. They left in three groups on February 4, 5 and 6, and on each occasion were surrounded at Peking Airport by Red Guards who harassed them, spat at them and sometimes struck them. The children, of course, were badly frightened; a year later some of them would still awaken screaming in the middle of the night, the Russians told me.

By the end of 1967, the excesses of xenophobia had ended and, in fact, Chinese authorities had made it clear that violence of any kind against foreigners would not be tolerated. The diplomats (including the Russians) were convinced that the Chinese meant what they said. All the embassies, even the East European ones, had their usual number of women and children. All, that is, except the Soviet Embassy.

For Moscow, the issue had become more a question of politics than of safety. After all, if the women and children had been brought home because their lives were endangered in Peking, then wouldn't it be equally true that to allow them to return to Peking would be a tacit admission that Moscow considered they no longer were in danger? But this could hardly be admitted by the Soviet leaders when *Tass* and *Pravda* were steadily publishing reports that China was in chaos, that pitched battles were raging back and forth across the country.

Thus the wives and children had to stay in the Soviet Union except for rare and brief "vacations" in Peking. These were not easy to organize, since the children could not have their schooling disrupted in the Soviet Union, and many of the women were working and couldn't easily get leave from their jobs.

It was interesting, by the way, that the Russian Chargé d'Affaires had his young grandson, on whom he doted, spend the whole summer in Peking. And that was in 1969, when fighting had broken out along the Sino-Soviet border and when Moscow was issuing dire warnings that the Chinese were about to attack the Soviet Union.

Without women, the Soviet Embassy was a gloomy place.

[215]

But with a little imagination, one could picture what it must have been like in the old days when the Chinese and Russians were the best of friends.

Probably no other embassy in the world has such a magnificent setting. The grounds cover more than one hundred acres in the northern outskirts of Peking, just beside the old city walls. Around the Embassy itself, high thick walls effectively close off the sounds of the city. Inside are thousands of trees and bushes giving the grounds the appearance of a giant secluded park. It is the only place in Peking—other than the wooded area beside the Forbidden City where Mao and other Chinese leaders live—where one can hear birds sing throughout the day. A small river—about twenty feet wide—meanders through much of the property and on warm summer evenings in past years couples in rowboats drifted along the slow-moving stream. In two places, the river has been widened to make small lakes which were the haunt of Russian fishermen in warm weather; in the winter, lights were strung around the lakes and they were the scene of gay skating parties.

The buildings and facilities were extensive, and in some ways had a touch of almost Tsarist splendour. The reason for this was quite simple: the Russian and Chinese Governments had agreed that each would build the other's embassy, and the Chinese were obviously determined not to be outdone by their friends in Moscow. They weren't.

The domed building, just inside the front gates, houses all the administrative offices of the Embassy. But it is so large that it also contains a twenty-foot-wide bank of marble stairs leading to a giant chandeliered and mirrored hall with polished parquet floors. It could serve as a ballroom. And adjoining this room is a modern, air-conditioned theater which, with its balcony, is able to seat about three hundred people—on well-upholstered chairs equipped with earphones for translations.

Another building (where we attended the New Year's Eve party) is equipped with an auditorium with stage and screen, as well as classrooms for a children's school. There is also a miniature hospital (the Russians had their own doctor and dentist) complete with a small laboratory and beds for six patients. Trade offices are housed in a large, separate building—though there has been less and less for the commercial officers to do: in just four years, from 1964 to 1968, total Sino-Soviet trade dropped from almost $500 million to $95 million. Residential quarters for the staff are contained in five apartment buildings, complete with air-conditioning. And, of course, there are also recreational facilities: outdoor basketball, badminton and tennis courts, an Olympic-size swimming pool with four diving boards and a small wading pool for children. The ambassador's residence, built just on the edge of the river, has its own swimming pool.

The gem of all the buildings, though, is a small house faithfully reproduced in Chinese style, with ornate enamelled cornices and delicately carved doors. The Chinese theme is continued inside, with the traditional rich rosewood furniture, huge vases, scrolls and high carved wood screens inlaid with ivory. This building, which the Embassy staff used for intimate dinner parties, must alone be worth at least $1,000,000. Historically, it is also fascinating, having been built on the site of a Russian Orthodox church erected more than one hundred years ago when the Emperor granted this same stretch of land to a group of Russians who wanted to settle in China.

Before the public split between the Soviet Union and China in 1960, there were many warm and cordial parties in this house attended by high-ranking Chinese officials with their wives. In those days nothing was too good for a Russian fortunate enough to be posted to Peking. Even hunting expeditions were organized for those Russians who were sportsmen, and they were taken not only around Peking for shooting but even as far away as Manchuria to hunt for wild boar and deer.

At that time, too, there were many Russians in Peking. First, there were the Embassy staff and families totalling more than four hundred persons. Among senior staff alone, there were five first secretaries (the British had one). Then there were several hundred Soviet technicians and advisors working in Chinese factories, and a number of Russians attending university in the city.

Diplomats from other countries who were in Peking during that period claim there was considerable antagonism toward the Russians among the general Chinese population, though it was well concealed until the Cultural Revolution. These diplomats may well have been expressing their own frustration at being kept at arm's length by both the Chinese and the Russians, but they argued that the Russian experts treated the Chinese arrogantly and ridiculed everything they did. This, said the diplomats, was particularly irritating to many Chinese technicians who had been trained in the West and, besides feeling they knew as much as or more than the Russians, were aware that the salaries of the Soviet technicians were five and six times higher than theirs—and the Chinese Government was paying the bill.

No doubt there is some truth in this, and it must have been equally irritating to the Chinese to know that the Russians were selling China only machinery that was badly outmoded or no longer useful to the Soviet Union.

On the other hand, I know that not all Chinese who came into contact with Russians ended up hating them. I was strolling through Peking's People's Market one day with a

Soviet diplomat when a smiling Chinese man rushed up to my companion and embraced him, Russian-style. They talked happily in Mandarin for about five minutes. Then the Chinese man fished a worn wallet out of his pocket and produced some photographs for the Russian to look at. After they said good-bye, the Russian explained that he had last seen his friend seven years ago when they were both attending Peking University. The pictures were of his children.

This obviously was a casual encounter. During the Cultural Revolution no Chinese would take the risk of privately arranging a meeting with a Russian when it could result in his being accused of being a spy, an offense that could bring a death sentence.

Among diplomats in Peking, the Russians had the reputation of having valuable sources of information in the capital, but I saw no sign that this was true. What they did have, though, was a great many people who spoke Chinese and who worked very hard at their jobs. Every night and day these Russian diplomats would fan across the city in their cars to read wall posters and to walk along the streets and wander into shops to listen to what the ordinary Chinese were talking about. All these scraps of information were pieced together in the Embassy to produce reports on what was happening in China.

They could also draw upon whatever information was gathered by other East European embassies: Hungarian, Polish, East German, Mongolian, Bulgarian and Czech (the Rumanians and Yugoslavs were close-lipped around the Russians). The Polish and Mongolian Embassies were exceptionally good sources. The Poles maintained a consulate in Shanghai and were able to supply news about China's largest city. The Mongolians, once they put on the proper clothes, could pass as Chinese and circulate unnoticed in the city.

It was through the Mongolians that the Soviet Embassy

every day received a copy of the *Peking Daily,* which foreigners were forbidden to buy. And the Mongolians also passed along to the Russians the preliminary draft of the Chinese Communist party's new constitution on the same day that it was being distributed to Chinese in Peking.

The Russians had one other possible avenue of information: the Russian women who had married Chinese men. These women, some of whom were in their late twenties, were tangible evidence that the friendship between the Soviet Union and China had indeed been very warm in bygone years. For while the Russians had sent a few students to Peking University, the Chinese had sent a great many students to Moscow University. Because it was useful to both sides, these student exchanges continued until the Cultural Revolution, despite officially frigid relations between the two countries. It was early in 1967 that the Chinese Government advised foreign countries to withdraw their students because China's universities were going to be "busy" with the Cultural Revolution. Moscow promptly ordered the Chinese students to leave the Soviet Union. Peking's decision apparently was designed mainly to get rid of the Russian students, who were, of course, reporting to the Soviet Embassy on what was going on in the schools.

In any case, long before 1967, romance was blossoming between the exchange students in both Peking and Moscow.

I heard many amorous stories—no doubt coloured by time —from East Bloc diplomats who had been students years ago in Peking. At that time, of course, dances were held every Saturday night at the university and the Chinese girls curled their hair and even wore skirts instead of baggy cotton trousers. Despite the freedom of those pre-Cultural Revolution days, when it was permissible for Chinese girls to have dates with foreigners, I never put much stock in tales of sexual escapades. The Chinese Communists had instilled such moral rectitude in most young people that, as one diplomat told me, to attempt to kiss an unwilling Chinese girl was tantamount to rape as far as the Chinese were concerned.

The same diplomat, by the way, once dated a Chinese girl who was remotely related to the Emperor's family. He decided to test her socialist loyalties and asked her how she could really be in favour of the revolution when it had deprived her of status and title. She replied that no thinking person could not be in favour of communism because it had wrought such great and beneficial changes in China. "Besides," she smiled gently, "if it had not been for the revolution, I would never be speaking to you at this moment."

He took this as the supreme compliment but later, when she brushed him off, he wondered.

In Moscow, where mixed marriages were less frowned upon, a number of the Chinese students married Russian girls and later brought them home to China. There were perhaps twenty who settled in Peking but retained their Soviet citizenship, and these women could provide interesting "inside" information to the Soviet Embassy: not only were they involved in the day-to-day life of the ordinary Chinese, but because their husbands were highly educated men they also had knowledge of upper level changes concerning politics, education and industry.

Certainly, the Soviet Embassy had no problem gaining access to this source of information. Once a week, the twenty women would arrive in a group at the Russian Embassy to see the new movie (flown in every Saturday from Moscow) being shown to the Embassy staff; it was their one opportunity to be among their own people, however briefly, and to see and hear something other than Mao Tse-tung's quotations and the constant thunder of Chinese revolutionary music (the Russians brought in films such as *War and Peace,*

[221]

Romeo and Juliet, Ballad of a Russian Soldier, The Cranes Are Flying and *Anna Karenina*).

But the dilemma for the Soviet diplomats was this: even if they could get information from the women—who stayed closely together on their visits and out of self-protection undoubtedly would inform on one another to the Chinese—could the information be believed? As Russian citizens, the women could go to the Embassy whenever they liked. But that, as the diplomats well knew, was a theoretical privilege. The reality of the situation was that the Russian women would not be coming weekly to the Embassy and thereby risking reprisals against the husbands and children, unless their visits had official Chinese approval. And why would they get such approval, the Soviet diplomats asked themselves. There could be only two reasons, both of which would disqualify the women as sources: first, they had been instructed by the Chinese to give misleading information; second—and more likely—they had been ordered to report on what was going on *inside* the Russian Embassy.

The result was that the Soviet diplomats treated the women with some wariness and, let it be said, considerable sympathy. But they left them alone.

And what really *did* go on behind the high walls of the Russian Embassy? None of us, of course, really knew. At one time the Chinese had at least some idea. When the Cultural Revolution began in mid-1966, there were about one hundred Chinese employed in the Embassy as translators, drivers, cooks, amahs and gardeners. Presumably, they turned in a daily or weekly report to their superiors on everything they saw or overheard while working at the Embassy, and these fragments of information were pieced together to provide some indication of what the Russians were up to.

But in early 1967, the Chinese employees (acting under orders) went on a one-day strike and joined demonstrators

[222]

outside the Embassy who were parading in protest against alleged Russian mistreatment of Chinese students in Moscow. The next day the Chinese employees turned up for work as usual, and to their surprise were not allowed into the Embassy; the Russians, delighted at being given the excuse, had fired them all.

The Chinese found themselves outside looking in, figuratively and literally. The Peking authorities had foolishly lost their access to the Soviet Embassy (the Russians had long before brought in their own electrical engineers to "de-bug" every building on the grounds).

To replace the Chinese employees, the Russians brought in about fifty muscular young men who in fact were members of the Russian Army. In some ways, life was probably more pleasant for them in Peking than it would have been in the army. Their chores around the Embassy were not onerous, and to fill in their spare time they organized their own basketball, volleyball, water polo and badminton leagues. But still, it was a lonely life. I often saw five or six of them sitting around the swimming pool on a hot summer afternoon, some wearing cowboy hats and plucking on guitars while others were stretched out in the sun with their portable radios, listening to Radio Tokyo or Radio Australia playing American jazz.

Their problem was girls or, more correctly, lack of girls. After all, one can organize only so many basketball games, so many volleyball games, so many cold showers. Not that Peking didn't have European girls. The French, British, Dutch and, of course, Scandinavian missions managed to be well-represented by good-looking girls, but the young Russian Army men were forbidden to go outside the Embassy except on approved assignments—usually to chauffeur a diplomat or to pick up food at the Chinese market. In any case, all the Western foreign ministries had issued orders that girls employed in embassies were not to date *any* East Bloc diplomat or journalist for fear they might get themselves into a compromising position and be blackmailed into handing out classified information. This rule, incidentally, was broken with some frequency in Peking.

Despite the Soviet Embassy's problems, female and otherwise, living conditions were not all unpleasant for the diplomats. Their apartments were larger and more comfortable than they would have had at home. Through a preferential rate for the ruble—a hangover from the old days of Sino-Soviet comradeship—their pay stretched further in Peking than it would have in Moscow and, most important, there were things to buy. The Chinese had special shops where foreigners could buy shoes, fur coats and beautiful materials that could be cheaply tailor-made into stylish suits and dresses. Indeed, East Bloc diplomats stationed in North Vietnam, North Korea and Mongolia tried to arrange to spend a few days every six months in Peking for "consultations," the official excuse for a shopping spree. Besides buying clothes, they would also take back trunks full of Chinese tinned foods to help supplement the sorry diet in Hanoi, Pyongyang and Ulan Bator.

There were of course drawbacks to being a Russian diplomat in Peking, aside from the fact that if you were married you would rarely see your wife and children. For one thing, the Soviet Foreign Ministry is not too keen on moving its diplomats about. Thus a Russian diplomat posted to Peking could expect to stay there for at least five years and possibly much longer; most other foreign ministries keep their diplomats in a "hardship" posting for a maximum of two years (three years for an ambassador). Even after six or seven years in Peking, when a Russian's transfer came due, it was more than likely he would be sent to Moscow for a couple of years and then be reassigned to Peking for another long spell.

At that, there were pitfalls in asking for another posting. Certainly, you would be confined to Southeast Asia and you might end up in a capital infinitely worse than Peking. The best posting was Tokyo, but the chances of getting there were slim since almost every Russian diplomat in the Eastern section of the Foreign Ministry had already applied for Japan. Or so they told me.

Anyway, if you were a specialist on China and could speak the language—and almost every Soviet diplomat and journalist in Peking could—then the possibility of another assignment was very remote indeed. The truth of the matter was that the Soviet Foreign Ministry was short of Sinologists.

At one time, when relations between China and the Soviet Union were friendly, Russian students were eager to enroll in Chinese programs offered by their universities. But at that time there weren't many studies offered, for the simple reason that the Government didn't see much need for them.

Now the Soviet universities have intensive courses on China, but there are few students who volunteer for them.

Another source of diplomats were the students who attended university in Peking as part of the exchange program. Most of them have been siphoned into the Foreign Ministry because they are able to speak Mandarin, even though their Chinese university training was in such non-diplomatic courses as geology or music. At that, there were only about eighty-five Russian students who studied in Peking, according to a Soviet diplomat who himself attended Peking University. In any case, that source has dried up since the Cultural Revolution.

But the feeling among Russian diplomats that they were "condemned" to spend much of the rest of their lives in China, plus the long separations from their wives and children, were only two of the difficulties they faced in Peking.

[225]

14

My wife and I were walking along Wang Fu Ching, one of Peking's main shopping streets, when we noticed a little Chinese girl tagging along behind us. She was about six years old and very pretty, her face softly oval, her eyes velvet black and her cheeks brushed with pink by the cold wind.

She followed us all the way to the car, but hung back until we got in and closed the doors. Then she ran over to the car window, whipped from her pocket a little red book of Mao Tse-tung's quotations and shook it at us shouting, *"Da da, su chow!"*

It was a phrase we heard thousands of times during our stay in China: "Down with Soviet revisionism." We also became used to being mistaken for Russians, though at no time did we feel in danger. In fact, only the more daring of the children ever said anything at all to us about the Soviet Union, despite our strange eyes and pinkish skin. Still it gave us a slight taste of what it was like to be a Russian in Peking.

On another occasion, the *Tass* correspondent invited a number of people, including us, to dinner at a Chinese restaurant. We arrived at 7 P.M., to find the rest of the guests standing outside the door. Inside was a great commotion; all the waiters and cooks had gathered to form two lines through which we would have to pass to get to the private dining room at the back of the restaurant. They were shouting revolutionary slogans at the top of their voices and waving their little red books.

"Come on," said the *Tass* man, "let's all have dinner at the Hsin Chiao Hotel." Which was what we did. The next day, though, he received a call from the restaurant proprietor who was quite injured that the Russian should so impolitely cancel his dinner party at the last moment.

Was the restaurant operator serious? Perhaps, but the Chinese do have an acute sense of humour.

One day the Soviet Embassy was having some trouble with its sewer system. A telephone call was made to the Chinese Diplomatic Service Bureau, which handles the supply of all workmen to the embassies, asking that someone be sent out to find what was wrong and repair it.

"Ah, but that is not necessary," said the Chinese voice smoothly at the other end of the line. "The Soviet Union has proved to the world that it knows more about sewers than any other country. I suggest that you repair it yourselves."

Even the *Russians* thought that was funny, though they finally did have to fly someone in from Moscow to fix the Embassy's broken-down sewer.

This sort of diplomatic hair-pulling went on at a minor, albeit official, level. What nobody knows, including Russian diplomats who have been in China more than a decade, was the cumulative effect on the average Chinese of years of anti-Soviet propaganda.

The Russians cling to the hope that the Chinese citizen who is thirty years of age or older will not forget the Sino-

[228]

Soviet friendship of years past though he must conceal his feelings in the face of present Peking policy.

That policy is clear enough: China has two enemies, the United States and the Soviet Union.

With the United States, China is determined, unforgiving, suspicious but also practical. The Americans are, after all, old adversaries. The Soviet Union, on the other hand, was a comrade from the earliest days of the Chinese Communist party. But now, again in the Chinese official view, the once close ally has willingly sacrificed both China and the world Communist movement to accomplish an accord with the United States. At the expense of China, the ·"jackals from the same lair" have agreed to divide the world between them.

The bitterness of betrayal goes very deep in the Chinese psyche, but so also do the emotional ties with the Russians.

There is, first of all, the ideological bond of the past. Although China has declared itself the center of true world communism, Lenin and Stalin are officially revered figures. One can buy paper-cuts or silk scrolls of the two Communists in any Chinese handicraft shop, and huge portraits of them are erected in Peking's Tien An Men Square every May 1 and October 1.

Indeed, one can still see on Peking television reruns of an old Russian-made film on the October Revolution, with the voices dubbed in Chinese. Lenin figures predominantly in the movie, of course, and one catches the occasional glimpse of an actor playing Stalin. The film has not been shown in the Soviet Union for many years.

But there are other visible and more permanent signs, the residue of the tide of Russian influence that flowed across China from 1949 to 1960.

On the outskirts of Peking, next to the zoo with its famous pandas, is an enormous and ornate building called the Peking Industrial Exhibition Hall. There are probably few

[229]

Pekingese who do not remember that its original name was the Soviet Exhibition Center. When it opened in 1954, its two main features were an exhibition of Russian economic and cultural achievements and the Moscow Restaurant (now closed).

The Chinese have their own car and truck factories, but one still sees many Soviet-made trucks and taxis cruising along Chinese streets; and Russian Ilyushin planes carry Chinese passengers on long flights over the vast country, and the Chinese Air Force flies MIG fighters. Signs in public buildings such as airports and post offices are in Russian as well as in English and Chinese, and in many shops the clerks will know at least a few words of Russian. Most of the larger and relatively new buildings, such as hotels, bear the stamp of Russian-inspired architecture—massive and stolid buildings with ornate, high-ceilinged lobbies containing marble pillars and wide staircases.

Much more important, of course, was the effect of Soviet technical aid and advice to China. Russian methods, machinery and equipment formed the industrial base of the new China after 1949 when Mao Tse-tung came to power. But the great capital construction program on which China had embarked had not been completed when in 1960 the Soviet Union suddenly withdrew more than 1,000 technicians and halted the supply of equipment to half-finished factories. (Today the Soviet Embassy in Peking has a huge wall map of China on which are pinpointed all the factories built with Russian aid.) It almost ruined China's delicate economy.

Now visitors to a Chinese factory usually are shown an idle machine that has been pushed to a corner; and they are told that it is old and useless Soviet machinery that was foisted upon China, the implication being that the Russians sent faulty equipment to hinder China's growth. And, of

[230]

course, this is blamed on Nikita Khrushchev, who indeed did give the order for the Soviet aid to stop.

The truth is not quite that simple.

For one thing, much of the machinery was sent in the early 1950's when the Soviet Union was still recovering from the effects of the Second World War and had little modern technical equipment to spare. Despite that, a good bit of the machinery is still being used. In 1969, for instance, electricity was still being supplied to the west end of Peking by steam turbine generators made in the Soviet Union (though in that same year they were being replaced by Swedish generators). In any case, if the Russian machinery was faulty or outdated, the blame should be placed as much on Stalin as on Khrushchev.

There is evidence, however, that Mao's real quarrel is with Soviet Union policy toward China—whether inspired by Stalin, Khrushchev or its present leaders. For this policy has basically always run counter to Mao's three great ambitions for himself and China: to make an independent China strong economically and militarily, to achieve world power status for China, to have Peking (Mao) recognized as the true center of genuine unsullied communism.

No Soviet leader could accept any one of these propositions, never mind all three.

From the very beginning, Stalin showed great caution and suspicion in dealing with the newly born People's Republic of China. What he wanted was to ensure that China became one more vassal state that could serve as a buffer on the Soviet border.

Thus when a triumphant Mao paid his first visit to Moscow—just two and a half months after the new China had been founded—he found no warm embrace of true proletarian brotherhood awaiting him. Instead, he was greeted by tough negotiators who were as cold and calculating as

[231]

the Shanghai moneylenders that Mao's army had just eliminated.

For Mao was, indeed, looking for money to rebuild a war-devastated China; but his only collateral was communism, and he soon discovered that was not enough. Stalin, as was revealed some years later by Khrushchev, treated a weak China with disdain (just as foreigners with the upper hand always have) and drove the kind of hard bargain that would have brought a smile of admiration from any Industrial Revolution capitalist.

The arduous negotiations went on for two months after Mao's arrival—an unheard-of length of time for two friendly Communist states—and Mao already had returned to Peking when the Treaty of Alliance was finally signed on February 14, 1950. In 1962, Mao said that Stalin had held up the signing for two months because he did not trust the Chinese and feared they would pursue an independent policy.

What did the Russians give their Chinese comrades? As little as possible.

In money, the Chinese were to receive only $60 million a year for five years, an inconsequential sum compared with what the United States was giving to a number of friendly countries. Not only that, but Russia was lending the money, not giving it, and it was to be totally repaid with interest. In addition, the Soviet Union was keeping the special rights in Kwangtung and Manchuria it had won from the Chinese in the 1890's, lost to Japan in 1905 and then regained as part of the spoils of the Second World War. On top of all this, the Russians achieved control of a number of Sino-Soviet companies that were to be set up to find and develop oil and mineral resources in China.

The harsh terms of the treaty must have angered Mao, but there is little reason to suppose that they surprised him. As shrewd a tactician as Mao could not have gone to Moscow with any confidence in Stalin unless he was blind to history. And Mao was blind in neither mind nor eye.

It was Stalin who ordered the Chinese Communists to cooperate with the Nationalist Government in the early 1920's; it was Stalin who rejected Chinese Communist fears that Chiang Kai-shek could not be trusted; it was Stalin who insisted that the Chinese Communists concentrate their strength in the cities, where in 1927 they fell easy prey to a sudden slaughter commanded by Chiang (Chou En-lai was among the few fortunate enough to escape from Shanghai); it was Stalin who immediately thereafter ignored Mao's splintered forces and refused to give them aid; it was Stalin who instead turned to Chiang Kai-shek and gave him $250 million in military supplies (up to 1939) plus Russian advisors to help in the battle against Japan; it was Stalin who in 1945 signed a treaty of friendship and aid with Chiang Kai-shek; and it was Stalin who later told the Chinese Communists they could not defeat Chiang Kai-shek and urged them to dissolve their own government and form a coalition government with the Kuomintang.

By the time this last piece of advice was given, Mao had learned a great deal about the Soviet Union. He ignored Stalin's counsel, and won the war against Chiang Kai-shek by gathering his strength from the countryside instead of from the cities as the Bolsheviks had.

Curiously, almost as though he could not bear to admit he had been wrong, Stalin kept the Soviet Ambassador with Chiang Kai-shek long after many other countries, including Great Britain, had withdrawn their diplomatic recognition of the Nationalist Government. Not until October 2, 1949, one day after Mao had formally declared the founding of the People's Republic of China, did Stalin transfer his ambassador to the Chinese Communist Government and give it the prestige of official recognition.

[233]

Then there was Stalin's shadowy role in the Korean War.

In his book, *War Between Russia and China*, Harrison E. Salisbury compiled a convincing amount of circumstantial evidence to show that the Korean War was prompted by Stalin, *without* Mao's prior knowledge, in order to bring the whole of Korea under Soviet influence and thus apply maximum military pressure against China.

Whether or not that was true, several high-ranking Chinese Army officers have made a point of telling Western diplomats in Peking that the Soviet Union was responsible for the Korean War. In addition, the fact that Han Suyin, a frequent visitor to China and a friend of some highly placed Chinese officials, mentioned the same theory in her book, *China in the Year 2001,* also means that Peking wants it known that Stalin was to blame—unofficially, of course.

The Korean War created an unwanted hardship for China. The new government had its hands full instituting massive reforms, trying to bring some order to the economy, and taking over Tibet. Peking apparently thought it could avert involvement in Korea by warning that if the United States went to the Yalu River then China would consider its own security threatened and would intervene. General Douglas MacArthur paid no heed (a mistake the United States did not repeat in Vietnam), and Chinese "volunteers" entered the battle.

It was a costly business for China, though it could be argued that China gained prestige by establishing itself as a military power. Nonetheless, it must have irritated Mao that China was engaged in a war because of Stalin's manipulations, while the Soviet Union sat on the sidelines. True, Russia supplied arms and equipment to North Korea and China but, as a Chinese general acidly pointed out to a Western diplomat in Peking: "The Chinese people had to

[234]

pay for every piece of material received from the revolutionary Russians." (In 1965 China completed repayment of all Soviet loans, worth a total of 1,406 million new rubles.)

In retrospect, it would seem that despite Peking's official glorification of Stalin and condemnation of Khrushchev, it was the latter who at least made some attempts to reach an accord with China.

In 1954, Khrushchev and Bulganin met with Mao and Chou En-lai in Peking and a number of important agreements were reached.

Port Arthur and Dairen were restored to the Chinese (Stalin had conveniently overlooked his written promise to give them back by 1952). The iniquitous joint exploitation companies already had gone. And the Chinese Communists had also recovered the Manchurian territories, though indeed there was not much to recover: the huge industrial complex established by the Japanese over their forty-year occupation consisted mainly of empty buildings, because Stalin had systematically shipped home millions of dollars' worth of equipment and machinery.

But Khrushchev was trying to overcome the past. He promised to build fifteen more factories (and speed up delivery of equipment to 141 already promised). The following year the Soviet Union agreed to build China's first nuclear reactor for peaceful purposes, and Chinese physicists were enrolled in Russian nuclear institutions. That same year, 1955, China and Russia signed a pact to build a railroad linking Sinkiang Province in northwest China with the capital of Soviet Kazakhstan. The railroad was never completed.

Other cooperative moves were initiated. In 1956 the three-year Joint Sino-Soviet Scientific Expedition began to survey the basin of the Heilungkiang or Amur River and chart mineral resources of the area. Up to that year about fifty

Russian scientists had been sent to China to help create specific courses and schools of scientific research in China. But from 1956 to 1960 this figure swelled to 800.

In addition, between 1954 and 1960, China received an enormous amount of scientific and technical data: more than 10,000 blueprints and designs for a variety of machinery and factories, a large quantity of laboratory and research equipment, and over 240,000 books which became part of the Peking National Library.

In that period, the year 1957 was significant. In October the Soviet Union and China signed a secret agreement (revealed by the Chinese in 1963) under which the Russians were to give a "sample atomic bomb and technical detail for its manufacture."

The following month Mao went to Moscow for the fortieth anniversary of the Bolshevik Revolution, accompanied by important military and political aides. The Soviet Union then seemed to the world to have stepped dramatically ahead of the United States: the Russians had successfully fired an intercontinental ballistic missile, tested new hydrogen weapons and, most spectacular, had startled the world by launching Sputnik into space. Mao, obviously exhilarated by these triumphs which he apparently felt belonged to the whole Communist world *including* China, asserted in a speech: "The east wind is prevailing over the west wind. That is to say, the forces of socialism are overwhelmingly superior to the forces of imperialism."

(He also made an emotional speech, to be recalled during the Cultural Revolution, to Chinese students studying in Moscow: "You young people, full of vigour and vitality, are in the bloom of life, like the sun at eight or nine in the morning. Our hope is placed on you. . . . The world belongs to you. China's future belongs to you.")

There is some speculation that Mao's optimism was also

due to Soviet pledges of help with missile technology and construction. I once asked a Soviet military expert in Peking if he thought the Chinese really possessed a workable nuclear delivery system. "We *know* they have," he grunted sourly. "We helped them build it." Interestingly, China's fourth nuclear test, in October, 1966, was of a warhead carried about four hundred miles by a guided missile thought to have been an adaptation of the Russian "Komet" missile.

All of this was to come much later. As 1957 ended, though, Mao had Russian assurances that China would soon have atomic weapons. And this would provide the key to some of Mao's cherished dreams: recovery of the offshore islands occupied by Chiang Kai-shek and elevation of China to great-power status. These dreams were not shared by the Soviet Union, as Mao was soon to learn.

In late July, 1958, Khrushchev and Defense Minister Marshal Rodion Malinovsky visited Peking. What transpired at their meeting with Mao has never been revealed, but the Chinese leader undoubtedly must have told them of his plans to attack the islands of Quemoy and Matsu in August. It also seems probable, in the light of subsequent events, that Khrushchev warned Mao that the Soviet Union was not prepared to back a Chinese attack with anything more than words. He may even have tried to persuade the Chinese to give up their plan completely; if so, he failed.

Twenty days after Khrushchev and his Defense Minister left Peking, batteries along the Chinese coast opened fire on Quemoy.

The action could be construed as an attempt by Mao to pull off a colossal bluff. He may have reasoned that since the attack began less than three weeks after his meeting with Khrushchev, the Americans would deduce that it had the approval and support of the Russians. This delusion would not be destroyed by Khrushchev who, for the sake of Communist solidarity, was prepared to give public verbal support despite his private misgivings (years later the Moscow press described the attack as a "provocation").

The question was: would the United States bow to a China that seemingly was backed by Soviet nuclear weapons? A suspenseful world did not have to wait long for the answer. Washington announced that it would honour its commitment to defend the offshore islands and that in doing so it would use nuclear weapons if necessary.

Mao had lost his gamble, and the crisis slowly fizzled out. But another crisis, far more important to the unknowing world, was slowly forming in the Moscow-Peking relationship.

For both Khrushchev and Mao, it was a time of reappraisal.

It was now clear to the Russian leaders that despite their offers of friendship, despite their attempts to patch past difficulties, despite their pledges to give economic and technical assistance, they had no hope that China under Mao would become a Soviet satellite. The Quemoy-Matsu affair had proved that even with limited resources Peking was determined to pursue its own goals regardless of what Moscow wanted.

Already, with the Chinese-sponsored Bandung Conference of Asian powers in 1955, there was evidence that Peking wanted to extend its influence in Asia and, with its Asia-for-Asians policy, indicated that it did not regard the area as within Moscow's sphere of interest. To repudiate this theory, Russia mended its fences with India, and Khrushchev made ostentatious visits to a number of Asian countries.

For Moscow, the crux of the problem now was that China considered itself at least the equal of the Soviet Union. This, to the Russians, was not only patently untrue but also intolerable. But should they help create a new superstate that would challenge Soviet influence in Asia and also upset the already delicate and complex balance of power between Russia and the United States?

The most immediate and important issue was weaponry.

Sometime in late 1958 or early 1959, Moscow apparently informed Peking that it would not supply nuclear weapons and missiles unless they were under the control of the Soviet military. This presumably was what the Chinese meant some ten years later when, while listing the various "crimes" of the Soviet Union against China, they angrily denounced the Russians for trying to install their own military forces under their own command on Chinese territory.

Meanwhile, the Chinese leadership was itself going through a bitter reappraisal—and a raging fight, as was learned during the Cultural Revolution—of the future of Sino-Soviet relations.

Khrushchev's refusal to back China's Quemoy-Matsu ploy had proved to Mao once and for all that Moscow saw only a subservient role for Peking in the world communism movement, and that China would have to rely only on itself to achieve the nationalistic goals implicit in Mao's 1949 statement, which was more of a promise to the Chinese nation: "China has stood up."

In August, 1958 (a fateful month of a fateful year for China), again just a few days after the Mao-Khrushchev meeting, the Chinese leaders met in Peitaho, a resort on the Yellow Sea not far from Peking. In response to Mao's urgings they approved the institution of the commune. The Great Leap Forward was born, a monumental experiment that was expected to mobilize the country's vast manpower and raise industrial and agricultural production so rapidly that China would be a formidable and truly Communist power within a few years.

China at that point had completed the first Five-Year Plan,

modelled essentially on the Soviet experience. Progress had been steady but slow—apparently too slow to suit Mao. In addition he could see the class society beginning to regroup itself, particularly in the countryside. But Mao's impatience at the slowness of orthodox (and foreign) economic planning must also have been spurred by his realization that China and the Soviet Union were rapidly heading toward a collision which a weak China could not survive. The Great Leap Forward, if successful, could give Mao the means to defy and even challenge the Soviet Union.

At first, it seemed the Great Leap Forward had exceeded even Mao's wildest expectations. In April, 1959, Chou En-lai reported that industrial production had increased 65 percent in 1958, and that production of grain, cotton and tobacco had more than doubled. Not until the summer did the Chinese leaders learn that it was all an illusion created by hundreds of thousands of cadres and managers who had falsified their reports in order to show the party they had met its high production demands.

In the first months of 1959, when he was no doubt heady with the apparent success of his economic experiment, Mao had to face the threat that either he accept Russian direction of China's foreign policy or lose Russian help in making the atomic bomb. The answer given by the self-confident Chinese leader became evident in June when Russia cancelled its agreement to give China a "sample" atomic bomb and manufacturing information.

Among the Chinese military there was great opposition to Mao's decision to become "self-reliant." A number of leading army officers, many of whom had experienced something of modern warfare during the Korean War, were unconvinced that Mao's guerrilla tactics were still relevant. They wanted a modern army trained by modern methods and equipped with modern weapons. And this, they believed, was possible on the short term only through the cooperation and assistance of the Russians. In addition, their concept of a "professional" army did not coincide with Mao's idea that soldiers should devote much of their time to "civilian work" such as political study, and industrial and agricultural labour.

Mao and the modernist generals clashed in the summer of 1959, with the immediate cause probably being Mao's plan to attack India along the Himalayan frontier. Not only was India being cultivated as a friend by the Russians, but the attack (in late August) would come a few weeks before Khrushchev's meeting with President Eisenhower at Camp David. This, the Russians later said, was a deliberate attempt to wreck Soviet efforts to achieve an understanding with the United States.

Mao won the fight against his dissident generals. In September it was disclosed that Defense Minister Peng Teh-huai had been replaced by Lin Piao, who was to ally himself with Mao.

That same month, when the border attack was launched, Mao and other leaders were beginning to realize how badly they had been misled by imaginative economic reports of the progress of the Great Leap Forward. But at that point, Mao could not have foreseen how disastrous that situation really was, nor that China would be visited by three years of enervating pestilence, flood and drought, nor that Khrushchev would seize the opportunity to weaken China even further by withdrawing all Russian experts and technicians in 1960, nor that the combination of these things would result in his losing control of the party and of China's destiny.

Meanwhile, Defense Minister Lin Piao was transforming the army to conform with Mao's views of military affairs. Officers were pulled down from their lofty position. Badges and insignia of rank were forbidden; admirals and generals wore exactly the same uniforms as sailors and privates. Soldiers went to work in the mines, the factories and the paddy fields. Military training was downgraded; soldiers and officers instead spent countless hours on the "living study and application of Mao Tse-tung's works." He ordered the printing of a little red book, the *Quotations of Mao Tse-tung,* so that every soldier could study the Chairman's writings at any time of the day or night.

Whether it began as his intention, by 1966 Lin Piao had created the vehicle Mao would use to regain control of the party and the country. He also won his reward, being named Mao's eventual successor at the party's ninth congress in 1969. The story of how he lost that honour in 1972, as well as political power, may not be fully known for many years. Perhaps he was too vehement an opponent to Mao's decision to try to reach an accord with the United States. Lin Piao, considered one of China's most brilliant generals, fought in the Korean War and was considered to be the most xeno-phobic of China's leaders.

15

THROUGHOUT this book I have used the term "foreigners" to mean diplomats, correspondents and businessmen who more or less had in common the fact that their presence in the country was tolerated but rarely welcomed. This was during the Cultural Revolution, of course, when any Chinese who showed friendship or sympathetic interest toward a foreigner was likely to be criticized and lose his position or worse. Before then it was possible to form friendships with the Chinese—journalists and translators visited each other's homes for family dinners—and high-ranking members of the Government frequently spent social evenings at foreign embassies in Peking.

The Swedish Ambassador, Lennart Petrie, was visited one evening by the Vice-Mayor of Peking, Wu Han, a cultured and artistic man who talked for an hour about China's most famous painters. When Petrie mentioned that he had a collection of scrolls, Wu asked to see them and would not be put off by Petrie's apology that most of them were stored in his bedroom closet. While Petrie unrolled the scrolls, Wu sat on the edge of the bed and explained the finer points of each of the paintings. Wu, incidentally, wrote a play that was criticized in 1965 as being a covert attack on Mao Tse-tung. Most historians regard that as the opening shot of the Cultural Revolution, and Wu was one of the first Communists to fall from power.

During the pre-Cultural Revolution days, the outspoken and ebullient Foreign Minister, Chen Yi, was a frequent dinner guest at the embassies. On one occasion, at the Norwegian Ambassador's residence, he gloomily stared at an abstract painting for several minutes. Finally the Ambassador asked if he liked it. "It's the ugliest painting I've ever seen," he finally announced.

The Chinese were also able to take a joke then. The former Canadian Trade Minister, Alvin Hamilton, who had a hand in Canada's first wheat sales to China, visited Peking with his wife after he was out of office and was lavishly welcomed. His host at a number of parties was a blunt old cadre, but Hamilton had such a good time that he decided to give a party for the Chinese who had been his companions during the visit. He stipulated that all of them, including the cadre, must bring their wives. They all did, and Hamilton was surprised to see that the cadre's wife was a beautiful woman about twenty years his junior. In his toast to the guests, Hamilton said that he had thought the cadre was a tough, hard-boiled man but now that he had seen his wife he realized who really was the boss in the family. The Chinese, including the cadre, doubled up with laughter.

During the Cultural Revolution the only Chinese leader who had contacts with foreigners, except at the official level, was Chou En-lai. The Premier was well-known for his habit of working late hours, and I often saw his curtained black Zim limousine in the small hours of the morning parked at the back of the Great Hall of the People, where his office was located. When other cars—usually Chinese-made Red

Banner limousines—were also parked there, it meant the leaders were meeting. One such occasion was the night that Chou En-lai returned from Ho Chi-minh's funeral in Hanoi. The leaders were apparently discussing not only the North Vietnamese political situation, but also a Soviet proposal that Premier Alexei Kosygin visit Peking to discuss the Sino-Soviet border dispute. Three days later a four-hour meeting was held between the two premiers at Peking Airport.

Chou En-lai, Mao Tse-tung and other top officials live in the western section of the old Imperial City, only a short distance from the Great Hall of the People. Three soldiers carrying rifles with fixed bayonets stand guard at the entrance, an arched open gateway set in the high vermilion walls which surround the whole area. Walking by, one could catch a glimpse of willow and bamboo trees and the blue waters of the manmade Central and Southern Lakes created at the beginning of the Ming dynasty. Palaces and smaller buildings that were built along their shores for the Imperial family and their court are now occupied by the Chinese Communist leaders. The area is closed to the public and little is known about these residences. A Chinese I knew in Peking told me that he was among a group of young students honoured (he didn't tell me why) by an invitation to visit Chou En-lai at his home some years ago. He said he couldn't remember the furnishings of the house—a statement I doubt —but that the grounds were like a park with grass (a rarity outside the walls), flower gardens and many trees. All the old buildings had been restored, he said, and had decorations painted with brightly coloured enamel in the traditional Chinese style.

Another Chinese told me that his cousin was a member of Mao Tse-tung's domestic staff and that the leader of China's 750 million people was very proud of the small

[245]

kitchen garden he planted and maintained himself beside his house. He said the Chairman was a very good gardener; in fact, he grew far more vegetables than he needed, and gave the surplus to his servants.

Premier Chou En-lai was the leader seen most frequently by foreigners, though he could hardly be described as easily accessible. He usually was the man who met visiting delegations when they arrived at Peking Airport and he also attended the National Day receptions given by the various embassies—if the country was on friendly terms with China. Because of the protocol involved, journalists did not get too close to him during receptions, though on one such occasion I drank a toast with him. There wasn't anything exclusive about it, but because it happened on the third day I was in China, I was mightily impressed. The reception took place in the huge dining room of the Peking Hotel, and after the formal speeches, Chou En-lai and the Foreign Minister, Chen Yi, went to each of the fifty tables in the room and clinked glasses with the guests. "Mesdames et messieurs, your health," he said and raised the glass to his lips but did not drink. Chen Yi, however, was trailed by a waiter carrying a full bottle of champagne and took a healthy gulp at every table. He was enjoying himself. Chou En-lai seemed to like these receptions, tapping his foot in time to the music played by a Chinese Army band, eating dinner with gusto, and afterward carefully picking his teeth with a toothpick behind cupped hands in the European style.

Journalists were able to get close views of Chou En-lai and lesser Chinese leaders at Peking Airport. We were allowed to join the ambassadors, who formed a line on the tarmac to meet the visiting dignitaries and the Chinese who were welcoming them. There were no obvious security restrictions, and I often took photographs of the Premier from a distance of about two yards. Indeed, I sometimes took Katharine and Regina along with me.

Once they accompanied me when a North Vietnamese delegation was arriving. As usual, we stood behind the row of diplomats. But as Chou En-lai walked along the line shaking hands with the ambassadors, a North Vietnamese woman at the end of the line noticed Katharine standing behind her. She took Katharine's hand and pulled her into the line. The Premier stopped short when he saw her and looked questioningly at the protocol man at his elbow. The aide shrugged his shoulders but then Chou En-lai noticed that the North Vietnamese woman was holding Katharine's hand. He smiled down at her and continued his way along the line.

There were two ambassadors (from friendly countries) who had a unique relationship with the Premier. About once or twice a month, often after 9 P.M., one of them would receive a telephone call asking him if he could be at the Premier's office at 10 P.M. The lateness of the hour and suddenness of the call did not signify a political crisis. Indeed, only rarely was there an urgent matter to be discussed, and more often than not the conversation had nothing to do with the state of relations between China and the ambassador's country. Sometimes Chou En-lai would ask the ambassador's interpretation of a political event in another country, such as an election, but frequently it seemed that the Premier had called the meeting simply because he had an hour to spare and wanted the intellectual stimulation (and relaxation) of talking about international affairs with someone who had lived abroad and did not view all events through Marxist eyes.

As could be expected, he had a precise and pragmatic evaluation of the workings of Big Power politics in areas such as the Middle East, but his grasp and understanding of internal politics in countries such as the United States rather surprised the ambassadors. He admitted his incomprehension, though, of the attitude of the American people toward Senator Edward Kennedy after the Chappaquiddick accident. He was also exceedingly well-informed about public opinion

[247]

abroad and would quote from an editorial in *The New York Times* or the *Times* of London published the previous day. These conversations, by the way, were not tête-à-tête. A Chinese translator was also present, though the Premier's knowledge of French and English was sufficient to allow him to comment on an ambassador's remarks before they had been translated. But there were also five secretaries ranged behind Chou En-lai. They apparently were economic and political experts on international affairs, since he would frequently turn from his desk to ask for a statistic or for clarification on a particular point.

Chou is one of the oldest of the top Chinese leaders (he was born in 1898, Mao in 1893), but he has stayed remarkably fit. His eyes are clear, his voice firm and confident, his walk purposeful. He looks ten years younger than his age despite his long hours of work since the Cultural Revolution. His only apparent physical handicap is his inability to straighten his right arm completely, a result of an injury during the Liberation War. In 1969 he had a mole just under his right ear removed and told a diplomat, "The doctors have been after me for years to have it cut out and I finally agreed. Now they've found another one they want to get rid of, but they'll just have to wait until I have more time."

He is, as his photographs attest, a man of striking appearance and he has considerable charm and personal magnetism. Once, in the Great Hall of the People in Peking, I saw him walk along a long line of blue-clad workers, shaking hands with men and women so excited that they were literally jumping up and down. The American Ping-Pong players and journalists who visited China discovered he has both charm and a sense of humour; but he is also a very tough-minded negotiator, as President Nixon no doubt found out.

Unlike most other Chinese leaders, Chou is also a fastidious dresser. His suits, usually grey, are cut in the Chinese style with high closed collars and are always carefully tailored and well-pressed. Other Chinese sometimes seem completely unconcerned about their clothing. While standing beside the armed forces chief of staff, Huang Yung-sheng, for instance, I noticed that his long underwear had gathered in folds around his ankles, easily seen because his trousers were about three inches too short.

Most of the Chinese leaders also wear caps at all times in public, and I often wondered if they regarded it as a proletarian virtue to sit through a banquet with their caps tightly pulled down to their ears. Not Chou En-lai. He almost never wears a hat in public, not even in Peking's bone-chilling winter weather. Perhaps it was a touch of vanity—his thick hair is only slightly grey—but I have seen him stand for more than an hour on a windy tarmac at Peking Airport in ten-degree temperature without a hat. Often he would not even wear a coat, preferring to leave it in his limousine. On one occasion, when it was pouring rain, he wore neither hat nor coat and impatiently waved aside an aide who was trying to shelter him with an umbrella.

There were other foreigners in Peking besides diplomats and journalists. Sometimes they came on a visit, but we would almost never see them though their arrival and departure would be glowingly reported in the Chinese press. These were officials of Marxist-Leninist parties from non-Soviet countries. They would be given the royal treatment in Peking, taken on tours of factories and schools, entertained at lavish dinners and—final and most important honour—stand for a formal photograph with Mao Tse-tung and other Chinese leaders. All of this would be recorded in the *People's Daily* and impressed on the minds of hundreds of millions of Chinese, though some of these Marxist-Leninists were probably hardly known by name in their own hometowns.

I met only one of them in China, the Australian, Jay

Gould, a stocky middle-aged woman with blond short-cropped hair. We happened to be on the same train travelling from Canton to the Hong Kong border. I was with Katharine and Regina; she was with several Chinese officials. But the only reason I remember her at all is that she asked to borrow an old New York *Herald Tribune* (international edition) that I was reading. She was, she said, completely out of touch with what was going on in the world because she had been in China for a few weeks—which seemed to me to be an admirable commentary on the English-language news bulletins which the Chinese gave visiting guests.

She settled back in her chair with the newspaper, but then suddenly sat bolt upright. "Look at this," she said, angrily shaking the newspaper at the Chinese. "Jackie's getting married. How could she do a thing like that?"

Her Chinese comrades looked at her blankly. "Who is Jackie?" ventured one of them.

"Jackie Kennedy," she snorted, but it was clear the Chinese still didn't know who she was talking about. "You know, President John Kennedy's wife. She's marrying an old Greek. Isn't that terrible?"

The Chinese grinned with polite embarrassment and Mrs. Gould dived back into the newspaper. Regina and I looked out of the window so they wouldn't see us laughing.

Peking also had a number of foreigners who were neither visitors, diplomats nor correspondents. Some were East European women who had married Chinese during the days of balmy Sino-Soviet relations. Others were like the White Russian couple I knew who had lived in China more than thirty years. It was a pleasant enough life for them. They taught Russian at Peking University, lived in a small Chinese house and had a circle of foreign and Chinese friends. Their lives changed with the Cultural Revolution. The university closed though, strangely, the Chinese continued their pay. Their friends vanished. They were terrified every time they heard drums outside their home, thinking that this time the revolutionaries were coming for them. They were too frightened even to play their "bourgeois" piano, which for three years stood silent in their living room. Finally, in 1970, they were allowed to emigrate to Sweden.

Then there were the foreigners, usually from friendly countries, who had been hired by the Chinese on a one- or two-year contract to work as language teachers or as translators for Communist publications distributed abroad. When the schools were closed in early 1967, the foreign teachers and students were told to go home. Most of the translators, however, stayed on and it was from some of them that I heard firsthand accounts of how the Cultural Revolution affected that peculiar group of people whom the Chinese called Foreign Friends.

They lived together in a compound which we called The Golden Cage, in the western section of Peking; and a strange and sad lot they were. They came from a variety of countries, and all were Communists. They also had in common the fact that they were either stateless or could not return to their country for fear of imprisonment. Some had come to China because it seemed to be the only "pure" Communist state in the world; others had no other place to go. They lived in comparative luxury in large modern apartments and were paid a salary (most of them worked in foreign language propaganda departments) that enabled them to buy valuable antiques and tailor-made clothes. They were also free to go where they liked in Peking. Often they attended embassy parties where they were treated as honoured guests because of their "inside" knowledge of Chinese affairs. Mostly, however, they stayed within their own tightly knit community, which was almost like a small village where everyone joyfully greeted marriages and new babies. Some played bridge regularly once a week, and these partnerships could be separated only by death—or the Cultural Revolution.

It was not surprising that the Foreign Friends responded enthusiastically to Mao Tse-tung's directive, "It is good to make revolution." Aside from the fact that their future depended on retaining the favour of their hosts, most of them had lived in China for so long that they considered themselves Chinese rather than foreign. Through the years they had vigorously joined every other Chinese political movement, and they were prepared to do so again. But this time, it was not just a simple campaign. For one thing, they were not sure who or what was supposed to be attacked. But they did the best they could, emulating the Chinese by putting up posters in the compound criticizing colleagues who had shown capitalistic tendencies. However, the Chinese staff in the compound was having its own revolution. Soon the superintendents were running the elevators and washing floors while the former elevator operators and cleaners were placed in charge of the compound.

Whether because of real or fancied insults, these newly promoted Chinese began to criticize their former Foreign Friends—something that had never happened before.

You say you love the Chinese people, they complained, and yet you wear dresses and suits and ties like the Western imperialists and the Soviet revisionists. The foreigners quickly put away their bourgeois clothing, and appeared wearing newly purchased blue cotton tunics and trousers. This didn't satisfy the Chinese, who denounced them for wearing new clothes like a landlord instead of the humble apparel of a Chinese worker or peasant. And so the frightened foreigners washed their new suits frequently to encourage fading and wore them unpressed. Some were more imaginative and, as one Foreign Friend wryly told me: "Almost overnight, patches were in style."

[252]

Still the criticism continued and, as it became clear that the Cultural Revolution had overtones of xenophobia, the Foreign Friends began to panic. They marched on the British Office and stood outside shouting insults at the same young English girls who had lent them books every week from the British library. They began to fight physically among themselves over who was more loyal to Mao Tse-tung. And they even petitioned the Communist party headquarters to withdraw their privileges and allow them to dress, eat and live the same way as the average Chinese citizen.

Finally, their pathetic antics were brought to the attention of Foreign Minister Chen Yi. He chided them for their misbehaviour, and turned down their request for a lower standard of living with the kindly admonishment that they could not survive if they tried to live like the average Chinese.

In the end, their revolutionary fervor did them little good. By mid-1969 the Chinese were "suggesting" that they should leave China. Some, such as the Russian who had fought in the Spanish Civil War and come to China more than thirty years ago, simply refused. "Where would I go?" he asked. Others went the rounds of the Peking embassies and submitted applications for landed emigrant papers—not altogether reluctantly. Most were anxious to get out of China, and who could blame them? It was difficult to feel secure when four of Peking's best-known Foreign Friends had disappeared: Americans Sydney Rittenberg and Israel Epstein and the latter's British wife, Elsie Chomedly-Fairfax, and Michael Shapiro, also British. Nobody seemed to know what had happened to them, but it was suspected they had come to grief for supporting Wang Li, the head of the Propaganda Department who had been purged for allegedly plotting with Peng Chen and Liu Shao-chi to overthrow Mao Tse-tung.

At the beginning of the Cultural Revolution, Rittenberg was in good standing. He had accompanied Anna Louise

Strong, the American who was undoubtedly China's most famous Foreign Friend, on a visit to a Red Guard headquarters where she was made an honorary Red Guard. Anna herself, who died peacefully in Peking at the age of eighty-six, escaped attacks from the Red Guards, though in 1968 a wall poster appeared saying "Down with Anna" and reporting that she had been thrown in jail. I didn't bother writing a story because I had seen her that same day, going into a beauty salon for foreigners. She was a tall woman, greyhaired and rather heavy but evidently feeble, since she walked very slowly and had to be helped by a young Chinese man. The story of her imprisonment, incidentally, was carried out to Hong Kong by a diplomat and flashed around the world. Miss Strong later angrily denied the report in her monthly "Letter from China," but she didn't mention Rittenberg or the Shapiros.

There were at least two other Americans in Peking, defectors from the Korean War. I did not see either of them, but I know they were married to Chinese girls and had applied for emigrant papers at one of the Asian embassies. They were turned down.

The Polish Embassy and the British Office also had some people turn up looking for help to get out of China, but they were not Foreign Friends.

Two Chinese men, one of them claiming to be a student at the Peking Academy of Music, climbed over the iron fence of the Polish Embassy one night and asked for political asylum. The Poles were not quite sure what to do with them. The two men pleaded they would be killed if they were turned out, but the Poles figured they probably were criminals, if not spies. Anyway, to give them asylum would mean they would become permanent residents of the Embassy since there was no way to get them out of the country. Embassy officials were still pondering the problem in the small hours of the morning, when the Chinese Foreign Ministry telephoned to say that it was known that two "escaped law-breakers" had hidden in the Embassy compound. Soldiers had surrounded the Embassy, said the spokesman, and if the escapers were not found in twenty minutes the troops would conduct a search inside. The Embassy handed the men over to the soldiers, who tied their hands behind their backs and then forced their arms upward so that they had to walk with their heads bent down almost to the level of their knees. Then they marched them off into the night.

The other case had a happier and—considering the political situation at the time—amusing ending. A British diplomat arrived at the office compound one morning and was startled to see a man hiding behind one of the garages. He claimed to be a North Korean (both he and the diplomat spoke Chinese) who had managed to cross the border into China and work his way down to Peking. Now he wanted the British to arrange an exit visa so that he could go to Hong Kong. The Britisher didn't know whether to laugh or cry.

"My dear chap," he said, "of all the embassies in Peking you couldn't have picked a worse one. It's far safer for you out on the street than inside here. As for exit visas, we haven't been able to get one for almost a year. We can't get even ourselves out of China, never mind North Koreans."

The North Korean was skeptical—he hadn't heard about the British Mission being sacked by the Chinese—but he was finally persuaded to leave. That night he scaled the wall again and headed for Hong Kong, or so the British assumed since he wasn't there the next morning.

16

It has not been my intention, nor is it now, to present this book or any part of it as a definitive study of the Great Proletarian Cultural Revolution; that work I gladly leave to the Sinologists and other scholars who eventually will assemble the jigsaw puzzle of events into an overall picture of what they think happened, and why. The purpose of this book has been to tell you what it was like for a group of foreigners, particularly one family, to live in Peking during what surely was one of the epic periods of Mao Tse-tung's rule, if not of Chinese history. However, it is necessary for me to touch at least briefly on some of the reasons for the Cultural Revolution in order to place into proper context the experiences I have already described, as well as the revolutionary reforms that began to take shape during our last months in China.

It always seemed to me that the years 1966–69 were as much a revelation as a revolution—for the outside world as well as for the Chinese people themselves. Until then, certain "truths" about the Chinese Communist leadership had been accepted in the Western world and, indeed, had been installed in history books. These truths or assumptions were very logical deductions based on *available* information. They were often also quite wrong, as we learned during the Cultural Revolution.

We know now that the party leadership was rent by bitter disagreement over national domestic policies. And we also know that Mao Tse-tung did not choose Liu Shao-chi as his eventual successor, turning over to him the chairmanship of the People's Republic of China as a symbolic laying on of hands. Indeed, Mao wasn't at all interested in voluntarily relinquishing the position to anyone, nor was he interested in devoting all his time to theoretical matters as head of the Chinese Communist party, as was commonly believed.

"I was dissatisfied with the decision, but I could do nothing about it," said Mao, according to Red Guard posters.

In fact, the move left him with very little real power. The extent to which he had lost the confidence—and in some cases the loyalty—of the party's administrative superstructure and large sections of the machinery of state (i.e., the State Council) was indicated by the severity of the Cultural Revolution purge. Of the forty heads of government ministries, only twenty retained their positions. The toll was probably just as high among senior party members, though the continuing "rehabilitation" of fallen officials will probably reduce the final tally considerably. Nevertheless, it was not until the beginning of 1971 that the new politburo was able to re-establish the first provincial party committee (in Mao's home province of Honan), almost five years after the start of the Cultural Revolution.

The humiliation and frustration Mao Tse-tung experienced when his power was "usurped" was summed up in what will probably become the most remembered and quoted sentence from the Cultural Revolution. It appeared in a Red Guard poster which reported Mao as saying that Liu Shao-chi and Party Secretary Teng Hsiao-ping "treated me as if

[258]

I were their dead parent at a funeral" and "never bothered to consult me about vital matters." There seems little doubt that Mao actually did make this eloquent statement.*

One of the interesting things about the poster, though, was that it had Mao admitting that both Liu Shao-chi and Teng Hsiao-ping *did* consult him on various policy matters—although in Mao's opinion the matters were not of extreme importance. From this, and from the fact that Mao issued various theoretical pronouncements during the years before the Cultural Revolution, it seems reasonable to assume that there was no plot to overthrow Mao Tse-tung or to stage a *coup d'état* in the true meaning of the word.

It could be argued, of course, that this would have been impossible in any case because of Mao's wide public appeal and because of his backing from the army under Lin Piao. But it could be just as easily argued that Liu Shao-chi and his colleagues made no real effort to push Mao out of the limelight or limit his indirect control of the army for the simple reason that they never considered themselves in any political danger. They may have assumed that Mao would bow to party discipline, just as they had in the past when a vote of the Central Committee went against them. They did not reckon with Mao's conviction that he, in fact, was *the* party.

But why the Cultural Revolution? Why did Mao Tse-tung launch communism's greatest rectification movement—a party

* Prince Kinkazu Saionji, who returned to Japan in 1970 after living ten years in Peking, said that American journalist Anna Louise Strong related the following incident to him: "An Australian friend called on me and told an interesting story. When he saw Chairman Mao yesterday, Mao told him happily that he just managed to escape from becoming a Buddha. Do you understand what he meant by that? Well, you see, Liu Shao-chi and his confederates tried to put Mao nicely on a shelf like a Buddha so that people would just kowtow to him while the Liu Shao-chi clique managed the affairs of the State in their own way, which was not Mao's way. They were, however, too optimistic." *The New York Times*, October 26, 1970.

euphemism for purge—when he must have known that in so doing he risked plunging the country into a civil war that could destroy it?

Some observers, notably those in Formosa, have argued that the Cultural Revolution was prompted by nothing more than the wounded vanity of an aging megalomaniac who vengefully set out to demolish those who had slighted him regardless of the consequences to the Chinese people. This reasoning, however, requires one to accept the premise that Mao views personal power as an end in itself. It is far too simplistic an explanation, contradicted by the fact that Mao's whole history has been that of a man virtually unaffected by self-ambition but relentless in his pursuit of greatness and ideological purity for the Chinese nation. Perhaps this is a form of self-aggrandizement, but Mao's insistence that the politically correct Lin Piao be named in the party constitution as his eventual successor is a further indication that his real concern was what would happen to China in the decades after his death.

Mao's preoccupation with the future of China has led other observers to suggest that a main reason for the Cultural Revolution was to enable China's young people to "temper themselves" in a real revolution of their own, and thus acquire the same qualities of self-sacrifice and discipline that had inspired Mao's generation of revolutionaries. Parallels were drawn between the Red Guard exodus to Peking and the Long March of 1934–36. Certainly, the Chinese leaders often seemed worried that China's young people were soft, that they were not motivated by revolutionary fervour, that they didn't really understand the evils of capitalism because they had never experienced the bad old days. For this reason, in the early sixties, a travelling exhibit was organized of clay statues arranged in tableaus to show hardships in pre-Communist China.

Commented Han Suyin: "To one like myself, to whom these representations had once been living persons, the very fact that now *statuary* had to keep the memory of the past alive was most moving and disturbing. Symbolic of the progress achieved, of the vastly better living standard, they were also symbolic of the dangers of the new ignorance among the young about what Old China was really like. For these shuffling, ragged beggars, these skeletal children, could no longer be found in China." (Han Suyin, *China in the Year 2001*, C. A. Watts & Co. Ltd.)

Conceding all these arguments, it still seems true that Mao created the Red Guard movement out of necessity and not because he regarded it as an educational process for young Communists.

Mao had three main strengths in his fight to regain power.

First, he had the support of Premier Chou En-lai, one of the best-known and respected Chinese leaders. Chou understood the workings of the apparatus of government better than any person in China and could be counted on to keep the delicate economy functioning during the Cultural Revolution and afterwards, when the pieces would have to be picked up and put together again. His acknowledged reputation as an administrator would also inspire confidence in many old-time Communists who might otherwise reject the Cultural Revolution as the work of impractical, overzealous theoreticians. In addition, Chou En-lai had built up his own power base within the State Council over the years, though it apparently was far less solid than outside observers had suspected; possibly he even felt his position as Premier threatened. Indeed, the wholesale purge of top officials throughout almost every ministry suggests that, contrary to some speculation, Chou En-lai was never in any danger during the Cultural Revolution and in fact welcomed it as an opportunity to root out those people in the government who had

[261]

given their allegiance to Liu Shao-chi instead of to him. Whatever the case, it is true that Chou En-lai emerged from the chaos with seemingly greater power and certainly with every logical contender for his position neatly eliminated.

Mao Tse-tung could also rely on the support of Lin Piao, the Defense Minister who had worked so assiduously from 1959 to 1966 to indoctrinate the great mass of soldiers with Mao's thinking and to convert or purge the army's top officers who did not accept Mao's theories of a People's Army. Despite the loyalty of the army, it was evident that Mao was determined not to use their weight of arms to force his enemies out of power. Perhaps he feared this would result in civil war (as it was, there were times when certain sections of the army seemed on the verge of revolt), but it seems more likely he wanted to preserve the army's carefully nurtured image as the defender and protector of the masses. To the Red Guards went the role of violent attacker. To the soldiers went the role of conciliator and peacemaker.

Mao Tse-tung's third and perhaps greatest strength was his enormous prestige among the Chinese people. Publicly, his preeminent position among China's leaders had never been challenged; he was still the revolutionary hero, the head of the Communist party, the saviour of China. On this simple fact was based the strategy of the Cultural Revolution. With Mao's public approval, the Red Guards began by criticizing school administrators and minor government officials with wall posters and in public meetings. But since the basis of the criticism was that the officials had not followed the correct proletarian line of Mao Tse-tung, the campaign in effect elevated Mao and his teachings. If you did not accept criticism, then you were opposed to Mao. As bigger and bigger targets came into view, the elevation became adulation; badges of Mao, statues of Mao, pictures of Mao, quotations of Mao.

Mao's opponents apparently recognized what was happening at the beginning, but they were almost helpless to do anything about it. When the Red Guards started their campaign in the schools, party officials sent out work teams of experienced cadres to cut off the criticism and turn it against the Red Guards. Mao Tse-tung countered by writing his own wall poster urging the students to continue their criticism. The work team effort collapsed, since its members could hardly be opposed to Mao. With this defeat, Liu Shao-chi, Teng Hsiao-ping, Peng Chen and their colleagues must have become aware of the real nature of their dilemma. They controlled the party at the top level, the Central Committee, but among the millions of ordinary cadres and among the masses of the Chinese people, Mao Tse-tung was still the revered leader of the country. To attack him would be to prove the allegations of the Red Guards. All they could do was try to weather the storm, defending themselves as best they could. Some were more successful than others, but these were individual fights in individual provinces and cities. Quite obviously, no one had ever thought to lay out a concerted plan of attack or counterattack against Mao.

The tortuous path that the Cultural Revolution followed for more than two years is a fascinating and complex study in itself, and no doubt it will be the subject of many scholarly tomes. It will be interesting to see if they agree on when the Cultural Revolution ended. In Peking, most of us *sensed* that the revolution had ended during the summer of 1968. But by the spring of 1969 we were *certain*. The evidence was all around us. The political tension which penetrated every street and home in Peking had begun to lift; you could actually see it happening. Old men began to sit under the street lamps again in the evening playing checkers and cards; loudspeakers played ballet music instead of revolutionary marching songs; goldfish bowls magically appeared in apartment windows; people no longer wore the previously mandatory Mao badge; merchandise began to replace busts of Mao Tse-tung in store windows; the almost daily demonstrations virtually ceased; the rudest of the clerks in the Friendship stores disappeared.

But as normalcy returned to China, the main question still remained to be answered: Why the Cultural Revolution? What had Liu Shao-chi done that was anathema to Mao Tse-tung?

Certainly, there was no shortage of accusations in the official press and in Red Guard newspapers, though some were so outrageous that probably even the Chinese people didn't believe them. The catalogue of his sins included every conceivable administrative bungle or deliberate malpractice that occurred in China for two decades. If children were not educated, it was Liu's fault. If peasants were unable to have farm machinery repaired, it was Liu's fault. If China didn't have enough doctors, it was Liu's fault.

More seriously, Liu was accused of being a traitor to China and to communism. He was supposed to have ordered comrades to surrender to Chiang Kai-shek's forces in 1936 and betray the Chinese Communist party. Wang Kuang-mei, his wife, was alleged to have been an American agent sent to Yenan in 1947 by the U.S. Strategic Information Service. Her brother, Wang Kuang-chi, was accused of delivering secret information to the U.S. Central Intelligence Agency in Hong Kong in 1950. Coincidentally, some of Liu's associates were supposed to have been passing confidential information to the Russians.

It all made fascinating if implausible reading. We were presented with a picture of China's top leaders tumbling over each other in their eagerness to send the latest state secret to Moscow and Washington.

Equally unconvincing was the allegation that Liu Shao-chi

was a capitalist-roader, that is, someone who was directing China back to capitalism. As evidence, the Red Guards presented a display in Peking of things which they said they had seized in the homes of Liu Shao-chi and his colleagues. It was a strange assortment: piles of American five- and ten-dollar bills and British pound notes, pistols, Western suits, shirts and ties, playing cards (Teng Hsiao-ping was reportedly a bridge addict), bars of gold and silver, copies of various Western magazines such as *Time* and *Punch*, jewellery, Western-style dresses and high-heeled shoes and, horror of horrors, silk panties that according to an attached sign were the property of Mrs. Liu. Whether or not these various articles belonged to Mr. and Mrs. Liu and their colleagues, nothing that was done by the Government or the Communist party under Liu Shao-chi gave the slightest sign that China was on the slippery path to capitalism.

The one charge against Liu that had substance was that he was a revisionist—if one accepts Mao's definition of revisionism as the Soviet style of communism. Thus, Liu Shao-chi's name was not mentioned in the official press for more than two years. Instead, criticism was directed at "China's Khrushchev," though everyone knew this was in fact Liu Shao-chi. A book could be written (and probably will be) about how every move made by Khrushchev and his successors was in Mao's view inexorably resulting in the slow dismantlement of all the true principles of communism. And to Mao, these principles were embodied in the days of Yenan.

Then the revolution had still to be won, and everyone was consumed by the desire for victory. There was no talk of special pay bonuses, or heated living quarters, or better clothing, or more varied food. There were no special privileges for officers; they ate and lived as ordinary soldiers and were treated with respect, but not awe. The American author Edgar Snow described a concert staged by the army at the caves of Yenan and how the audience of soldiers shouted that they wanted Mao and a blushing Lin Piao to sing a song for them.

This spirit of equality and comradeship sustained the men as they endured death and countless hardships to bring the same spirit to the whole of China. Perhaps the dream was an illusion, but more than one observer from those days has written about how ordinary men seemed transfigured by a nobility of purpose and purity of selflessness.

In any case, as peace settled over the land, the traditional values of Chinese society began to regain their importance: the family, the acquisition of land, the veneration of ancient culture, the pursuit of scholarship for its own sake, the disdain of city dweller for peasant and of the educated for the uneducated, the benign tolerance of bureaucracy. In Mao's view, these were the very things that had throttled old China, and their growth was encouraged by the Soviet brand of pragmatic communism being followed by Liu Shao-chi.

Interestingly, each of these "faults" was severely criticized during the Cultural Revolution. In a private conversation with a diplomat, Chou En-lai admitted he too had been guilty of "bureaucratism," but boasted that he now had only five secretaries instead of twenty and that as a result he was able to "get more work done and have better control and understanding of what was happening on the lower levels of government." In 1970 Chou told Edgar Snow that officials in the central administration had been cut from 60,000 to 10,000 and that the number of departments would be reduced from 90 to 26.

It would, however, probably be an oversimplification to suggest that Liu's downfall was simply because he favoured orthodox Communist methods of economic and social development. Perhaps he also believed that China should resolve its ideological differences with the Soviet Union at least for the time being in order to gain military and economic help, a concession that the proud Mao would certainly be unwilling to make. That is only speculation, of course.

To discover what Liu Shao-chi's shortcomings really were, it is more profitable to examine the reforms that are taking place in China today. They are a more reliable guide to the reasons for the Cultural Revolution and, far more important, provide us with some idea of the shape that China is likely to take in the years ahead.

17

ANYONE who has read much about China written by Westerners is aware of the elusiveness of objectivity. There are writers who either hate or love China's form of government, and their writing shows it. Then there are others, perhaps the majority, who do not rejoice in communism but who have a grudging admiration or at least respect for what Mao Tse-tung has achieved for the Chinese people. But even these writers, most of them academics, and basically sympathetic to China, were unable to conceal their revulsion at the changes in education wrought by the Cultural Revolution.

It was a revulsion I shared, especially concerning the reforms in medical education. Literally, the Chinese seemed to have gone mad. They were talking about shortening medical schooling by two to three years, about training peasants to become "barefoot doctors" in three months and sending them out to treat patients. And reports that bona fide medical specialists were being abused were confirmed when a couple of foreign women told me they had seen their gynecologist scrubbing the floor in the Anti-Imperialist Hospital in Peking.

As the months went by, I discovered that the radical medical "reforms" being discussed in Chinese newspapers were not just revolutionary bluster, that the education policy-makers were quite serious about putting them into effect. I also became convinced that the reforms were no more extreme than China's problems, that in fact they were practical measures designed to meet the country's needs.

China had made tremendous strides in medical education since the Communists came to power in 1949.

In that year the country had only eight Western-style medical colleges and about 200,000 doctors trained in Western medicine. Between 1949 and 1962, China produced 102,000 Western-type physicians and 500,000 doctors trained in traditional Chinese medicine—that is, in the use of herbs and acupuncture. By 1964, Peking claimed there were 90,000 students in 80 medical colleges.

Impressive as these statistics were, however, they were overwhelmed by the fact that China's population was growing at the rate of from ten to twelve million a year. The country simply was not producing enough doctors to care for its people, and the gap between supply and need was growing wider every year.

The countryside was in particular need—as in other countries, Chinese doctors prefer to stay in the cities where the living is easier and modern medical facilities are available—and one of the Cultural Revolution's first medical reforms was directed at helping the peasants. Men and women who had showed an aptitude or interest in nursing the sick on communes were sent to medical schools for brief periods to learn how to treat simple ailments. The Chinese press claimed that some even were taught to perform minor operations such as appendectomies and the removal of cataracts, but it seems likely that most of them learned how to diagnose and treat common diseases and how to give emergency treatment to accident victims. They were also given adequate supplies of basic medical equipment, dressings and medicines. Interestingly, China had been a large producer of pharmaceuticals for the world market, but foreign buyers at the Canton Trade Fair in the spring of 1969 were told that none was for sale. The explanation was that pharmaceuticals were being stored in case of war, but most of them were probably being channelled to the countryside where the vast majority of China's population lives.

The Barefoot Doctors, as they were called, may not have been skilled general practitioners but they provided a valuable health service in remote parts of China where trained medical help was virtually unknown. The idea of producing paramedical training is now being taken seriously across the United States and Canada as a way to ease the doctor shortage.

The question of what to do about reforming the medical colleges was more complicated, but the Cultural Revolutionaries were agreed that the basic fault of the schools was that they were designed to meet the needs of foreign countries instead of China. Certain changes had to be made, they said: the length of schooling had to be shortened (another idea being considered in Canada), students had to be given time for political activity, more students had to be assigned to work in the countryside, medical training had to be shifted from its urban hospital orientation, students had to participate in physical labour, discrimination against students from worker and peasant families had to stop, less stress had to be placed on marks and rigid examinations.

I have listed all these criticisms because they were basically identical to those levelled against all institutes of higher learning. And what happened in medical colleges was fundamentally what happened in other schools.

At the time of the reforms, I had the good fortune to meet a young foreign student at Peking Medical College. He may

[271]

have been the only foreign student allowed to continue his studies during the Cultural Revolution; he was the only one I knew of. By the time we met, in 1969, many of the reforms had already been instituted. He himself was preparing to spend two months working in the countryside with his fellow graduates before returning to his native country. He said he was looking forward to the experience, but that they had been told to expect to spend a good part of their time training Barefoot Doctors.

My young friend was, to put it mildly, exhilarated by the changes that had taken place in Peking Medical College. Before the revolution, he said, classes were conducted with extreme formality. No one but the teacher was allowed to speak, and students spent much of their time staring at textbooks and blackboards. Most of the doctor-teachers had been trained in Western schools, and they transferred the Western teaching methods and curricula directly to Peking Medical College.

"It was ridiculous," he said. "Hundreds of thousands of Chinese were in need of medical help, and there we were dawdling along studying obscure diseases and treatments that simply had no real application in China. It seemed such a waste of time, and we often sat around grumbling about it but of course nobody dared to say anything to a professor. Our opinions were not wanted."

All this, of course, will sound familiar to anyone who understands student discontent in North American universities. In China, though, the Cultural Revolution gave the students the opportunity to upset the old order. Naturally, some of the entrenched professors resisted the change. They had their thinking changed through prolonged discussions and arguments with the students, though force was never used, according to my friend. But the students did take the opportunity for revenge on certain doctors who had been arrogant. They

[272]

were assigned to part-time work such as washing test-tubes or scrubbing floors to lose their "superior airs."

Student-faculty committees were chosen to frame new curricula and to consider writing new textbooks that would take into account the "practical" needs of a Chinese doctor. But while this was being done, new teaching methods were already transforming the once staid college system.

"It was tremendously exciting," said the young student. "The old professor-student relationship was broken down, and all of us were seized with what seemed to be a new freedom to learn. We didn't have to sit like mice during lectures. We could challenge the professor or the textbook, and for the first time we were listened to. The result was that the professors started to do their research because they knew they had to have more than just an answer; they had to have an explanation for their answer.

"But the most remarkable change was that we were actually allowed to do what we were being trained for. Bright students, regardless of their years in school, were invited on to the floor of the operating theater to watch surgery and to hand instruments to the doctor. Often some of us would stand on stools around the table so we could see what was going on. When the doctor was satisfied that a student was able, he would be allowed to open and close an incision—with the doctor standing at his elbow watching like a hawk. Those students who showed ability were progressively given more to do, suturing and so on until finally they performed simple operations.

"I haven't graduated yet"—he grinned—"but I've lost count of the number of hernia operations and appendectomies I've done. I only keep track of the number of babies I've delivered. I've had forty-three so far, and I hope to have fifty before I leave school.

He also described some serious operations he had performed under the supervision of a specialist, but they were too complicated for me to understand or remember. I asked him how he would compare his education to that received by a medical school graduate in the West. He said that his practical experience was immensely superior and that he believed he could practice medicine immediately, which was the object of the new Chinese training. But he added that he was very weak on theory, and would have to spend considerable time with his textbooks when he returned home.

Practical experience is all very well, of course, but with a shortened school system it cannot produce a neurosurgeon or a heart specialist. I made that very point at Dr. Sun Yat-sen Medical College in Canton when I met with the school's revolutionary committee, a group of teachers, students, soldiers and workers.

"We aren't considering the specialist training for the moment," said one of the teachers. "We are acting in accordance with Chairman Mao's instructions and putting our emphasis on the countryside."

"There certainly is merit in that," I said, "but surely you cannot just stop training brain and heart specialists, for instance?"

"Chairman Mao says we can't crawl at a snail's pace," said one of the students. "Before the Cultural Revolution brain surgery was done only by specialists. But now young doctors also dare to perform such operations and the results have been good."

I persisted: "But surely you do not just stop training specialists?"

Finally, the teacher added a qualifying comment: "After doctors have been working and have accumulated experience, they can return to school to acquire a complete knowledge in all fields."

[274]

In other words, the Chinese were not abandoning specialist training.

It is neither necessary nor possible to go into a detailed examination here of the changes taking place in other areas of higher education. Their purpose is basically the same: to produce as quickly as possible graduates with practical on-job experience who can apply their knowledge immediately.

What this will mean to the pursuit of research in China is difficult to predict, though it is known that in certain areas such as nuclear development the scientists have never stopped working. A Western ambassador asked Kuo Mo-jo, the President of the Academy of Sciences, if China had decided to forgo research generally for the time being.

"That would be impossible," he replied. "No country, and especially a developing nation such as China, can afford to neglect research."

In the area of economic planning, the Chinese leaders seem content not to proceed with radical innovations that are likely to disrupt production—at least for the present. Thus many of the reforms promised by the Cultural Revolution seem to have been postponed until the next massive political campaign. Private plots for peasants and material incentives for factory workers, for instance, were severely criticized by revolutionaries, but in early 1971 they were still in existence. Other reforms that were announced with fanfare turned out to be little more than experiments that were either drastically modified or discarded as unworkable. It could be said that this approach was in itself a reform of the Cultural Revolution, a sign of the leaders' willingness to adhere to the "mass line" principle of socialist democracy. A more likely explanation, however, is that many of these reforms were temporarily laid aside because they would unnecessarily irritate peasants and workers at a time when far

[275]

more important matters were at stake: a fundamental change in the direction of China's industry and agriculture. And with this change there was no room for compromise, regardless of how the masses might feel about it.

Basically, the new policy called for China to pin its faith for the future on the countryside. There were emotional as well as practical reasons for Mao Tse-tung to adopt this strategy. It was because he had bypassed the cities and depended on the countryside for support—contradicting the Soviet formula for a successful revolution—that Mao was able to seize power in China. And ever since, he seems to have had a deep distrust of the cities and the bureaucrats and intellectuals who inhabit them. It is interesting that the one identifiable group hit hardest during the Cultural Revolution was the December 9 Clique, the loose title given to Peking University students who took part in an uprising against the Japanese in 1935, became Communists, and eventually rose to influential positions within the party and government. They were recruited and guided by Liu Shao-chi and Peng Chen, who undoubtedly remained their patrons over the years.

Besides having confidence in the tenacity and devotion of China's peasants, Mao is also well aware of the importance of agriculture. It is the inescapable fact of China.

Agriculture occupies more than 80 percent of the population and supplies 50 percent of the national budget's income, 40 percent of the raw materials used in industry and 70 percent of the exports. Much has been accomplished by the Communists in the way of irrigation and flood control projects, but much more has to be done if agricultural production is to match China's increasing population in the years ahead. Nobody knows the exact size of China's population, not even the Chinese, who have conducted only one census. That was in 1953, when a population of 583 million was claimed. In 1961 the Government began using 650 million as the official figure, and in 1966 upped the total to 700 million, the figure still being used though it clearly is too low.

In 1970 United Nations demographer Dr. Carl Frisen estimated China's population at just under 760 million, and another expert, Dr. Leo Orleans of the U.S. Library of Congress, came fairly close to that figure with a projected total of 757 million. The encouragement of late marriages (twenty-five for women, thirty for men), sterilization, birth control clinics and the Pill (rather graphically called the "medicine of the 21 remembrances") is believed to have reduced the annual population growth to about 1.5 percent. This is quite low compared to other Asian countries (India's rate is about 2.5 percent) but it still means an increase of more than 11 million people a year.

Obviously, China must steadily increase its annual food production. Fortunately, the country had four consecutive years of good harvests (1967–70) and in early 1971 Chou En-lai said grain reserves were about 40 million tons. This, in combination with a vigorous campaign to store crop surpluses, means that the Chinese could survive two or three years of poor harvests without calamitous results. The long-term problem remains the same, however, and will increase rather than diminish in the years ahead: China must have more food.

The Communists have made considerable progress. From 1959 to 1967, China is conservatively estimated to have reclaimed about 2.3 million hectares of land, and to have added irrigation works to about 3 million hectares in 1956–67 to bring the total irrigated area to about 39 million hectares (Owen L. Dawson, *Communist China's Agriculture*, Praeger Publishers). Much of the most fertile land, however, is close

[277]

to exhaustion because of centuries of close cultivation. The Chinese have always used organic fertilizers, but chemical fertilizers must be used if production is to show an appreciable increase. Chinese economists told a Japanese visitor that if Chinese farmers used nitrate fertilizers in the same proportion as the Japanese, then China would have to produce 50 million tons annually. At the country's rate of production then (1961) economists estimated it would take fifty years to produce that amount (*Asian Dilemma: United States, Japan and China,* Center for the Study of Democratic Institutions).

China has indeed raised its production of chemical fertilizers from 1.7 million tons in 1960 to 14 million tons in 1970, but this remarkable increase does not alter the fact that China will have to continue to import costly fertilizers and also build many more fertilizer plants.

The problem of food supply is as old as the country itself— even the old expression meaning to have bad luck, "to break one's rice bowl," is tied to food—but it is typical of Mao Tse-tung that he believes the solution must be found in terms of people's thinking rather than in terms of production statistics alone. Thus the Cultural Revolution reforms in the countryside should perhaps be viewed as a grandiose plan, sweeping in concept, which is designed to transport China's peasant population physically and mentally into the Twentieth Century. If it is successful, China could move ahead dramatically in economic and political development in the next decade.

Anyone who travels in China cannot help but notice the tremendous difference in the standard of living between city and country. Starvation and bondage that amounted to slavery have been eliminated, but China's peasants still have little more than the barest necessities of life; and despite more than twenty years of Communist rule they still are a conservative, backward force, resistant to change, superstitious, content to work the land in much the same way as their ancestors did. Yet China's peasants number 600 million, the vast majority of the population. If they are not transformed, then China cannot be transformed.

One of the first moves in this direction was made in late 1968, when tens of thousands of young students from the cities took up the call to settle in the countryside. There had been similar movements in the past, but it soon became clear that this was not to be a short-lived campaign. Through 1969 and 1970 the exodus continued, including not only students but also workers, engineers, doctors and other educated adults. In 1971, with perhaps 10 million people already having left the cities, the stream toward the countryside was still continuing.

The program had a number of immediate advantages. It eased overcrowding and unemployment in the cities, effectively dispersed the troublesome Red Guards, and eliminated the educational bottleneck that would have occurred if the reopened upper schools had to find room for their former students—who had been out making revolution since 1966—as well as for the flood of new graduates from lower schools. More important, the program brought to the countryside an army of people who were politically motivated and, compared to the peasants, highly educated.

The impact they will have on rural life was illustrated in a Chinese report on 20,000 Peking youths who settled in villages around Yenan in 1968. Two years later, 2,600 had become cadres of production teams or brigades, more than 1,000 had become Barefoot Doctors and teachers, 600 had joined the Communist Youth League, and almost 100 had become Communist party members. No doubt many others became militia cadres and propagandists.

There was, of course, the danger that the peasants would object to having to feed and house arrogant and weak-muscled city dwellers, but Peking made it clear to everyone that the "ignorant" newcomers were under the authority of the "wise" peasants. In addition, Peking initiated campaigns to build small fertilizer plants on the communes, as well as small factories to produce simple farm tools and machinery and consumer goods. This provided suitable employment for young people as technicians, bookkeepers and machinery operators.

These various moves not only were intended to raise the rural standard of living, but also to make the communes as self-sufficient as possible—for Peking was deliberately adopting a policy of decentralization.

The communes were told they must operate their own school and health systems, paying for the latter through a form of medical insurance. They also were handed the financial burden of purchasing heavy machinery and operating repair stations instead of relying on the state. This, in fact, was not too much of a hardship since the communes had built up considerable reserve funds because of crop surpluses, and Peking did not increase the low commune tax rate. In any case, the purpose of the scheme was not so much to save money for the central government, but rather to implement Mao Tse-tung's theory that communes must be made responsible for buying and maintaining their own machinery or they would never become mechanized and technically oriented.

Besides these reforms, there has been a continuing campaign to send educators, doctors, technocrats and administrators to the countryside for periods of up to a year. Officially, they are supposed to do manual labour, but it seems more likely that much of their time is spent passing along their skills to commune members. In the process, they also learn something of the peasants' problems and needs, which in turn prevents them from becoming "divorced from the masses."

Even members of the Foreign Ministry get a taste of life on a commune. A diplomat in Peking complimented a Chinese official on the success of China's new pig-raising campaign and was told: "I've done my spell in the down-to-the-country movement, and I've seen enough pigs to last me a lifetime." (Far Eastern Economic Review, October 17, 1970.) Lo Kwei-po, a vice-minister of foreign affairs, also spent some time on a commune in early 1969. When he first failed to attend public functions, we speculated he had been purged. But he popped up on May 1 and strolled around Pei Hai Park in Peking, wearing a peasant's straw hat and shaking hands with foreigners. He looked much better for the rural experience, with much of his prominent belly having vanished.

One other point should be made about the reforms in the countryside. All of them—decentralization, the dispersal of small and medium industries throughout the country, the emphasis on self-reliance, the infusion of political and intellectual vitality from the cities, the improved medical and educational facilities—are excellent preparations for the "people's war" that Mao Tse-tung believes will be China's only salvation if there is a war. It is, of course, a defensive strategy.

But the reforms are also a dramatic shift away from what Lucian W. Pye has described as "an exaggerated pattern of investments in heavy industry and a refusal to exploit China's marginal advantages in light consumer goods." * Naturally, China will continue to emphasize heavy industry that produces supportive materials such as steel, chemicals

* Lucian W. Pye, The Authority Crisis in Chinese Politics, The University of Chicago Center for Policy Studies.

and oil for light industry, agriculture and defense requirements; but Peking's apparent interest in light industry and, presumably, labour-intensive consumer products presents fascinating trade possibilities.

Could it be that China's concern for African countries— a high point was the agreement to finance and build the $412 million Tanzanian-Zambia railway—is based on economics rather than politics? Does the continent which Peking once regarded as being ripe for revolution now seem more attractive as a market for China's relatively unsophisticated manufactured goods? And as a source of the minerals and food that China will need in the decades ahead?

There is also the question of whether the China of tomorrow will be run by the army. The military gained new prominence during the Cultural Revolution when Mao Tse-tung had to rely on the army—honed to political perfection by Lin Piao after he became defense minister in 1959—to stop the fighting between factions and restore order to schools and the economy. In the process, army officers not only took over the management of factories, communes, schools and other institutions, but also became a political force. The chairmen of nearly all the provincial and municipal revolutionary committees were military men. And the army also dominated the party's Central Committee. Other officers moved into executive positions in the various administrative levels of the government.

In his interview with Edgar Snow in 1970, Chou En-lai denied that the army had taken a dominant role in the party and government. He said it hadn't happened and never would. But of course, the Chinese Communist leaders have always tended to regard the army as a political rather than purely military force. This attitude stems from the days of Yenan when political leaders were in fact military leaders —Mao Tse-tung, Lin Piao, Chou En-lai, Chen Yi. The military and political roles were interchangeable even after victory in 1949, with officers moving into civilian jobs and then back into military positions.

Whether Mao Tse-tung can re-create and relive the days of Yenan is another matter; 1971 is not 1949. Fortunately for Mao Tse-tung, his presence is so overwhelming that the experiment will probably be successful while he lives. It is after his death that China will have to find its own answers.

18

THERE was still one more change caused by the Cultural Revolution that we, as a family, noticed during our last days in Peking.

We had not been looking forward to leaving China. We had a number of close friends we would probably never see again, since they came from distant countries. We had also discovered that despite the frustrations and irritations of living in China, we would miss the Chinese people and the beautiful city of Peking. And the knowledge that we probably would never return to China exaggerated our melancholy. In the weeks before our departure we were like students cramming for an exam, walking for hours through Peking's parks and streets, trying to fill our minds with the sights and sound of the city. On clear nights we went into the old part of Peking to see for one last time how the moonlight softened the roofs of curved clay tiles. We were, I'm afraid, quite sentimental.

There was another reason to be concerned about leaving; it meant we would have to face the customs department. And I could remember only too well what my predecessor, David Oancia, had gone through.

Three days before he was to leave Peking, he was told to go to the customs department at the railway station where two large crates containing his belongings were waiting to be shipped to Canada. There, while we watched, five customs men pried open the crates and took out every article. Clothing was examined minutely, every pocket was turned out and seams were carefully fingered for hidden material. Hundreds of colour slides were put to one side, and he was told they would be sent by mail after they had been inspected (they eventually were.)

One by one, each of David's music records was taken out of its jacket and stared at by a Chinese, to what purpose I do not know. Books were leafed through page by page, and a number on Chinese politics were confiscated. Strangely, one of these was *Who's Who in Communist China,* a book which the customs department had permitted David to bring into the country. All his papers, including letters, were also sifted through. One customs man became quite excited when he came across a newspaper clipping. He called over his colleagues and they decided it must be important, though they obviously didn't seem to know why. I could see why they were confused. The story was innocent enough, but the heading had been written by a punster: "Once Mao, dear friends, into the breach." I imagine the Foreign Ministry is still trying to decipher it.

At five o'clock in the afternoon, they finally finished their inspection. David and I were tired and cold and angry. For five hours we had been standing in an unheated railway shed watching them, and it was difficult not to believe we had been part of a Chinese make-work project. After all, these very same crates were not packed by the Oancias, but by a special team of Chinese supplied by the Government; the packers surely examined every item carefully. But at

[286]

that time, of course, the Cultural Revolution was still booming along and the Chinese hardly trusted each other, never mind foreigners.

Naturally, Regina and I wondered if our belongings would get the same treatment when we left China. They didn't. In fact, hundreds of colour and black-and-white photographs were packed by the Chinese without a questioning look. Indeed, the only thing that seemed to interest them was Katharine's collection of Mao Tse-tung badges. She had been gathering them for about a year and had collected about three hundred, each different. The Chinese packers were mightily impressed and insisted on wrapping each separately in tissue paper. It took them about half an hour to do that little job. But eventually the crate was packed, nailed down, hauled off by a truck and—we later learned—was on its way to the port of Hsinkang. We never did hear from the customs department.

Unlike the Oancias, we had no problems leaving China. I applied for the exit visas and received them a week before we were to go. The Oancias, on the other hand, were granted their exit visas only two days before they were to leave. Not only was the wait nerve-racking (at that time Reuters correspondent Anthony Grey was under house arrest and exit visas were denied all the British diplomats in Peking), but it also meant that their last two days were frantically busy. Without exit visas they couldn't wrap up their affairs with the Bank of China or buy airplane tickets from Peking to Canton. And at that time, too, personal luggage accompanying air travellers had to be taken to the main air transit building and cleared by customs on the day *before* the flight.

I later met David Oancia several times in Hong Kong, where he was on leave of absence from *The Globe and Mail,* and we could never decide whether his difficulties were due to the exigencies of the Cultural Revolution or whether the Foreign Ministry was subtly letting him know that his work as a journalist in China had not been appreciated.

By the time we left, the political situation was calm and, an extra bonus, the Canadian and Chinese Governments were discussing diplomatic recognition.

I picked up our exit visas at the Foreign Ministry, where two smilling young Chinese men shook hands with me and wished me a pleasant trip. Then I walked across old Legation Street to the Public Security Bureau, a grey brick European mansion set behind high walls. As I pushed open the big green wood gate and walked through the courtyard to the back door—which was used as an entrance to the house—I felt quite cheerful. I would be seeing the Dragon Lady for the last time.

She was the person responsible for giving final approval on exit visas, and it was quite obvious she would have liked nothing better than throwing away her little rubber stamp and locking up every foreigner in sight. Perhaps her grandfather had been killed in the Boxer Rebellion, but whatever the reason, she didn't like foreigners and managed to intimidate those who had to appear before her. She had the uncanny knack of looking down her nose at me through steel-rimmed spectacles though she was no taller than four feet. Her hair was cropped short and had only a few streaks of grey, sticking out from under her brown cotton cap. She must have been in her fifties. She was also quite thin: her police tunic hung in folds from her shoulders, and her baggy blue trousers were so large that she seemed to walk without bending her knees. I had never seen her smile.

I went in the back door, passed through the enclosed veranda filled with racks of political pamphlets, and entered the "office." It was a large room, damp and cold. The fireplace had been boarded up. The walls were whitewashed and bare of adornment except for the usual posters of Mao Tse-tung. There were two plain hard-backed chairs and a battered wood table, behind which sat the Dragon Lady. She looked as though she had eaten something disagreeable.

"Sit down," she ordered, these being the only two words she had ever spoken to me during our many encounters.

She looked even unhappier when I handed over our passports, but she reached for her rubber stamp and thumped an official approval on each one. It was just at that point that I happened to glance down and see her feet sticking out. This important official of the Public Security Bureau of Peking, who probably could have had me thrown in jail, was wearing yellow nylon ankle socks and bright green plastic sandals. What other police force in the world? I thought, and smiled. To my surprise she smiled back, stood up and stuck out her hand.

"Good-bye," she said, and we formally shook hands.

It was a good omen. There was to be no delay in our departure from Peking. In fact, as things turned out, the Chinese practically hustled us out of Peking—causing us some embarrassment among friends who had driven out to the airport to say farewell.

It was the custom among foreigners to meet at the airport restaurant for a small party when a friend was leaving. The restaurant, a large room with windows overlooking the landing strip, had about forty big round tables covered with white linen. The foreigners would pull some of the tables together, and sip beer or tea while waiting for the plane to leave. The Chinese staff didn't seem to mind, perhaps because the restaurant was never busy; there was only one international flight a week (to the Soviet Union) and probably no more than ten domestic flights a day. The airport was a remarkably quiet place, considering the fact that it was serving China's capital city with a population of seven million people. The restaurant wasn't exactly the most cheerful place for a party—on its walls were large photographs of a power station, some portraits of Mao Tse-tung, and a billboard bearing one of Mao's quotations (conveniently translated into English and Russian) about the perfidious imperialists and revisionists.

The airport itself, located about twenty miles northeast of Peking, is a modern yellow brick building with a wide bank of steps leading to the entrance. Just in front is a pool with several fountains that are turned on when visiting delegations arrive, and turned off as soon as they leave. The large main lobby has rows of padded chairs, candies, tins of tea and souvenirs. During the Cultural Revolution, a small stage was set in the middle of the lobby, and travellers had to sit through performances of revolutionary music and dancing put on by airport employees. By 1970, the concerts had stopped.

We arrived at the airport in plenty of time, showed our exit visas to the Chinese police, who sit behind a grille like bank-tellers, and headed for the restaurant. We didn't get there. A somewhat agitated Chinese girl bustled up to us and said we must get on the plane immediately. I didn't argue. If all the passengers were on hand, Chinese planes would sometimes leave early to miss bad weather.

But it soon became clear that the plane wasn't leaving early. About three hundred Chinese students were lined along the tarmac, holding flags and placards and beating drums. Obviously somebody of some importance was leaving Peking, and it wasn't us. We peered curiously out the window, and saw two burly foreigners waving Mao Tse-tung's little red book of quotations as they passed the cheering students. They climbed on board the plane and settled in their seats. I asked the stewardess who they were.

"El Fatah fighters," she beamed. I hadn't even known that officials of the Palestinian guerrilla organization were in town.

We looked anxiously for our friends as the plane began to move, but there were so many people standing along the tarmac that we couldn't pick them out. We took out our blue Canadian passports and pressed them to the window. We couldn't see our friends, but we knew they would see us. Our window would be the only one on the plane that didn't have a bright red book of Mao's quotations flashing up and down.

Canton, our last night in China. At dusk, we strolled along the street near our hotel. Only Katharine was not sad; she could hardly wait to get to Hong Kong the next day. But Regina and I were like two tourists who had just arrived in China. We nudged one another when we saw a pretty child, or a pedicab, or a woman with a shoulder-pole hurrying along the road. But only one sight during those last hours in China has stayed in my mind.

We had stopped by a coal-yard. All the workers had gone home except an old woman squatting on the ground, her back to us. On one side of her was a small pile of coal dust, on the other a pan of water. She cupped her blackened hands, dipped them into the pan and splashed water on the coal dust. Then, as though making a snowball, she packed and patted the wet coal dust into the shape of a briquette and put it on the ground beside her. Already she had made about fifty of them, and they would lie there in neat rows to await the drying sun of morning.

Suddenly, the sound of music broke the stillness and we

swung around just in time to see a young man go past on a bicycle. He was steering with one hand and holding a transistor radio to his ear. I looked at Regina, and I could see she was thinking the same thing. We turned and walked back to the Tung Fong Hotel to pack our suitcases and get ready to go home.